Praise for *Managing Nothing*

"Conversation is the best way to promote reflexive inquiry within groups, between groups and across organizations. Reflexive inquiry keeps an organization alive and relevant over time and in almost all conditions and states of a market. This is particularly so in a volatile, dynamic state, presented by markets these days and the knowledge society that is fast developing. Sudhir Varadarajan has found this compellingly validated in the IT industry where he was engaged for nearly two decades. Reflexive inquiry keeps people fresh in their approaches to problem solving, giving the impression that problems manage themselves, as if there is nothing to be managed. It can be developed in an action research mode. Sudhir Varadarajan's experience is presented via a lucid, precise and smoothly flowing narrative. It is definitely a good addition to the literature on problem solving."

— Professor P.N. Murthy, former faculty at IISc, Bangalore and IIT, Kanpur and Advisor to TCS

"In this book, Sudhir Varadarajan presents an innovative account of the problems encountered in the development of the IT industry in India. Although focusing on India, the book provides more general insights which are relevant to IT industries in other countries, indeed, to other industries globally. The book is innovative because it moves beyond the usual abstract accounts of industry development to give a rich, reflexive narrative account based on the author's own experience from which relevant generalizations about industry evolution emerge. The book provides a critique of the dominant discourse and takes up the theory of complex responsive processes as a way of reflecting on experience. It is concerned with how managers make strategic decisions in paradoxical situations. The author proposes that paradoxes can be dealt with by managers and employees by directing their attention to small differences in day-to-day complex workplace interactions—in other words, micro-politics."

—Professor Ralph Stacey, Complexity Management Centre, University of Hertfordshire, UK

"A well-thought-out account of the defining period in the growth and development of the Indian IT industry. Dr. Sudhir Varadarajan provides first-hand experience as to how the Indian IT giants have grappled with the challenge of rising up the 'value chain'. Through a narrative inquiry he shows that the complexity of human interaction in global IT services not only challenges prevalent views on sourcing, consulting and innovation, but also creates possibilities for new forms of participation from suppliers and clients. This has implications for client CIOs, IT and sourcing managers as they seek to co-evolve their IT organizations along with the supplier landscape to address the digital challenge."

—Richard Cribb, Managing Director, Ofsure, a UK-based independent advisory company

Managing Nothing

Sudhir Varadarajan

First published in India in 2015 by:

Dr. Sudhir Varadarajan
vsudhirs@outlook.com

Print Book ISBN: 9789384439514

eBook ISBN: 9789384439491

Publishing facilitation: AuthorsUpFront

Cover design: Neena Gupta

Foreword

The Indian IT industry has come a long way since the difficult days of the 1960s and the 1970s. Its contribution to the national and the global economy is a matter of great pride to the country. There is and will continue to be immense potential in Information Technology. However, it is yet to touch the lives of those whose language is not English. The majority of Indians read, write and work in their own language. The next stage will entail, apart from continuing innovation, computerization of Indian languages.

The future of the Indian IT industry lies in meeting the digital challenge, both at the global and national levels. At the global level the industry needs to find ways to work with clients to enable them to transform their organizations in all aspects. This has implications for Indian IT firms: they will need to look beyond outsourcing and develop new forms of symbiotic relationships with their clients. At the national level, there is the challenge of Indic computing, which is critical to drive digital transformation in a diverse country like India. Indian IT firms would do well to realize that this can be as big a market as the export-oriented IT services business. Both these challenges are bound to create new thinking and work for our people.

Dr. Sudhir Varadarajan's **'Managing Nothing'** is a timely reminder of why reflexivity in management is critical to promote new thinking to deal with paradoxical situations. Through a narrative enquiry into his own experience in developing strategic capabilities, Dr. Varadarajan draws attention to the complexity of human interaction in global IT service networks, and urges leaders to take a fresh look at everyday interactions to evolve new practices that are relevant to a hyper-connected digital world. I believe this perspective could open up new kinds of participation from service providers and clients, and provide a different way of working in the future. This book is a good addition to the debate on the Indian IT industry in particular and to managerial practice and education in general.

Dr. F. C. Kohli
Former Deputy Chairman
Tata Consultancy Services

Contents

Foreword   v

Preface   ix

I. Invitation to Reflexive Inquiry

1. Indian IT Services: A Case for Managerial   3
    Innovation

2. Within the Obvious: Understanding   29
    Complexity and Change in Indian IT
    Services

II. Early Attempts to Move Up the Value Chain

3. Grand Vision, Lost in Translation: Struggle   51
    to Institutionalize Integrative Thinking

4. Differently Abled: Evolution of Consulting   117
    and Domain Practices in Indian IT Services

5. Scale Takes Over: Glimpses into the Politics   154
   of Strategic Realignment

III. Challenges of Scaling in Global IT Service Networks

6. Putting the Heart in the Mouth: 179
   Co-evolving Client Access and Innovation
   in a Multi-Sourcing Context

7. Making the Familiar Strange: Triggering   214
   Strategic Conversations in Key Accounts

8. Out of Sight, But Not Out of Mind: 259
   Enhancing Knowledge Intensity in Offshore
   Operations

IV. Grappling with the New Normal and Digital World

9. Hollow Whole: Strategic Marketing in Indian   279
   IT Services

10. When NOTHING matters! Innovation in a   305
    Disrupted world

Epilogue   347

Appendix: Interactions with Sample Accounts   355

Bibliography   399

Preface

I am one of the three–four million people working for the Indian IT industry. I joined the industry in February 1991 immediately after completing my post-graduate programme in Industrial Management from IIT Madras. I chose to join one of the earliest software product firms in India (based in New Delhi) primarily because of their vision and focus on product development. This choice was also easy because the largest IT firm then, for some peculiar reason, indicated that students from our particular programme in IIT Madras were not suited for their type of work; and the other IT firms (two of them are leading players today) did not present any compelling vision, although interactions with their recruitment team suggested that they had a very smart and talented workforce.

However, within 1.5 years of joining the software product firm and after working on two very interesting engagements (an integrated management system for small and medium businesses in India, and a next generation MS-windows based product for law firms in the North American market), I started feeling that the world of IT was very constrained, especially in terms of extracting meaning from data. The innovation that was unfolding in the area of user experience was interesting, but not as strong as my interest in systems engineering[1] and management of public goods.[2] I was also not enamoured by the overseas opportunities that started emerging from the early waves of the offshoring tsunami. In mid-1992, much to the surprise of my friends and family, I decided to leave the IT job to pursue a PhD at IIT Madras. In the next couple of years this decision was severely tested when I got to see the real scale of the offshoring tsunami and how it had catapulted my friends in the industry into the league of global citizens. I realized that I was perhaps going against the trend, but I was keen to follow my passion.

After completing the PhD programme in 1996, I joined a very unique R&D centre of one of the leading Indian consultancy firms, little realizing that I had re-entered the IT industry and a terrain where I would spend the next two decades perennially swimming against the stream, and often without sufficient experience in the area of work, whether it be technology, process, domain, and now writing this book. I wondered if this was due to some hidden desire that was pushing me into uncharted areas, or the nature of work in the Indian IT services industry. I reflected on both these aspects from time to time. Every time I did this a new interpretation of my work appeared to emerge and encouraged me to pursue the new path. However, since 2010 I noticed that it was becoming increasingly difficult to make sense of what I was doing, i.e., package my experience into a coherent

---

1   I was introduced to this inter-disciplinary perspective in IIT Madras and it made a deep impression on me, courtesy Professor L.S.Ganesh.

2   In economics a public good is a good or service where individuals cannot be effectively excluded from use and where use by one individual does not reduce availability for others, for example, fresh air and national security.

story that would motivate me to take a new path. There didn't seem to be any cause-effect at all. It looked like I had hit the law of diminishing returns. I wondered if I was actually having fewer positive experiences or was I taking a more balanced view of reality? These questions forced me into a reflexive inquiry, why was I doing what I was doing? I also realized that this inquiry would be incomplete if I did not probe into a related question, why were *we* doing what *we* were doing, both from a social and historical perspective.

I started by revisiting the documents and notes that I had put together at different points in time over the past 15 years. One of the earliest documents was an internal paper that I had written at the turn of the millennium (April 2000) to make sense of the struggle we were going through, as part of an R&D centre, in institutionalizing integrative thinking among IT professionals, consultants and managers in one of the large Indian IT services firms. I shared it with my manager and was pleasantly surprised to note that he also had the habit of writing about his experience and sharing it with his peers. However, these papers did not seem to make sense to most senior managers. They were engrossed in the agenda of scaling the organization into a global IT services firm, riding the wave of global outsourcing.

Over the next five years I got to participate in some of the strategic initiatives that were emerging from pursuing a global agenda, for instance, developing business consulting and key account management. When I continued with this reflexive practice, I started noticing for the first time that there was a palpable difference between what we were doing and how we were talking about it. While what we were actually doing seemed messy and unpredictable, most conversations amongst us (professionals and managers) seemed to be guided by a strong belief that a powerful group of leaders can objectively analyse situations and align internal and external stakeholders to achieve desirable outcomes. This belief was at the heart of the dominant managerial paradigm. When I documented and shared my observations with some of my colleagues who were in sales and delivery roles, most of them seemed to relate to the problematic aspects of the dominant management paradigm but felt that something must be right since the firm was successful in the marketplace.

In 2008 I wrote another note pointing to the same difficulty. It was regarding the irony of communicating the importance of knowledge management to the IT professional, a knowledge worker, as part of the knowledge management initiative. I shared it with most of the stakeholders of the initiative. This time there seemed to be more understanding among people at the operational level, but it did not provoke any real rethink among senior managers. The response I got from the sponsors of the initiative was "how can we scale up your approach". I struggled to explain to them that instead of asking this question why don't they participate in what was emerging? It didn't seem to make sense to them as they were now busy restructuring the firm into independent business units to propel the next phase of growth under a new leader.

However, my views seemed to generate some interest among a couple of senior leaders in a relatively smaller firm. They made me an offer to join them. I joined this firm in mid-2008. Within six months I realized that I had jumped from a frying pan into the fire. Two major crises rocked the firm—first, the global financial crisis and second, a major financial fraud. The firm survived after the government intervened and facilitated a transfer of ownership. Once the new management took over, they initiated an exercise to right-size the firm. There was lot of uncertainty as to who would survive this right-sizing exercise. The group I belonged to was dissolved, but I was retained. I was asked to be part of one of the domain practices. I was in a dilemma over whether to stay or to look for alternatives. I decided to go through the crisis. My main motivation for continuing at that time was to see whether such a crisis (external and internal) would help shake up the thinking within an Indian IT services firm and move it in a new direction and possibly a differentiated capability in the future. It was around this time (September 2009) that I wrote a paper discussing the prevalent state of affairs and the possible directions we could take. I shared it with some of my senior colleagues. It did not invite much response. After four extremely difficult years of rebuilding the domain practice and the confidence of the teams to more effectively engage with clients, partners and analysts, I started feeling that the outcomes were not commensurate with the quality of effort put in. In fact there didn't seem to be any cause-effect pattern at all. It appeared as though the non-linearity or leverage was working in the reverse, i.e., a huge effort was required to make a small shift. In August 2013 I wrote another note trying to make sense of this situation. In the process of writing I realized that one thing that seemed to persist in the near-death scenario was the nature of everyday conversations and patterns of relating among people from different groups. Employees and managers in the firm (existing and those who joined anew) spoke the same language—scalability, predictability—and exhibited similar patterns of power relating as in my earlier firm even though this firm was in a crisis situation. We all seemed to be prisoners of the dominant managerial paradigm. When I noticed that clients, partners and management students were also in the same boat I started thinking about documenting these experiences in the form of a book that could, by chance, urge other managers and professionals (current and future) to reflect on the way we understand and participate in IT services organizations, especially in developing higher-level capabilities where the cause-effect process is not clear and outcomes most often appear like nothing. I also thought that this would be a good way of thanking all my sponsors and colleagues at various stages of my work across different firms for knowingly or unknowingly allowing me to explore a path that led to the realization that NOTHING in the IT industry is worth understanding.

In mid-2014 when I garnered the courage to take time off from work and write this book, I found support from different quarters. Some of the industry veterans, academicians, former clients, and friends across different firms offered to share their experiences, review and provide comments on the manuscript despite their busy schedules and commitments. I draw inspiration from Dr F.C. Kohli, regarded as the father of the Indian IT industry, who at the age of 92 continues to have a very strong passion to apply IT to address the complex socio-economic challenges facing the nation. His insistence that the IT industry can still make a strong contribution to the country by focusing on computing in local languages pushed me to ask a question "do I as a senior professional in the IT industry know enough about my local context to be able to contribute to it?" This in turn led me to a fascinating discovery of the complex interactions between the East India Company (the earliest joint stock and global corporation) and the Kaniyatchi system (local practices for sustainable agriculture, water and land management) in the Madras Presidency during the 18th century[3] and some clues

---

3   I had an exposure to the fascinating literature on the socio-political history of the Madras Presidency during the 18th century through the works of Tsukasa (1986), Sivakumar and Sivakumar (1996) and several others.

about my roots, values and my fatal attraction for the messy problem of developing higher-level capabilities.

I express my profound gratitude to Professor P.N. Murthy, a towering personality in the field of engineering and management education, for reviewing the entire manuscript and sharing valuable insights that enhanced my understanding of the different challenges. I would like to thank Professor Ralph Stacey, founding member of a very unique Centre for Complexity Management at University of Hertfordshire (UK), for challenging me to constantly reflect on what I was doing and introducing me to a body of literature that has had a profound impact on my work since 2005. I cannot thank enough G. Sekar, an industry veteran with a strong sense of humour and practical judgement, for putting himself in the shoes of the author and giving very valuable feedback in the early stages of this book. I would also like to thank several other senior leaders and friends who encouraged me to tread this path and provided their feedback, notably Professor K.V. Nori (Distinguished Professor, IIIT Hyderabad), Professor L. Prakash Sai (IIT Madras) and Professor V. Santhakumar (Azim Premji University).

I appreciate the suggestions provided by my former clients, a senior leader in the UK financial services industry and Richard Cribb (presently Managing Director of Ofsure, UK). Richard was also instrumental in introducing me to the publishing world. I would like to thank Manish Purohit, Arpita Das and the team at Authors Upfront for helping me explore the world of self-publishing, another new terrain.

Last but not the least, I thank my wife Sumathi for being my clementine mirror, my son Anant Vardan for nudging me to appreciate the dynamic stability of the solar system which played a crucial role in my decision to embark on this book, my father-in-law Professor K. Venugopal (former Director of Remote Sensing, Anna University) and the extended family for their constant support.

My thoughts today, to use Randall Collin's (2004) term, are "a moving precipitate" of the interactions I have had with various people (associates, clients, partners, and academia) in the Indian and global IT service networks and several others through their books and research papers. This book is my way of giving back to the industry and the networks that I participated in. The intent is to inspire better inquiries and ways of participation in the ongoing conversations in global IT services.

Section I

Invitation to Reflexive Inquiry

"By three methods we may learn wisdom: The first is by reflection, which is noblest; the second is by imitation, which is easiest; and the third is by experience, which is the bitterest."

—*Confucius*

Chapter 1

Indian IT Services: A Case for Managerial Innovation

The phenomenal rise of the Indian IT industry from about $4 billion in 1998 to about $120 billion in 2014 has transformed India into a hub of the global sourcing industry and the epicentre of the global technology industry[1] (NASSCOM, 2014). The industry today comprises about 16,000 firms spanning software, IT services and IT-enabled services like Business Process Outsourcing. It employs 3.1 million people[2] and contributes about eight per cent of India's GDP. NASSCOM (National Association of Software and Services Companies) predicts that the industry could scale to $300 billion by 2020.

Indian IT services,[3] which is the main focus of this book, is the

---

1   A number of leading IT firms like IBM, Microsoft, Google, Motorola and Apple have their development centres in India. Some of these firms also do R&D work out of their India centres.
2   The industry provides indirect employment to about 10 million people (NASSCOM, 2014).
3   IT services include custom application development and maintenance, package implementation, infrastructure management services, systems integration and IT consulting. The top IT firms also offer services like Business Process Outsourcing, but that is not the focus of this book.

largest and fastest growing segment of the industry. In FY2014, the IT services revenues touched $64 billion and grew at 14.3 per cent over the previous year (NASSCOM, 2014). About 80 per cent of this revenue came from exports. This segment has played a pivotal role in the rise of the Indian IT industry. Blessed with a talented workforce,[4] it has shown great resilience in dealing with different types of challenges[5] and show sustained growth over the past three decades. The senior managers of Indian IT services firms are highly regarded by analysts, media persons, policy makers[6] and the Indian society at large for orchestrating this phenomenal success by adopting innovative managerial practices for skill development, employee engagement, performance management, corporate governance, growth and profitability.

While the industry continues to attract global clients in search of better operating models,[7] a highly aspirational workforce, and consistent government support at national and regional levels, questions have been raised about the effectiveness of the business model[8] in sustaining future growth and improving equity and

---

4 IT services predominantly employ engineers (graduates and post-graduates). In the past six years, some firms have been taking the route of transforming non-engineering graduates into IT professionals.

5 The Indian IT industry has faced several challenges over the years: first, in making offshoring work and second, in scaling up the model. Challenges have come in the form of connectivity and technological limitations, socio-political issues like job losses and protectionism, cultural differences, intellectual property, data privacy and security, geo-political issues like terrorism, and the after-effects of the global financial crisis.

6 I think that the success of the export-oriented Indian IT services and its skills development initiatives has in some ways also inspired the "Make in India" policy of the new government in 2014.

7 Most of the Fortune 1,000 firms have some kind of sourcing relationship with Indian IT services firms. Today other segments (tier-2 firms) are also attempting to exploit the benefits of offshoring.

8 Cost-competitiveness has been a key driver for the success of Indian IT services firms. India is supposed to be seven–eight times cheaper than source locations and 30% cheaper than the next nearest low-cost country

inclusiveness in the domestic economy. For instance, Sharma (2014), who traced the historical evolution of the Indian IT industry,[9] argued that the future of the Indian IT industry depends on three key factors: availability of quality manpower; capability of the IT industry to move up the value chain; and growth in domestic IT consumption. He expressed a concern that on all three counts, the industry's future growth was subject to uncertainty. Economists have reasoned that while the industry's export-led growth contributes to the improved balance of payments situation of the economy, its impact in terms of equity and inclusiveness has not been commensurate with the nature of support it has received from the government (D'Costa, 2011, Barnes, 2013). They have urged the industry to pay more attention to equity and inclusiveness, and also the government to rethink its support for the industry. Similarly, Agrawal et al. (2012) argued that it is imperative for the industry to focus on inclusive growth and holistic development of society in its journey forward. Industry professionals Rahman and Kurien (2007), through a detailed analysis of the global IT services industry, raised a more serious concern. They observed that most stakeholders, i.e., leaders, employees and clients, were taking a myopic view of the industry and were not thinking enough about the future. So, what have leaders and managers[10] actually been doing?

(NASSCOM, 2014). The dominant model is based on addition of headcount. In the past 10 years efforts have been made to move to fixed-price assignments and asset-based services. But, these still make up a small proportion.

9   Sharma (2009) provided a detailed historical account of the Indian IT industry starting from the early 1900s. He argued that the government's role in seeding and nurturing first the electronics and hardware industry, and then supporting the IT services industry at different points in time was crucial to the success of the industry.

10 In this book I use the terms "leaders" and "managers" interchangeably. However, there are subtle differences in the way Indian IT firms interpret

The challenge of innovation and leadership

The challenge of moving up the value chain, i.e., developing strategic capabilities like product development, consulting and innovation, is not a new one for the Indian IT services. Some of the firms have been grappling with this problem for more than three decades. The dilemma that most firms faced in the early days was whether to move up the value chain in the context of the global export market or in the domestic market.[11] Both options seemed difficult. In the domestic market the willingness to exploit IT was limited. The global markets were primarily looking at Indian firms for technically skilled resources. In such a scenario, most firms chose to follow the demand. Since the demand was coming from the global IT services market, they started focusing on exports. Establishing credibility in the international market was pretty tough in the 1970s–80s. In the 1990s the model started to scale up rapidly with the help of government support and strong alignment of interests of global clients and employees. It was from early 2001 (post Y2K and the dot com bust) that

---

these terms. For a start, most firms have democratized the concept of leadership, i.e., everyone is called a leader. The term "Manager" is reserved for roles with some source of power. A number of middle-level designations carry the term manager —Delivery Manager, Relationship Manager, Practice Manager, Alliance Manager. As a consequence, we have a situation where an IT professional becomes a Team/Module/Project Leader, before becoming a Programme Manager (also pointed out by Revuru, 2012). Senior managers differentiate themselves through designations like Director, President, Executive, mirroring the terms used by clients. And at these levels people can exhibit the characteristics of manager or leader identified in management literature.

11 Until the turn of the millennium, IT spending in India was very small. Governments and public sector institutions which constitute a major segment were concerned that introduction of IT could result in job losses. Things started changing from the late 1990s with the government and regulatory bodies like RBI mandating computerization in governance, banking and several public services. Today this is a sizeable market that is of interest to global players like IBM, HP, Microsoft, Amazon, Google and Facebook.

most firms started feeling the pressure of increased competition, client expectations and aspirations of employees. As a result they explored opportunities to move up the value chain.[12] They invested in initiatives to develop high-value consulting, domain-specific products and accelerators/tools. Some firms took the inorganic route (M&A) to acquire higher-level strategic capabilities like consulting and product development.[13] They also launched initiatives to improve performance management, knowledge management, sales force transformation and global branding. The belief was that these initiatives would improve the positioning of Indian IT services firms in the eyes of global clients (board-level), and lead to larger deals and higher revenue realization.

However, the decision to develop strategic capabilities in the context of global markets threw up an important paradox[14] for the Indian IT services firms. They not only had to change their positioning as a cost-competitive player, but also sustain that positioning in the face of increased competition,[15] i.e., pursue differentiation (value) and cost-leadership (scale) strategies simultaneously.[16] Most IT firms and their managers struggled

---

12 This happened largely in the context of existing client relationships. This is in line with innovation in services as observed by Holzweber et al. (2010), where they note that innovation management in services is dependent on management and relationship with top-clients

13 For instance, TCS acquired a core banking product firm; Satyam acquired consulting firms like Citisoft, Bridge Strategy and S&V; HCL acquired Axon; and Infosys acquired Lodestone.

14 A paradox is two or more self-contradictory statements that conflict with pre-conceived notions of what is reasonable or possible (Stacey, 2003). One cannot separate it in space or time.

15 A number of global firms such as IBM and Accenture significantly enhanced their offshore presence in India, thus neutralizing the cost-advantages of Indian IT firms to an extent.

16 Such paradoxes are not unique to the IT industry. They have been observed in other sectors as well. For example, Heracleous and Wirtz (2014) throw some light on the case of Singapore Airlines.

with this paradox. Attempts to solve this paradox with the logic of "both ... and"[17] did not seem to succeed in a big way. Indian IT services firms found it difficult to quickly scale up strategic capabilities either through internal initiatives such as recruiting and training fresh engineers/MBAs, hiring senior professionals, creating separate R&D/competency groups; or by creating a separate subsidiary/acquiring a high-end services firm. These initiatives also led to a new problem, integration issues that demanded deeper management involvement. In some cases where they managed to demonstrate a differentiated capability, clients either couldn't reconcile this with what they saw in their everyday interactions or used their bargaining power to demand such high-value services for free,[18] thus making the differentiation strategy appear counter-productive. These experiences led most managers to focus on cost-leadership, i.e., follow Porter's (1980) advice on competitive advantage and strategy.[19] The underlying rationale was that IT service was a scale business[20] and since Indian IT

---

17 Poole and van de Ven (1989) suggested four generic ways to deal with paradoxes, three of them relate to resolving contradictions by separating them in space, time or through a higher level synthesis. Stacey (2003) argues that these arguments draw upon Kant's logic of "both ... and" to deal with duality. Since they eliminate the conflict, they cannot truly change the identity of the core and cannot be termed as transformational.

18 Clients adopt sourcing strategies that segregate vendors into different buckets and rate cards. A typical segmentation divides vendors into consulting partners versus offshore providers. A vendor who straddles both the spaces creates challenges for this model.

19 According to Porter, firms can protect and sustain their competitive advantage by adopting one of the three generic strategies: cost-leadership, differentiation and focus. However, they should not try and combine two strategies, for instance, cost-leadership and differentiation. This would be difficult and could leave the firms in the middle. This is a reflection of the Aristotlean approach to handling a paradox. According to Stacey (2003), the Aristotlean way assumes that paradox is a contradiction and contradictions are a reflection of faulty thinking. So, the solution is to eliminate the contradiction.

20 Alvesson (2004) observes that there is a general belief among knowledge-intensive firms such as IT services that size and fame are key indicators of

service had a very small share of the global IT services market, they should focus on increasing scale by targeting untapped geographies and vertical segments, and reducing unit cost by increasing offshoring, moving to tier-2/3 cities, converting non-engineers into IT professionals, and platform-BPO.[21] Another argument that was subtly used to enhance the legitimacy of cost-leadership was that it was the only way to accelerate employment generation and spread the benefits to wider sections of the society, thus taking care of concerns regarding equity and inclusiveness, and enabling continued government support. In other words, instead of channelling the tension created by the paradox into a new identity and strategic capability, managers sought to further scale up the existing model under the rationale of cost-leadership and speed. In such a scenario, initiatives to move up the value chain got equated to NOTHING, i.e., insignificant in terms of value in comparison to the total revenue and incommensurate to the quality of effort, and therefore not worth pursuing. As a result they have been largely used for marketing purposes.[22]

Some ambitious and path-breaking attempts to tackle complex socio-economic issues of the Indian economy

---

success and reliability, and communicating to the stock markets. However, there is no clear evidence of economies of scale.

21 Platform BPO refers to a service where the service provider delivers business services to multiple clients using its own proprietary technology. This trend has increased since 2008 (due to the global financial crisis and advancement in technologies like cloud) as it provides an option for clients to reduce capex and shift to leaner balance sheets. However, the long-term implications of such strategies for the service provider are yet to be fully understood

22 A glance at the websites, recent presentations, interviews and analyst reports of leading Indian IT firms would suggest that most Indian IT firms claim to pursue both cost-leadership and differentiation. If this is true, then Indian IT firms could end up in a low profitability regime with neither scale nor differentiation. Are firms not aware of Porter's prescription? Then why are they mixing it up? One explanation is that firms may be using the rhetoric of differentiation to shape perceptions of clients and analysts.

through innovative use of IT such as, Dr Kohli's initiative in Adult Literacy[23] and Ramalinga Raju's initiative in Emergency Management Research (EMRI), also did not seem to alter the dominant line of thinking. The adult literacy initiative came after Dr Kohli retired from TCS, and the new management largely treated it as corporate social responsibility (TCS, 2009). The initiative also did not receive the desired support from other national initiatives, thus limiting its impact in terms of rural transformation. The erstwhile Satyam's CEO Ramalinga Raju took a more strategic approach with EMRI. This initiative also got strong support from several state governments. Since their launch, emergency services (108) have saved numerous lives and scaled to cover more than half of India's population, registered a significant impact indeed. However, Ramalinga Raju's attempt to use the EMRI initiative to improve political alignment and further his non-IT business interests in the domestic market appears to have led him into an undesirable web (Bhandari et al., 2011). His ability to grapple with an undesirable paradox, i.e., passionate commitment towards a social initiative while perpetuating a financial crime on investors, came under pressure during the global financial crisis. He tried to solve it through a higher level synthesis, i.e., merger of two firms. When shareholders resisted, he couldn't handle the paradox any longer and ended up owning the fraud saying he "didn't know how to get off the tiger without getting eaten by it". This derailed the plans to exploit the global business opportunity in emergency management and destroyed the identity of the firm.

---

23 Dr F.C.Kohli along with Prof. P.N.Murthy and Prof. K.V.Nori designed an innovative IT solution that could significantly reduce the time and cost involved in improving adult literacy (Kohli, 2005). It leveraged the legacy computers to deliver the core ability to read a newspaper in a very short span of time. Pilots were conducted in eight states and covered a population of 120,000 as of 2009.

In summary, the discussion above shows that there are two contrasting views about moving up the value chain. While the broader expectation is that Indian IT firms should move up the value chain and contribute to growth and equity in the domestic market, the industry appears to have moved in a different direction. It attempted to move up the value chain in the context of the global market and when faced with a paradox treated such initiatives as nothing and resorted to scaling the low-cost services model; this was an unfortunate conclusion. Will the industry change its view and address the broader expectation in the future? Dr Kohli, who is regarded as the father of Indian IT, argues that it is possible (Kohli, 2014). He observes that while in the early days pioneers like TCS had to solve the export puzzle to stay alive and develop the industry, today most of the top firms have the resources and experience to apply IT to improving productivity in the domestic economy. He argues that if firms and governments invest in developing Indic computing (Indian language computing)[24] and apply it in different spheres of human activity, then the domestic market for IT could be as big as the current export revenues of Indian IT.[25] It can also trigger more variety and innovation in the ecosystem.

However, it is doubtful if most Indian IT firms[26] will move in

---

24 CDAC, some IITs and groups have been doing some work in this direction. Please see http://telecentre.eletsonline.com/2006/07/software-in-indian-languages-will-speed-up-computerisation-process-in-india-5/ (downloaded 31 October 2014). Also, see an article by Kamthania (2014).

25 Dr Kohli has been arguing for computerization in Indian languages for over a decade. http://www.itsmyascent.com/hr-zone/IT-challenges/152624 (downloaded 31 October 2014). http://articles.economictimes.indiatimes.com/2002-09-18/news/27350726_1_hardware-industry-software-computerisation (downloaded 31 October 2014).

26 Vidhyasagar (2007) points to TCS R&D efforts in this direction. TCS also has sponsored research at IITB. Global Technology companies like Microsoft and Google have taken initiatives in this direction. It is critical for their core business.

this direction given that at present there is no major push from the government for Indic computing; Indian society in general and workforce in particular see greater social and economic value in learning a global language like English;[27] analysts expect the firms to deliver growth and profitability every quarter; and their own experience in developing strategic capabilities has meant nothing. Leaders will argue that focusing on the domestic market in the absence of demand represents a nationalist ideology, not economics or business sense (blissfully ignoring that they urge their teams to focus on demand creation in the global market). As global companies and good corporate citizens that are responsible to shareholders, they would go to any country where there is demand for IT. Managers should note that this view is also not free of ideology. They may be consciously or unconsciously using contentious ideas like shareholder value[28] to further their own interests and those of certain segments like the Indian middle class.

The real issue that needs attention is how managers make strategic choices in the light of paradoxical situations and prevalent ideologies. Managers must understand that firms will need to continuously evolve new capabilities to stay relevant in any market they operate in.[29] For instance, one of the key

---

27 Prof. S.V. Raghavan (President of CSI) observes that "although it is understood that Indic Computing is a topic of immense importance for a country like ours, it is rather surprising to notice that not many contributions were received on this theme" from professionals and students.

28 Ho (2009) shows how the concept of shareholder value is a reflection of the ideology of investment banks.

29 The Dynamic Capabilities View popularized by Teece & Pisano (1994) argues that the competitive advantage of firms depends on their dynamic capabilities, i.e., their ability to learn, integrate and reconfigure internal resources and competencies to market needs. Such dynamic capabilities are firm-specific, evolve over time, and are dependent on the underlying organizational and managerial processes or routines. Athreye (2005) and Holzweber et al. (2010) throw some light on such capabilities in Indian IT services.

questions being asked today is whether Indian IT services firms can attain a leadership position in the emerging global digital revolution, where capabilities in innovation and integration of technologies like mobile, analytics and cloud are extremely important. Such questions will continue to emerge in the future and strategic choices will have to be made. Managers also need to understand that eliminating the paradox is not enough. New paradoxes will keep emerging. This is due to the inherent complexity of interactions between clients, service providers and other stakeholders as they grapple with differences in intent, bargaining power, an ambiguous and intangible nature of services, and levels of knowledge-intensity. The globally distributed nature of work adds to the complexity of interactions by dissolving organizational and cultural boundaries and enabling interplay of different ideologies that produce new tensions among people.[30] The result is a complex evolving Global Service Network (GSN) that produces paradoxes and complicates choices, as illustrated in Figure 1 below.

---

30 For example, employees of an IT services firm are distributed across different locations and time zones and report to at least two managers who may be from different organizations and cultural backgrounds.

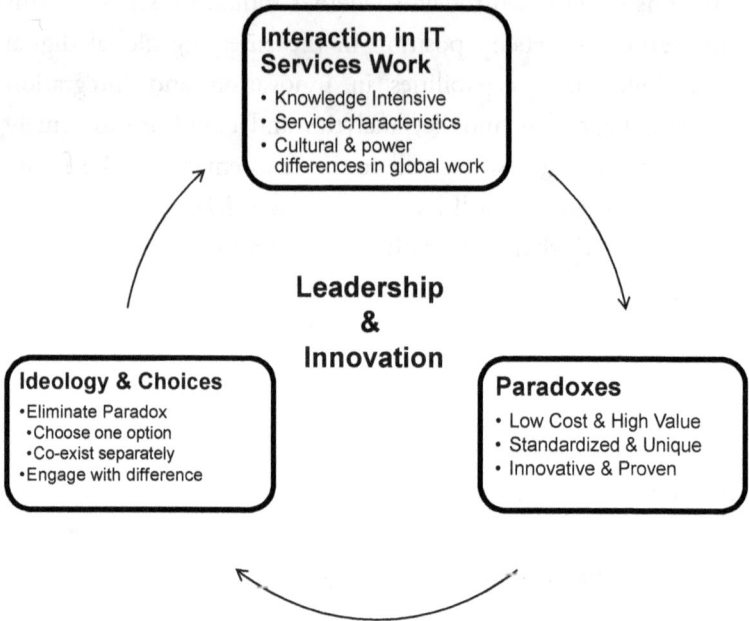

Figure 1: Interplay of nature of work, paradoxes and choices

Therefore it is imperative that Indian IT services firms find ways to handle paradoxes[31] while staying clear of doublethink.[32] Unfortunately, management ideas that are based on assumptions

---

31 Heintzman (2003) points to several authors such as Kim Cameron, James Collins and Jerry Poras, Paul Evans, Richard Tanner Pascale who have drawn attention to the paradoxes and dualities of organizational life and have argued that a central, if not *the* central, challenge of modern organizational leadership is the management and reconciliation of dualities. Tracy (2004) argues that it is not contradiction or paradox, per se, that is productive or unproductive, good or bad, liberating or paralysing, but rather, that employees can react to contradiction in various ways, and that their framing techniques of workplace tensions can have various personal and organizational effects.

32 Doublethink is the act of ordinary people simultaneously accepting two mutually contradictory beliefs as correct. For example, people will accept that it is difficult to predict outcomes of our actions, and also argue that we must plan for the long term, we simply need to be more agile and flexible (Stacey, 2012).

of linear causality and elimination of paradox are not well suited for handling complexity and change in GSNs.[33] It is important for leaders and managers to seriously think about managerial innovation[34] to evolve new capabilities to stay relevant in the GSNs.

Purpose and motivation of this book

The present book entitled "Managing Nothing" points to a certain way of dealing with paradoxical situations and managing in GSNs. It calls for managers and employees to pay attention to the small differences that emerge in ordinary day-to-day workplace interactions among people,[35] i.e., the micro-politics of everyday work, which as mentioned earlier is the fundamental source of complexity in GSNs. And, paying attention to what one is already doing does not require separate workshops, specialized groups, and additional costs. It can also generate some bandwidth in an otherwise time-constrained everyday work routine. One may wonder why managers are not practising this, if they aren't already.

An analogy might help further explain why workplace

---

33 Management concepts are largely built on very strong cause-effect logic [Desired Results=Strategy*Execution]. If the desired results are met, then one can retrospectively say that the company had great strategy and execution capability—the stuff of best practices and case studies. If the desired results are not met, then either strategy or execution is flawed. A typical response in such a situation is to juggle with strategy or execution levers hoping that things might improve. They largely treat complexity and paradox as undesirable and try to eliminate it.

34 Hamel (2007) in his book on Future of Management had called for leaders to focus on management innovation. He argued that what ultimately constrains the performance of an organization is not the operating model or the business model, but the management model.

35 It draws upon Hegel's dialectical way of dealing with paradox, i.e., staying with the tension through a process of social knowing, a process of forming social selves, and a process of the movement of thought (Stacey, 2003).

human interaction is an extremely important, yet poorly explored aspect of our organizational life. Human interaction is central to organizational life, much like breathing is central to our biological life. Patterns of human interaction shape individual and organizational behaviours in the same way as breathing patterns influence our bodily rhythms. How many of us understand and practise these? A majority of managers and employees tend to view human interaction from a narrow perspective, i.e., as opportunities for exchange of information and to check for alignment of interests—are you with me or are you against me? Very few try to consciously observe and engage with the small differences that emerge during repeated interactions between people, differences that carry the potential for transformation in new directions.[36]

It took about 10 years of action research[37] experience for me to arrive at the paradoxical conclusion that I need to pay more attention to the obvious aspects of day-to-day interactions, and another 10 years to experience it first-hand. The richness in our day-to-day interactions remained "rationally invisible"[38] to me due to (a) my grounding in engineering, management and systems perspectives; (b) a tendency to look beyond the obvious

---

36 Research on people-intensive services has shown that interactions between the client and provider can create opportunities for transformation in relationships. The service-recovery paradox shows that fixing a service failure can lead to much higher customer loyalty compared to a situation where there was no failure.

37 Action Research emerged out of a need to bridge theory and practice. It involves elements of reflection and understanding why something is working or not. There are similar suggestions made for practitioners to reflect on their work and improve their practice (Schon, 1983). Since I originally started as a researcher I adopted the action research style. However, over time I tried to shift the focus to reflecting on the practice.

38 A term coined by Shotter (1993) to denote our tendency to ignore many aspects of reality.

as a consultant,[39] and (c) the prevalent patterns of interaction in multi-sourced GSNs. And, I realized that I was not alone in this situation. My interactions with several other people in GSNs such as colleagues, clients, competitors, partners, and analysts revealed that this situation is endemic. As managers or consultants most of us seem to rely more on concepts such as values, visions, strategies, scorecards, structures, processes, resources, for managing our organizations. And we hope that all these concepts will somehow shape the interactions among stakeholders and generate predictable outcomes. When it works we call it "leadership" or frame it as a "best practice". When it does not work we blame the individuals or re-search for better concepts to predict and control behaviours. But, most often we end up in highly constrained patterns of relating, feeling stuck or feeling unable to act, to the point where inaction may be the only way to express our free will.

I have grown increasingly disenchanted with this way of working. My experience since 2001 was telling me that while management concepts are necessary, they may not be sufficient to shape our interactions. I wondered if human interaction was more natural and central to how we think and act. And revisiting the theory of Complex Responsive Processes by Professor Ralph Stacey and his colleagues at University of Hertfordshire around 2005 helped clarify the importance and complexity of human interaction (Stacey, 2001; Shaw, 2002). Guided by this theory and related literature, I started looking more closely at our day-to-day interactions in organizations such as meetings, reviews, workshops, informal events, and during lunch/coffee. I also tried

---

39 McKenna (2006) refers to a tendency among consulting firms to project an image as the "Newest Profession".

to understand how these operated in interfaces such as supplier-customer, strategy-operations, sales-delivery, business-technology, and support-core. I looked at these interfaces in different types of GSNs: industry verticals—banking & financial services, insurance, manufacturing, retail & travel; service lines such as traditional ADMS and testing, package implementations and high-value consulting; and accounts of different sizes varying from $2 million to $100 million. I did this in a spirit of action research while enacting different roles in two different organizations. This journey across the value chain of IT services firms has given me sufficient clues about the fact that paying attention to local interactions can generate possibilities for exploring new directions in GSNs. This book is an attempt to make sense of this experience.

Through a narrative and reflexive inquiry[40] into the micro-politics of everyday interactions in Indian IT services, I will show how the pursuit of higher-level strategic capabilities such as integration, consulting and innovation has over time got equated to NOTHING. I will draw attention to how managers and employees actually interact and think about these challenges in everyday work. How they explore or close conversations on strategic choices? What ideologies and beliefs guide such strategic choices? How are these translated into change initiatives? What kind of rhetoric is used to implement such change initiatives? How are such change initiatives interpreted by employees (knowledge workers) at different levels, in a setup where they are distributed across different locations and time zones, and are not under the control of one manager or one organization?[41] How asymmetries in power

---

40 "Reflexivity is thinking about how we are thinking, asking ourselves who we are, what we doing together, why are we doing it" (Stacey, 2012).

41 Employees in IT services may be controlled by two–three managers such as, the Project Manager, Practice Manager and Sales Lead in the Geography.

with stakeholders such as clients and industry/financial analysts affect these choices? How it could bring their ideologies into this mix? For instance, clients themselves may be influenced by contentious ideas such as "shareholder value" or "employee liquidity" or "performance culture" promoted by Investment Bankers and Management Consultants.[42] I will also show how paying attention to the ordinary day-to-day interactions can lead to new forms of strategic advantage and possibilities for turning the dominant discourse on its head.

This inquiry is not intended to be a diagnostic study about any firm or its managers. The intent is to show that a narrative and reflexive inquiry, unlike other forms of abstractions, has the potential to bring out the richness in everyday ordinary work and point to alternative formulations. This book should encourage managers to pursue such an inquiry so that they can provide "intelligible formulations" to complex situations that may have become a "chaotic welter of impressions for others" in the organization.[43]

Why should anyone be interested in this inquiry?

First, the questions that I am reflecting on are highly relevant for the future of the Indian IT services. While these questions have

---

These vary by location of the employee—onsite or offshore. Employees in these locations align with relevant sources of power to reduce conflicts or further their own interests.

42 Ho (2009) argued that the industry-wide restructuring that happened in the Americas can be linked to the liquidity culture within Investment banking firms. Similarly, McKenna (2006) and Macdonald (2013) have shown cases where management consultants imposed their culture of performance on to their clients.

43 Shotter (1993) argued that the core ability of a manager was not in finding and applying true or false theories. It was instead to do with framing complex issues in a manner that can restore a flow of action.

been there for more than two decades and some progress has been made, firms predominantly treat higher level capabilities as nothing. My observation, like that of several others in the industry, is that the traditional sources of value are fast drying up and the demand for real knowledge-intensive work is slowly beginning to surface.[44] This calls for a deep reflection on how firms have approached strategic capabilities, i.e., managing NOTHING. It took a long time for me to realize that there could be more to this "nothing" than meets the eye. It was only in the process of writing this book that I have been able to see the evolution of strategic capabilities in a new light as properties emerging out of the patterns of human relating. I hope this book will inspire similar attempts among those interested in this issue, however insignificant or unconnected that experience might appear. "A reflexive inquiry can clarify the difference between 20 years of experience and one year of experience repeated 20 times" (Bolton, 2009).

Second, my experience involves looking at these issues during critical transitions in management and market across three different types of firms.

1. One of the earliest software product firms in India and its attempt to move into services business that failed. I had a very short stint at this company but observed this critical transition over a period of one and a half years.

2. A firm from a reputed business group that has grown to be one of the top global IT services firms. Its journey from 1998 to 2008 under a new leader shows how the

---

44 The muted Q4 2015 results of most Indian IT firms have triggered a fresh debate on the future of the Indian IT industry. Analysts suggest that it may be more than a currency-related issue. It may be a symptom of the difficulty to adapt to new realities.

strong momentum for its core IT services business made it difficult to develop distinctive capabilities and largely moved to a cost-leadership model that has been very successful and highly profitable.

3. A firm that sought to differentiate and grow very fast by adopting a fractal organizational model, brand building and inorganic strategies, but suffered a fatal injury and eventually got acquired by another firm. As the industry matures and consolidates, new forms of organizational arrangements will emerge in GSNs that will challenge the identity of people. The perspective put forward in this book will aid people in making sense of such challenges.

Third, my observation is that there are a number of people in the industry such as clients,[45] leaders, managers, employees playing different roles who are constantly trying to evolve new work practices, but feel that their span of control is limited. They believe that change has to start at the top. On the other hand senior managers are realizing that their control is limited to defining policies or rules and it does not guarantee full co-operation and control over outcomes. This is the paradox of control, emerging out of the complexity of human interaction.[46] The message for both is that there is no magical way of setting

---

45 A similar challenge exists for client organizations that have adopted multi-sourcing. How do client managers enhance their internal capabilities in the wake of outsourcing? How do they make sense of and assimilate the best practices of different vendors? How are these shaped by the underlying patterns of relating within client organizations? Similarly, analyst firms face the challenge of making sense of emerging trends in the industry through a process of interacting with different stakeholders such as clients, product vendors, IT service providers, where they have to constantly differentiate between what people say and what they actually do.

46 This is the paradox of control discussed in the works of Ralph Stacey.

pre-conditions and hoping that change will happen. Yes, one can do a lot to control the pre-conditions through interventions like policy, structure and resource allocation. It can surely stifle certain activities, but it may not be sufficient to enable identity change or transformation. Transformation depends on how managers and employees participate in the ongoing conversation and take a reflexive view of what is really happening and asking why we are doing what we are doing. In addition it is important to recognize that not all the people in a GSN will have the appetite for change at the same time and in the same way, but could be open to change at different times and in different ways. The themes discussed in this book will point managers and employees towards such possibilities.

Fourth, grappling with these issues has also pushed me to explore the prevalent workplace interactions and managerial practices. It is clear that effective participation in everyday interactions in GSNs requires better skills in paying attention to the present moment, the interaction process and rhetoric-responsive ways[47], and spontaneity/improvization. And such skills develop out of repeated participation in everyday interactions. The possibility of learning these skills collectively can be a major source of motivation for IT professionals. This book will point readers to such practices. While the book is written about the specific context of Indian IT, the issues are relevant for leadership in most organizations.

---

47 Shotter (1993) argued for the centrality of rhetoric-responsive ways in managing people and organizations, and the limitations of the recursive-representational methods promoted in management theory.

Organization of the book

The book is divided into four sections and 10 chapters. Section I provides the introduction and theoretical foundation. Sections II, III and IV discuss the three key elements of Managing Nothing. These three sections are written as a socio-historical narrative and organized in a timeline starting from 1996 to 2015. Each chapter discusses one type of strategic capability. The readers can either read a chapter/section in isolation or the whole book from beginning to end.

Section I comprises two chapters:

- In Chapter 1, I have outlined the background, purpose and structure of the book.
- In Chapter 2, I will throw light on the nature of complexity in Indian IT services by drawing upon relevant literature. I will show how complexity in Indian IT services emerges from interactions among people as they grapple with different characteristics of the work such as levels of knowledge-intensity, intangible nature of services, and global distribution of work. I will then use the theory of complexity to show why it is useful to understand Indian IT services as complex evolving Global Service Networks, and point to a certain way of living with paradoxes that relies less on abstractions/best practices, but more on observing and amplifying the differences that emerge out of patterns of interaction among people.

In Section II, I reflect on my experience in participating in some of the early attempts to move up the value chain in one of the leading Indian IT firms from 1996 to 2004. I will show how the firm invested in building higher level capabilities as early as 1980, but struggled to institutionalize and develop a distinctive model due to differences in the way leaders experienced their reality, especially the paradox of cost and value and the conflicting demands of domestic versus global markets. The firm eventually chose to pursue cost-leadership in the global market. I do this in three chapters:

- In Chapter 3, I discuss the challenge in institutionalizing integrative or design thinking to change the way consultants think about problems. This is a case where the leader embarked on a vision, as early as the 1980s, to set up an R&D centre to develop and institutionalize a holistic approach to problem-solving in its services business—management consultancy and computer consultancy (IT services). This resulted in some very high-profile management consultancy engagements in the domestic market, and established the firm as a thought leader. However, significantly higher growth of the export-oriented IT services business, changes in leadership in the mid-1990s, and the dissolution of the management consultancy division in the late 1990s led to attempts to realign the R&D unit to the IT services business, only to be met with a lot of resistance. The unit was almost dissolved in 2001. Why and how did visionary leaders, powerful personalities, and intelligent professionals go through this kind of struggle, when at a high level everyone seemed to agree that it was a good thing to do?

- In Chapter 4, I discuss the struggle to develop a consulting model that could complement the core IT services business. It started with a decision to dissolve a viable management consulting unit and absorb it into the core IT services business in 1998. This decision (a sort of creative destruction) resulted in a loss of identity of the management consulting unit and some professionals. Over the next three–four years some small groups tried to fill this void, but they did not scale up. Five years later the leadership of the firm re-discovered consulting as a strategic growth area and launched a consulting practice in 2005. When industry analysts evaluated the status of consulting in Indian IT, it was clear that this firm had lost an opportunity to create a distinctive model. How and why did this attempt at creative destruction[48] go wrong?

- In Chapter 5, I provide a glimpse into the politics of organizational realignment that took place from 1998 to 2004. It started with an attempt to adopt a consensus type of leadership and creative destruction of some competencies that led to chaos and confusion. It lasted for about three–four years, but the firm kept growing very fast. A new leadership team with a strong legitimacy for scaling up the business through cost-leadership emerged in 2003. In this environment, the pursuit of higher level capabilities was subtly reduced to NOTHING or considered not worth pursuing seriously. How did this transition happen?

In Section III, I discuss the journey from 2004 to 2008 when leaders who rose from the ranks of the IT services firm, aggressively pursued the goal of becoming a global firm and initiated a number of global management practices to transform sales and delivery. I will show how people in sales and delivery struggled with these

---

48 Creative destruction describes the process of industrial mutation that incessantly revolutionizes the economic structure from within, incessantly destroying the old one, incessantly creating a new one. This idea brought to light by economist Joseph Schumpeter was later promoted by Management thinkers and consultants as a practice for organizational change and innovation.

top-down interventions that did not seem to appreciate their reality. I will throw light on how I experienced and triggered some change in these two critical sources of power in existing client relationships (also called Existing Business Development, EBD). It involved understanding and facilitating change in constrained patterns of relating among three entities—the client, the employees in key accounts (sales/delivery and onsite/offshore staff), and senior management at onsite (sales) and offshore (delivery). During the journey I went through some fundamental shifts in my thinking and started to get a glimpse of the richness in the process of human interaction and emergence of novelty and change, two critical elements of innovation. I discuss this in three chapters:

- In Chapter 6, I narrate the experience in co-evolving client access & service innovation in a multi-sourcing environment, a complex web of interactions among different species where collaboration and competition can happen simultaneously. I will show how interactions with some client managers spawned new interactions with others and eventually led to the development of deep trust with the client organization, an alternative path in the face of the cost versus value paradox.

- In Chapter 7, I talk about triggering strategic conversations in key accounts—primarily sales and delivery staff at onsite—to help them make sense of the corporate initiatives that were launched by the senior management to move the organization into a higher orbit. I will also show how my attempts to explore interactions with onsite project teams led to some positive experiences and revealed some problematic assumptions that guided the thinking of the client-facing units.

- In Chapter 8, I dwell on another major change initiative (Knowledge Management) that was launched by the senior management in 2006; there was a quick realization that it was not yielding desired results in terms of the quality of knowledge assets produced. The issue was traced to lack of time, training and incentives to codify and share the knowledge. It was in this context that I tried to interact with knowledge workers across different client accounts to help make sense of what they were doing. These micro-interactions and improvizations led to more people joining the conversations and better quality of assets.

In Section IV, I discuss the challenges in re-building confidence in a disrupted organization to re-engage with a marketplace that also went through a major upheaval post the global financial crisis (2008–15). I focus on the challenges in New Business Development (NBD) that is important for future growth and signalling in the market. It is possibly the most turbulent and also most creative phase of my work. I discuss this in two chapters:

- In Chapter 9, I discuss the challenges with strategic marketing in Indian IT services and translating this into NBD opportunities. I draw attention to a deeply ingrained view in Indian IT firms—the dominant focus on process and inadequate attention to content, and how it impacts the ability to sense and respond to market changes. It also points to an ironical situation where a strategic task is outsourced to the weakest team.
- In Chapter 10, I talk about the managerial discourse that took place in the face of two disruptions—one

in the market and the other inside the firm. I will talk about how these disruptions put a support team (domain solutions team) at the centre of attempts to re-engage with the market. While the struggles to alter the power relations have not been entirely fruitful, the attempts to work across boundaries and connecting the dots led to the emergence of a concept that not only provided the firm an early mover advantage in the digital solutions landscape, but also helped in positioning the merged entity as a new force in the marketplace.

In the Epilogue I summarize each of the sections and present the three key elements of Managing Nothing as a way to explore managerial innovation in Indian IT services.

Chapter 2

Within the Obvious: Understanding Complexity and Change in Indian IT Services

The phenomenon of Indian IT services and the broader trend of IT outsourcing and offshoring has received a great deal of attention from academicians, practitioners, and policy makers both in developed and developing countries (Arora, 2001; Dossani, 2005; Athreye, 2005; Castells, 2006; D'Costa, 2011; Barnes, 2013). These studies throw light on different facets of this development, for example, advances in Information and Communication Technologies (ICT) and the Internet, globalization in services, availability of human resources and government policies. While this literature is useful to understand the interplay of various macro-level factors and the overall dynamics of the industry, it does not throw much light on the nature of complexity and management in Indian IT services firms.

In contrast, some scholars and industry leaders have been arguing that the phenomenon of offshoring in services poses new conceptual challenges and needs to be viewed differently.

For example, please see the works of Levy (2005), Doh (2005), Blinder (2006), Palmisano (2006) and Bunyaratavej (2011). It is this line of thinking that I will explore in this chapter, i.e., how do we understand the complexity of Indian IT services and what are the implications for change and management in Indian IT services? I will first provide an overview of the nature of work and organization of a typical Indian IT services firm and highlight terminology common to the industry. I will then show how the workplace interactions in a people-intensive business are shaped by the interplay of three key dimensions: the knowledge-intensive nature of work, the services characteristics of the work, and the global nature of work as shown in the Figure 2.

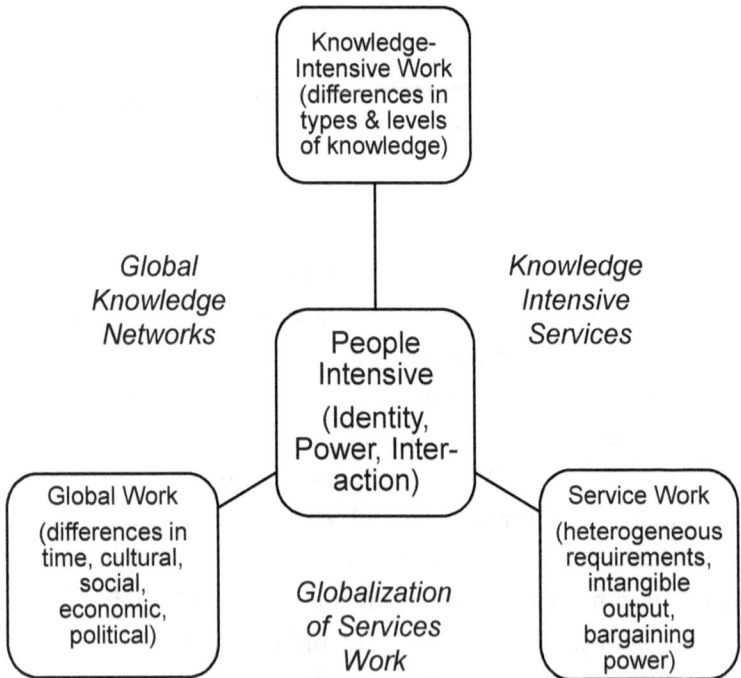

Figure 2: Factors shaping human interactions in Indian IT services

I will show how these characteristics add to the complexity and challenge conventional thinking about organization, management and change:

- as knowledge-intensive services firms that rely on professionals and processes to handle a variety of service requirements of clients from different industries, with different levels of ambiguity and bargaining power;
- as parts of global knowledge networks that maintain competencies in a variety of technologies used by clients across the world, and draw upon global partnerships to track and internalize latest developments in technology; and
- as global service firms where young and aspirational employees interact with customers from different geographies, time-zones and cultures that has implications for their notion of self and identity.

I will then draw upon the theory of complex responsive processes to propose a certain way of thinking about Indian IT services firms in which paying attention to the obvious aspects of day-to-day interactions becomes a central role for managers.

Elements of a typical Indian IT services firm

Let me start with a brief discussion of the key elements of Indian IT services, i.e., clients and why they source IT services, types of IT services, and IT services firms (including managers and employees). Clients try to solve different types of business problems using IT. The level of IT spend varies by industry; industries such as banking and financial services spend about 10–12 per cent of their revenues on IT. Other industries spend around three per cent of their revenues on IT. Client IT leaders manage the budgets by categorizing their IT work into Run-the-Business

(RTB) and Change-the-Business (CTB). RTB typically accounts for about 65–75 per cent of IT budgets and involves activities such as maintenance of IT infrastructure and applications and ensuring their accessibility and availability to the user community (business users, B2B customers, retail consumers). CTB accounts for 25–35 per cent of the IT budget and involves projects that are aimed at changing the IT landscape, developing new applications to suit emerging needs of business or re-engineering applications leveraging emerging technologies. Client IT leaders are under constant pressure to ensure that IT investments deliver value to their business and that IT costs are manageable and vary in relation to the demand. As a consequence, they are always on the lookout for models and partnerships that can allow them to do more with less, address time to market concerns, renew the skills of their workforce and drive technology-led business innovation. Clients therefore rely on IT services like outsourcing and offshoring to address some of these concerns. They adopt different types of sourcing models, hiring external contractors being one of the earliest forms. Since the 1990s, firms have tried to streamline their sourcing practices and adopt sourcing strategies[49] that cater to their interests. Multi-sourcing is one of the preferred strategies, where a client sources services from a set of vendors that have been identified and grouped under certain categories, for instance vendors for consulting/advisory work, vendors for infrastructure and vendors for application development and maintenance work. They have contracts with the vendors for time-periods ranging from three to seven years. The work-packages (request for proposals) are usually floated to these preferred vendors and

---

49 Gonzalez et al. (2006) provide a detailed analysis of outsourcing literature. Oshri et al. (2009) provide a good collection of research and case studies on global outsourcing and offshoring.

through competitive bidding they select the right vendor for a work-package. Recent advances in technologies like cloud and SaaS are also allowing clients to address these challenges in new ways.

IT services companies respond to these requirements by providing different types of services: consulting, application development (including package implementation) and maintenance, support services (including infrastructure like servers, networks and desktops, and business process services). These are either offered through resources on Time and Materials (T&M) basis or carried out as Fixed Bid projects. IT services companies have to manage demand and supply through the following organizational elements: sales, accounts, delivery centres, horizontal competency units (also called service practices) and verticals (also called industry or domain practices). The sales teams are responsible for giving projections on the demand and generating it. An account houses the projects pertaining to a particular client. The accounts may have offshore development centres (ODCs) and onsite components (mostly working out of client locations). Each account would have a sales head and a delivery head—the two primary sources of power in the organization. The sales head owns the client relationship and the top-line, while the delivery head owns the human resources and the bottom line. There are some variations and overlaps here and the boundaries are not water-tight. Sales teams leverage delivery staff to work on proposals and make presentations to clients. Based on their tenure and size, accounts are classified as existing relationships (more than one year) and new relationships (less than one year), large accounts ($50–100 million and above). Accounts are also grouped into different categories based on the maturity of the organization and work in a particular industry or region. In cases where there is a significant amount of work in a particular vertical, accounts are organized around verticals. For instance, all banking and financial services accounts are treated as an independent business unit. Otherwise, most of them are grouped by region (onsite) and by delivery centres (offshore). Horizontal competency units are the third source of power. They typically own certain skills that are niche and need focused efforts to develop and sustain the competency, for instance, Business Intelligence, Analytics, Content Management and BPO. They manage the product alliances, develop and maintain skills in that competency, and deliver projects for different client accounts. The vertical units (called practices or domain teams) house domain consultants, subject matter experts and product specialists in particular industry-native software products like core banking systems. These resources are typically deployed in projects as business analysts and product specialists. They are also called in to help with solution design for proposals. The horizontal and vertical units in some cases are only seen as competency development units, with no P&L responsibility. In addition to these units, there are back-office support units for sales, accounts, delivery centres and horizontal competency teams to take care of activities such as pre-sales (proposal making, collateral preparation and maintenance of repository) and PMO/operations support (pipeline management, resource forecasting, resource management, delivery metrics, and billing). Other functions such as strategy, finance and accounting, training, marketing and branding are usually centralized at the corporate level.

Indian IT services as knowledge-intensive services firms

IT services firms have been recognized as a particular type of Knowledge-Intensive Firms (KIFs) (Alvesson, 2004). KIFs differ from other organizations in terms of the nature of work, how it is managed and organized. The key characteristics of KIFs include: highly qualified individuals doing knowledge-based work; dealing with an intangible nature of services; need for extensive communication for coordination and problem-solving; a fairly high degree of autonomy; use of adaptable and ad hoc organizational forms; and information and power asymmetry. Indian IT services firms exhibit most of the characteristics of KIFs or as Holzweber et al. (2010) argue, they can be seen as knowledge-intensive business services.

The knowledge-intensive nature of the Indian IT firms is a source of one of its key challenges. For instance, employees of Indian IT services firms are expected to learn and develop different competencies on a continuous basis. It starts with the initial training where they need to learn a variety of software engineering methodologies, programming languages and competencies that are in demand in the market. Then they need to learn about the client's domain, business, software processes, and applications (that could be in a variety of technologies including legacy and with different levels of documentation), engage with client's staff or the outgoing vendor to capture knowledge and document it. During the projects, employees will be expected to demonstrate collaborative problem-solving skills. And finally, employees will be expected to learn and document their project experiences and train others. Most of these activities involve some form of abstraction, codification and transfer of knowledge. However, there are also tasks, in some support and testing projects that are considered routine or mundane. The demand-supply situations can result in a mismatch between competence of people and tasks that are allocated to them. This leads to frustration especially in cases where highly qualified and competent knowledge workers are assigned to mundane tasks or legacy technologies that may be critical for the customer and the business. Agrawal et al. (2006) note that

> the industry requires IT professionals to do what would contribute towards customer satisfaction but IT professionals want to work what would give them sense of learning and contribute towards keeping them relevant for the IT services markets in India as well as globally. The pulls from opposite directions are the cause of stress and frustration for IT professionals.

One of the offshoots of this tension is a rationale that the Indian software industry needs to move up the value chain to meet the aspirations of software professionals. In some cases, this aspiration has been twisted and given legitimacy by saying that clients are actually demanding such high-value work from the Indian IT firms. This not only shows the nature of bargaining power that employees have, but also how priorities can change in a people- and knowledge-intensive services business.

Another challenge emerges from the intangible and idiosyncratic nature of client services. It is well known that service industries rely a great deal on effective communication and interaction with the clients/users.[50] However, this has been a problem area for IT services in general and Indian IT services in particular. Rahman and Kurien (2007) observe that "the track record of the IT services industry seems to be poor compared to other customer-oriented industries, in terms of understanding and meeting customer needs, as well as in basic project delivery."

---

50 There is a vast literature on customer satisfaction and innovation in services. Please see Lind and Smud, 1991, Cook, 1999, Hertog, 2000, Sundobo et al, 2001, Sundbo and Gallouj, 2002, Lovelock and Gummesson, 2005, Sampson and Froehle, 2006.

One of the reasons for this problem is in understanding the business needs of its customers and translating them effectively and efficiently into IT systems that meet them.

> There is plenty of anecdotal evidence to suggest that the IT industry expects business to learn to speak its language and not vice versa. It is one of the many ways in which industry demonstrates its relative immaturity compared to other service industries that have learnt to communicate to customers in their language. A majority of the effort is spent on development, maintenance and operation of the IT applications. The proportion of time spent talking to and understanding customers in order to build the right applications is relatively low compared to other consumer oriented industries. *Those that do develop an understanding of the customer perspective are a minority and do not seem to be treated with the same importance as in consumer oriented industries.*

It not only points to the complexity of the task, where people need knowledge of multiple disciplines to understand the problem, but also a paradox since such higher-level capabilities may not be highly regarded in a knowledge-intensive firm.

A third challenge can be seen in the debate on services versus products. Most leaders in Indian IT services strongly believe that services are fundamentally different from product firms and therefore need to be managed differently. Feuerstein (2013) in a study of internationalization strategies of Indian IT service firms, observes that

> While the business model of IT service providers relies on a "relational approach", there is a considerable pressure for standardisation and formalisation of transactions in play, as clients try to fight the dependency on particular providers by spurring competition for standardised services and demand close control of the outsourced projects.

While this study shows how clients can influence decisions of IT firms, there are other reasons why firms focus on standardizing a services business. One of them is to reduce people-dependency. Employees with a good understanding of the systems and relationships with client managers can exhibit strong bargaining power.[51] The other being improved productivity and profitability. In essence, very few actually exploit the unique characteristics of services and the potential for innovation.

There are other ways in which power imbalances between Indian IT vendors and western client organizations shape the reality of Indian IT services (Ravishankar et al., 2013). The study shows how "asymmetric power relations appear to be deeply embedded and implicated in the very process of creation and development of practices within vendor organizations". They also point to an important area of further research—exploring patterns of intra-organizational variations in how employees view strategic initiatives. For instance, "empirical work could examine whether and why a group of middle managers may be cognitively predisposed to frame a strategic initiative as impression management in contrast to senior managers who may be more inclined to frame the same initiative as a capability development exercise". The discussion above shows that characteristics such as knowledge-intensity, service work, asymmetries in power and ideologies produce paradoxes in Indian IT services. An appreciation of these aspects is critical for understanding the

---

51 Knowledge transfer is another contentious topic in the supposedly professional IT services world. While the professional culture of the high-tech global industry assumes open communication and knowledge transfer processes, studies have shown that processes of knowledge transfer, regardless of the nature of culture and technology in a specific place as well as the nature of the knowledge itself, are highly embedded in socio-cultural structures (Zaidman and Brock, 2009).

complexity and change in Indian IT services. Next I will draw upon literature that throws light on the social aspects of self and identity in a global IT services context.

Indian IT services as global services firms

Sociologists from the National Institute of Advanced Studies who did an extended study of Indian IT firms observed that the export-oriented nature of the IT industry in India has significant implications for the nature of work and the modes of organizational control employed (Upadhya and Vasavi, 2008). "For instance, growth of offshoring is immobilising labour in new ways as work is increasingly performed virtually and online, i.e. labour is disembodied, yet connected. This is likely to alter the very experience of work and hence the subjectivity of the worker in significant ways." They also argue that culture has become central to the management of work and workers and this in turn shapes the subjectivities of employees.

> Panoptical management techniques introduced to control the work process are combined with extensive use of indirect or soft management techniques, which are aimed not only at motivating workers to put in extra effort and time but also at alleviating the stress and frustration that is created by the routine nature of the production process.

This combination of direct and indirect techniques of organizational control allows companies to extract the maximum work out of their employees and hence to maximize productivity. They point to an interesting contradiction in the process: "workers are expected to transform themselves into individualised, self-managed and self-directed entrepreneurial employees while at the same time they must perform within a tightly controlled and impersonal management system that tracks their every move and moment." Similar contradictions are highlighted by Nadeem (2011). He argues that globalization produces similarity and difference simultaneously. "On the one hand, offshore spaces of work are constructed in the Western corporate image. On the other, existing values and organizational forms cannot be extended to new social groups without being transformed in the process." In the face of such a contradiction the adoption of modern managerial practices like employee empowerment, flat structures and culture change has largely been superficial, mostly aimed at image building in the eyes of clients. Smart employees can feign compliance with some of the initiatives to further their own goals.

D'Mello and Sahay (2008) explore an important source of instability in global IT services work, mobility. They note that "mobility is an uneven and unpredictable process in which the hope of going in some upward direction is counterbalanced by risks of profession, market, industry, as well as norms of social relations and the individual conditioning and beliefs". They argue that the idea of "nets of social relations"[52] will be important to make sense of mobility in Global Software Work.

> These nets of social relations are inherently dynamic and changing, subject to diverse and sometimes contradictory temporal-spatial as well as cultural pressures and flows. Simultaneously, they are also local places where people assemble and continuously shift within social and professional networks across space and time. In this way, we can conceptualize global software work and global software organizations as increasingly locked and co-evolving cycles of continuous interaction with, as well as reacting to the global. Reflecting the inherent

---

52 An idea floated by Massey (1988).

tensions between stasis and mobility, space and place, these cycles and relations are seen to forge the life-worlds of IT workers, resulting in an itinerant state of existence that we call "permanent transience".

Through a similar study of global software development, Gibbs (2009) points to the important role of tensions in managing complexity and ambiguity in processes of global organizing. He observes that tensions such as autonomy and connectedness, inclusion and exclusion, and empowerment and disempowerment mirror the larger tensions between integration and differentiation inherent in globalization processes. Gibbs suggests that global team interaction needs to be viewed as an ongoing process of negotiating contested meanings in the form of tensions enacted from differing interpretations of work roles, values and processes due to the team's embeddedness in multiple contexts.

Indian IT services as part of global knowledge networks

In the process of servicing clients across the world and their unique technologies, Indian IT firms need to develop partnerships with a variety of Independent Software Vendors (ISVs). These relationships could be strategic global partnerships or need-based alliances. Since clients may choose different ISVs (sometimes multiple products of similar type exist in client landscapes), the Indian IT firms as service providers will need to develop and maintain competencies in different products. For instance, a global banking client could be using different CRM systems for different lines of business or regions. So, the IT service providers will have to maintain competencies in multiple CRM systems. This creates internal tensions within IT services firms. One of the tensions is in deciding which competencies to invest in. Managers show an inclination to invest in competencies where there is committed business. Clients on the other hand would want to understand the depth of competency before purchasing services. It is a typical chicken or egg situation for the owners of the competency. Similarly, another type of conflict emerges in the context of specific opportunities—which partner to align with for a particular opportunity? Firms that have accumulated multiple competencies use this variety to attract clients. On the other hand IT services providers who are constrained in terms of resources and do not have strong client access tend to maintain opportunistic relationships with ISVs and make investment decisions based on the trust they repose in the owners of the competency.

Another aspect of the relationship with ISVs is that they can go beyond a simple Go-To-Market partnership. In some cases, the IT services firm may actually be servicing the ISV's business or product development. Vice-versa, the IT services firm may license the ISVs product for its own use. In other words, IT services firms can have a 360-degree relationship with the ISVs, where traditional definitions of customer, partner or supplier become contestable. It also makes IPR a contestable issue. Knowledge in these partnerships emerges from the interactions among people and cannot be restricted by organizational boundaries. Trust becomes a crucial element in sustaining such relationships.

The discussion above points to the need to take a fresh look at the way we manage in Indian IT services. The conventional ideas of managerial control appear to generate new contradictions that are creating different kinds of stresses on individuals and their identities, and there is a suggestion that it may be better to conceptualize Indian IT services as an evolving network of relations. Interestingly, research on complexity has shown that such a network of relations among people can produce paradoxical situations. It is also emerging that mainstream management ideas that rely on assumptions such as linear causality are inadequate for dealing with such dynamically evolving non-linear scenarios.[53] Similar calls for rethinking organizations and management are emerging from leading thinkers.[54] I will discuss the complexity perspective next.

Indian IT services as complex responsive processes of relating

One group that has been developing a certain way of using complexity ideas to understand and facilitate organizational change is the Complexity Management Centre at University of Hertfordshire. Professor Ralph Stacey and his colleagues at

---

53 One of the theories that has shown promise to guide thinking in a fresh direction is complexity theory. Meyer et al. (2005) argue that "shifting industry boundaries, new network forms, emerging sectors, and volatile ecosystems have become the stuff of everyday organizational life." They urge scholars to transcend the general linear model and embrace ideas like field configuration, complex adaptive systems, and autocatalytic feedback. They recommend conducting natural histories of organizational fields, and paying especially close attention to turning points when fields are away from equilibrium and discontinuous changes are afoot. Similarly, Urry (2005) suggested that globalization could be conceptualized as a series of adapting and co-evolving global systems, each characterized by unpredictability, irreversibility and co-evolution.

54 We see similar thinking emerging in the field of management. For instance, debating on the future of management research, Birkinshaw et al. (2014) observe that "the challenges for the discipline can be addressed if we approach them with the right degree of reflexivity, openness, and level-headedness ... we have to get our hands dirty and closely observe and study, or even live with, people in organizations—rather than relying on arm's length, or at worst ivory tower, approaches that are based on lab data or proxies." Henry Mintzberg in an interview about his book *Managing* says that "our current knowledge of organizations is similar to the science of biology before biologists had names for different species of mammals. They were all mammals, just as consultants say the latest technique is good for everybody. It's as if we were incapable of distinguishing between bears and beavers. I think it's amazing how few people are actively researching managerial work—empirical studies of what managers do—as their main focus. Many people are concerned with organizational issues, but because they don't actually study what managers do, they lack insight into the essence of organizations" (Kliener, 2010).

this centre have been developing this perspective for more than a decade. They have brought together the ideas of complexity (Prigogine and Stengers, 1984, Kauffman, 1995, Allen, 1998 and several others), process sociology (Elias, 1991), philosophy of present (Mead, 1932), Symbolic Interactionism (Blumer, 1969), Conversations (Shotter, 1993, 2005), Interaction Rituals (Goffman, 1967, Collins, 2004) and Improvisation (Johnstone, 1999) to develop the theory of Complex Responsive Processes of Relating (Stacey, 2001, 2003, Patricia, 2002, Stacey & Patricia, 2006). According to Stacey (2012),

> Complex responsive processes of interaction describe what people are already doing in organizations. They accomplish their work by engaging in conversation; they engage in power relations of inclusion and exclusion; they make choices reflecting their ideologies; they abstract from their experience to understand what is going on; they carry out procedures and take up rules and other techniques ... the theory is useful not because it yields general prescriptions or general techniques. It is useful because it directs attention to what we are actually doing, matters which are rarely reflected upon. It is useful because it directs attention away from just the techniques to the processes in which the techniques are being used. The dominant discourse focuses attention on the techniques and largely ignores the processes of using them.

I think this is an important observation; the theory of complex responsive urges us to be aware and possibly eliminate some of the inconsistent abstractions that have crept into our ways of understanding and participating in social networks. Stacey also observes that leadership and management is the ability to exercise practical judgement.

The exercise of practical judgment is highly context-related. It is exercised in highly uncertain and unpredictable, unique situations. It cannot, therefore, be generalized or dealt with in the manner of second order abstractions. The exercise of practical judgment calls for wider awareness of the group, organizational and societal patterns within which some issue of importance is being dealt with. This requires a sensitive awareness of more than the focal points in a situation, namely awareness of what is going on at the margins of what is being taken as the focus. Practical judgment is the experience-based ability to notice more of what is going on and intuit what is most important about a situation. It is the ability to cope with ambiguity and uncertainty as well as the anxiety this generates.... Practical judgment is not an individual possession, competence or skill set. Practical judgment is, rather, social processes; interdependent individuals can only develop and sustain the skills of practical judgment through participation with each other.

This is a key observation and highly relevant to IT services organization where work is invariably part of a network demanding effective ways of participation. Practical judgement develops through narrative and reflexivity, participation in conversation to widen and deepen communication, spontaneity and improvisation and rhetoric and truth telling (Stacey, 2012). Stacey also argues that the assumption that one person or a coalition of senior leaders can create conditions, influence the game, and design the system to bring about improvement reflects an ideology. We can never act without ideology, but ideology can blind us and distort what we can see.

This theory has very strong relevance in an Indian IT services organization. I will show through the rest of the chapters that most of the challenges pertaining to developing higher-level capabilities have been shrouded in different ideologies and patterns of power relations thus affecting the responses to paradoxical situations. An understanding of Indian IT services from the perspective of complex responsive processes as Global IT Service Networks (GSNs) urges leaders, managers and employees to pay more attention to what is going on in everyday work. In other words look "within-the-obvious" aspects of local everyday interactions[55] and reflect on them to improve practical judgement of the collective which can pave the way for doing things differently. This counter-intuitive proposition is the most realistic and practical guidance for leaders and employees to participate effectively in the dynamic and paradoxical world of Indian IT services firms.

Conclusion

In this chapter I have outlined key perspectives about Indian IT services organizations and drawn attention to a line of thinking that needs greater emphasis. There is an increasing amount of literature pointing to how service interactions among people

---

55 The process of how meaning is created through participation in everyday talk is also emphasized by ethnographers who have actively probed the IT world (Cefkin, 2009). In an earlier work on sales talk in a global IT firm Cefkin (2007), observes that "The element of talk, with its potential for unruliness, plays a central role in this otherwise hyper-rationalized activity focused around numbers, accounting and calculability. I suggest that to understand such signification processes and the forms of meaning that emerge through them we must look beyond the content of enunciated statements to consider the forms they take over time. I propose that participation in the sales pipeline process, particularly the meetings, forms a part of sales-people's rhythmscape of work. By situating sites of expression in the notion of a rhythmscape, I point to the broader performance landscape in which employees participate, and experience their organization and the market more broadly. By doing so, we are reminded to recognize the multiple levels of meaning and signification embedded in ordinary workplace tools and practices, including those intended for other uses, when considering recommendations to and designs for tools, processes and interventions that support them." Similarly, Grounded Theory is also gaining ground in the world of software development (Badreddin, 2013).

with differences in knowledge, power, values, and ideology can result in a network of relations that can in turn contribute to paradoxes in Indian IT services. I have also shown how the theory of complex responsive processes can explain such a situation and guide leaders and managers to pay attention to the day-to-day interactions in the workplace to make sense of and explore possibilities for change. This line of inquiry forms the theoretical basis of this book.

Early Attempts to Move Up the Value Chain

"The words of truth are always paradoxical."

—*Lao Tzu*

Chapter 3

Grand Vision, Lost in Translation: Struggle to Institutionalize Integrative Thinking

In this chapter I discuss the challenges that a leading Indian IT services firm Digital Consultancy and Technology Services (DCTS) faced in institutionalizing integrative thinking[1] among its managers, consultants and IT professionals. It was one of the earliest attempts to move up the value chain in Indian IT services, involving some of the best leaders and thinkers, and backed by strong executive sponsorship for more than 15 years. A key belief that guided the initiative was that managers, consultants and IT professionals would be keen to acquire a higher level thinking capability, and that such capability could be institutionalized through training, and practice in the domestic market. This belief got severely challenged in later years, especially from the mid-1990s in the wake of high global demand for relatively simpler

---

1   Integrative thinking emphasizes a holistic approach to complex problem solving. Over the years several approaches have emerged with similar intent, notably, Systems Thinking and Design Thinking.

programming skills and the phenomenal rise of the firm's IT services export business. I was associated with this initiative between 1996 and 2000, a turbulent phase, when attempts were being made to realign the initiative to changing market realities and communicate its relevance to the new leadership. Personally, it was a very challenging time for me that pushed me to question the assumptions behind integrative thinking, managerial thought and organizational change. By the turn of the millennium most of my beliefs, professional and personal, were shattered.

Foundations of DCTS

Let me start with some historical background of DCTS. The firm started its operations as a shared electronic data processing centre for one of the reputed business groups in India. In the late 1960s it was christened as DCTS and given the freedom to tap into the nascent but emerging market for data processing and computer services. Around the same time, DCTS also got a new Managing Director (MD), a highly committed[2] and visionary leader, who had established his credentials in developing one of the group companies into a best-in-class business leveraging the power of IT.[3] Over the next three decades, he dedicated himself to building DCTS and the ecosystem around it, and establishing the platform from which consulting and knowledge-intensive IT services could take off.

One of the key elements of this platform was the strong commitment to a holistic and rigorous approach to problem-

---

2   Armed with a postgraduate degree from MIT and some work experience in the US and Canada, he returned to India in 1948 and committed himself to the process of industrial development of independent India.
3   In the late 1960s only three other electrical power companies in the world had gone digital.

solving. The MD strongly believed that holistic thinking was critical to produce solutions that are acceptable to multiple stakeholders; and that high technical competence has to be enhanced with sufficient peripheral vision for an engineer to become a successful consultant. He constantly tried to inculcate this perspective among his managers and consultants. One body of knowledge that he thought would be very relevant in this pursuit was Systems Engineering.[4] This belief can be traced back to his association with the Massachusetts Institute of Technology (MIT) in the late 1940s. It was in MIT that he was first exposed to concepts of cybernetics and systems while attending the lectures of Norbert Wiener.[5] MIT was also home to Jay Forrester who promoted the idea of applying IT to solve complex managerial and societal problems in a holistic manner using System Dynamics.[6]

Another key element of the platform was the importance of academic partnerships in developing a people- and knowledge-intensive services business (management consultancy and IT services). The MD had developed strong linkages with reputed academic institutions in India such as the Indian Institutes of Technology (IITs), Tata Institute of Fundamental Research (TIFR), and Indian Institute of Science (IISc) since his return to India in the 1950s and during his work at the earlier group

---

4   Systems engineering is an inter-disciplinary approach to complex problem-solving. It gained importance after the Second World War aided by developments in Systems Sciences and Cybernetics and the successful mission to moon.
5   Conway & Siegelman (2005) provide a detailed history of Cybernetics and why Norbert Wiener is regarded as the father of Cybernetics.
6   Forrester (1961) showed how systems dynamics could be used to model industrial dynamics and world dynamics. MIT is also home to Peter Senge. In the 1990s, Peter Senge popularized Systems Thinking by linking it with the concept of a Learning Organization.

company.[7] There were particularly strong linkages with IIT Kanpur which had taken a lead in the area of computer sciences.[8] He also built a strong rapport with several faculty members at IIT Kanpur, including one professor of aeronautical engineering.[9] In addition to developing the Indian academic ecosystem around DCTS, the MD also reached out to academicians in American universities while targeting the US market for IT services exports. One such interaction had brought him in touch with Professor John Warfield from George Mason University. The area of mutual interest was Systems Engineering. In the 1970s Professor Warfield had developed a methodology for group problem-solving called Unified Program Planning that leveraged a semi-mathematical technique called Interpretive Structural Modelling (ISM) (Warfield, 1976). In late 1970s the MD, in consultation with the Aeronautics Professor, invited Professor Warfield to conduct a series of workshops in India to demonstrate the method and its applications. Workshops were conducted in New Delhi, Mumbai, Pune, and Bangalore. These workshops seem to have convinced the MD about the value of institutionalizing such integrative thinking capability in DCTS. The workshops also highlighted the potential to develop a computerized tool to aid group problem-solving.

---

7   The academic connection also helped in gaining access to computers for a key digitization initiative in the earlier group company.

8   IIT Kanpur was set up with assistance from leading academic institutions in the US. In the process a number of faculty members developed good linkages with faculty in American institutions.

9   During one of the visits to IIT Kanpur, the Professor of Aeronautics had invited the MD to address his students to assuage their concerns about the limited options available for aeronautical engineers in India. In response the MD put a view that Systems Engineering capability was at the heart of aeronautical engineering, and this capability can be extended to different challenges. So, when he decided to start Systems Engineering discipline in DCTS, he immediately thought of the Aeronautics Professor.

DCTS developed the ISM software in the early 1990s. This tool became one of my best friends later on.

A design centre for knowledge-intensive services

Once the MD was convinced about the value in institutionalizing Systems Engineering in DCTS, he spent close to two years persuading the Aeronautics Professor and his wife to leave IIT Kanpur and join DCTS to give shape to the Systems Engineering programme. The MD also promised full freedom to the Professor in shaping this programme. The Professor, who was in his early 50s (a few years younger than the MD), joined DCTS in 1982. Once the Professor started thinking about the programme, he felt that Systems Engineering as a problem-solving methodology should be guided by a theory of change. Since he was convinced that the cybernetic concept of feedback could explain stability and change, he suggested that the centre be named the Systems and Cybernetics Centre (SCC). SCC became operational in 1982.

In parallel, the MD was also having discussions with academicians at IIT Kanpur, IIT Bombay, faculty at one of the American universities, and the Board and Chairman of the group (to which DCTS belonged) about setting up a Centre for Research, Design and Development (CRDD). This was set up as a formal R&D centre in 1982 in Pune.[10] The intent of this centre was to focus on "Design Thinking", which was recognized as a critical element in developing a differentiated R&D capability.[11] Software Engineering was a major thrust area

---

10 The Pune location was chosen for its proximity to academic institutions and was slightly away from the corporate office in Mumbai, but also reachable at short notice.
11 The idea to focus on Design Thinking was recommended by the panel of senior academicians after reviewing the state of R&D in the universities across the world and the industry within the country.

of this centre—mirroring the core business of DCTS. A Professor of Computer Science, in his mid-30s, who also had a stint at Carnegie Mellon University and IIT Kanpur and was passionate about industrializing software development, was invited to head the Software Engineering Centre (SEC). These two centres were seen as two key investments from the perspective of the MD. His vision was that a deeper understanding of Software Engineering and Systems Engineering would provide a strong foundation for developing good consultants and efficient processes for delivering holistic IT solutions to complex industrial and societal problems. However, he may not have anticipated that this vision would get challenged over time due to some small differences that crept in during the inception of the centres in terms of location, HR practices and target businesses. While SEC started operating out of CRDD in Pune, SCC started off in Hyderabad since the Professor of Aeronautics had some reservation in operating out of Pune. On the other hand while SCC adopted the mainstream DCTS rules, SEC had a separate set of rules and practices to attract and retain relevant staff. Another difference was in the choice of problems. While SEC started working with the challenges faced by the IT services unit, SCC devoted itself to the challenges faced by the management consultancy unit. These initial differences in location, HR practices and target businesses widened the differences between the centres over time.

Co-evolution of SCC and management consultancy

Over the next decade and a half, the Professor and Head of SCC devoted his efforts to addressing challenges in management consulting projects and institutionalizing the approach. One of the earliest clients that SCC worked for was an Indian university helping the latter streamline the examination system and reduce the time to publish results. This need apparently emerged during a conversation between the MD and the Chancellor of a reputed university (also the Governor of the state where the University was located). The Chancellor had inquired whether DCTS would be able to do this project in the small budget of $10,000 that they had at their disposal.[12] The MD did not seem keen and asked the Head of SCC if he was interested in taking up this study as a pro-bono exercise. The Professor took it up and was able to demonstrate that a good quality consulting assignment could be delivered within the given budget. This was appreciated by the stakeholders and led to more interesting studies. One of the studies that followed was for an Urban Development Authority, helping them corporatize without losing sight of societal objectives. Similar work was done for other departments and public bodies of the central government (Government of India) to help them adapt to the changing socio-political-economic conditions that were emerging in the mid-to-late 1980s. SCC also worked on engagements that involved trying to figure out why central government aid was not reaching people in different states[13] or helping some of the economically backward but resource rich states to drive industrialization. These were high profile and politically sensitive engagements. By the mid-1990s, SCC and the Head had contributed to about 40+ such high profile management consulting engagements and built a rich knowledge base on applying a systems approach to complex managerial and policy issues. This established DCTS as a thought leader in the domestic market. During this period, the Professor and Head also tried to institutionalize this practice in two ways. First, through an action research approach and leveraging his

---

12 In 1980s, the exchange rate was about Rs 10 for 1 USD.
13   A problem that is being addressed today due to technology advances in identity management and payments.

scientific and philosophical understanding[14], the Professor defined a holistic consulting methodology called Multi-Laws. It had a unique way of combining state-of-the-art systems models to address complex management consulting assignments.[15] Some of the popular modelling techniques and models used were the Cybernetic Model;[16] understanding Stakeholders, Needs, Alterables, Constraints (Sage, 1977); Interpretive Structural Modelling (Warfield, 1976); Viable Systems Model (Beer, 1979); Autopoiesis (Maturana and Varela, 1980); and Living Systems Model (Miller, 1978). Second, the Professor tried to create a set of evangelists for Systems Engineering by mentoring several consultants in DCTS. Some of these consultants later went on to hold senior leadership positions at DCTS. The Professor also developed SCC into a centre of excellence with a core team of 10–15 people and set up knowledge exchange programmes with academic institutions abroad.

The Head of SCC, due to his vast experience and his ability to quickly sense what was going on in a situation, also played another role—as a sounding board for the MD and other senior leaders of DCTS on various strategic issues. For instance, one of the dilemmas that DCTS faced in the early days was the nature

---

14 The Professor leveraged his understanding of Indian philosophy and inquiry systems such as Bhagavad Gita and Upanishads in giving shape to the methodology. It inspired Stafford Beer to re-interpret Viable Systems.

15 The Professor largely picked up models that he felt represented different laws of complexity, like requisite variety, hierarchy, stability and self-organization. This seemed like a more powerful way of combining different perspectives compared to methodologies like Total Systems Intervention (Flood and Jackson, 1991) or Multi-methodology (Mingers, 1995).

16 The Cybernetic Model appeared similar to the influence diagrams used in System Dynamics. However, it was not very rigid in terms of defining elements and relations. It was more seen as a natural model of a situation that could help understand the critical influences, feedback loops and get a sense of the spirit of the problem.

of participation in the domestic market. In the 1980s and early 1990s most firms including DCTS were highly export-oriented and did very little IT work in India. Some leaders argued that since there was very little IT spending in the Indian market at that point, it did not make sense to focus on this market other than for training. The Head of SCC used a systems perspective to present a different argument. He suggested that DCTS should make at least that much revenue in the Indian market to pay off its consultants for a year. That would not only provide it the necessary stability against external threats, but also expose their consultants to the unique challenges of applying IT in developing economies. After some deliberation the MD apparently started taking a serious interest in this direction. A shift in the government's focus on computerization in the late 1980s also helped matters. Today, DCTS is one of the strongest IT players in the domestic market with government initiatives and public sector institutions. Senior leaders valued the Professor for this practical judgement. However, this had an undesirable side-effect as well. Most leaders started associating SCC strongly with the Professor. It also set up an expectation gap that others in the SCC team had to cope with in their interactions. In addition, there was the challenge of constant attrition in the team.[17] A couple of consultants who had developed a liking for Warfield's "Interactive Planning" went on to start their own consulting firms. One consultant developed a deep interest in Indian philosophy and Vedic literature and went on to pursue that. As a result, the Professor was on the constant lookout for candidates who could help pursue the agenda of SCC. It was one such recruitment drive that I came across while pursuing my PhD at the Indian Institute of Technology, Madras (IITM).

---

17 Attrition was already an issue that was impacting the IT industry, and this effect was felt by SCC as well.

Joining SCC—destiny calling?

I first heard about SCC in 1992 from a senior in the PhD programme at IITM. At that time SCC was one of the few groups in India that was actively applying systems and cybernetic concepts to address public systems issues in a commercial context. There were other groups like the Administrative Staff College of India, Systems Research Institute in Pune, and some groups in IIT Delhi and IIT Kharagpur that were exploring these in an academic environment. In the winter of 1995 I came across an advertisement from SCC, but noticed that I had missed the last date for submission by about two weeks. All the same I applied and was pleasantly surprised when I was invited for an interview in February 1996. After getting through the written test,[18] the Professor and Head of SCC interviewed me and in March 1996 I got the appointment letter. It seemed like destiny calling. But, the letter stated that I was being considered for the position of Assistant Systems Analyst (Probationer) which is normally offered to engineers with one–two years of experience. I wrote back to the Professor that I would like them to reconsider the offer given that I was on the verge of submitting my PhD thesis and also had 1.5 years of work experience in software product development. When I went to meet the Professor, I also found the HR manager in the room. The HR manager pointed out that since I had not yet submitted my thesis and my software work experience was not relevant to SCC, they didn't see a justification in my request. I clarified to him that I had completed my synopsis (and draft of the thesis) and my PhD work was exactly in the area of interest to SCC. After a few minutes of discussion, the Professor suggested that I should consider joining and he would get the necessary

18 Standard test administered to check basic competence of IT professionals.

corrections done post my joining.[19] These were early indicators that SCC was not modelled like CRDD and SEC, at least from an HR perspective.

I joined SCC in May 1996 after submitting my PhD synopsis. About 10 people had joined at the same time taking the total team size to about 20. All of us, the newcomers, were put through a two-month-long training programme. Through the training process and interactions with the Professor and senior colleagues at SCC and also by poring over past reports, I got to know more about the unit and the nature of projects they had done in collaboration with the management consultancy division for public sector institutions in India. It was during this period that I also came to know about the MD's view of SCC being a design centre for the consultancy business, and it quickly fired my imagination. The possibility of combining research and consulting was very much aligned with my own interests. Not many consulting firms possibly had such R&D units to support consulting work in the 1990s, and certainly none were relying on systems sciences as a discipline. IBM, which is known for its leadership in R&D, came up with the ambitious programme of "Services Science" around 2004.[20]

---

19 The correction was done one year later (in 1997) and after much to and fro with the corporate HR Head. I was given a hike of two grades that seemed commensurate with the qualification and experience. However, in 1998 I realized that I had slipped one level below when the two grades were merged into one as part of a corporate HR plan. And I was denied further promotion until 2000 on the pretext that I had got a double promotion in 1997.

20 While this initiative was launched with much fanfare around 2004–5, it seemed to have given way to the Smarter Planet initiative a few years later. At the time of its launch, IBM's leaders stated that this initiative would help redefine the way services would be designed and managed in the same way that its earlier initiative on Computer Science education had done for the IT industry. I got a feeling that IBM was using this initiative to connect its R&D with its services business, something similar to what DCTS attempted.

I also got to understand the Professor's views on systems, cybernetics, multi-Laws and consulting more closely. A central aspect of his thinking was the strong focus on abstracting and modelling problems.[21] He believed that there was a clear need for consultants with superior thinking and modelling capabilities. I think the Professor and the MD were strongly aligned on this approach to management consulting and problem-solving.[22] The MD strongly felt that consultancy can never be complete unless consultants bring a measure of innovation and creativity to their solutions. Since the capacity to change or adapt is implicit in the concept of innovation, a consultant has to be a change agent. He believed that management consultants must keep abreast with new knowledge that appears in the literature, participate in building on that knowledge and follow closely the experiments that are taking place throughout the world. The MD was a voracious reader and kept himself abreast of both technology and management trends. I heard senior colleagues talk about meetings with the MD. He apparently used to challenge the management consultants every time he met them by asking what new books they had read and if someone blurted out some name, he would then go into the details of the book. One had to be really sure what he/she had read and understood. Such a focus also manifested in the form of investment in libraries, latest books and journals on technology and management, and very knowledgeable librarians in most DCTS centres.

---

21 It can be traced to his strong engineering and mathematics background.

22 The MD had a very high regard for Management Consulting and a professional approach to problem-solving. He believed that management consulting, if properly utilized, can benefit a wide range of governmental and non-governmental organizations and agencies. He expected consultants to make an organized and determined attempt to probe complexity through their analysis.

Another important aspect of the Professor's view and the Multi-Laws approach was the importance of understanding the uniqueness of a situation. According to him,

> Consultancy in general and management consultancy in particular, is about analysing, understanding, structuring and managing real world. Consequently the problem solving techniques should bear a close relationship to the societies in which the problems are posed. The level and nature of complexity in developing countries is significantly different from that of highly industrialised societies. In such contexts, techniques like the consensus methodologies have to be reinforced by cybernetic insights to learn about the problem. Further the intensity and nature of the need of the client for help in problem solving seems to force a new relationship between client and consultant.

Clearly he was trying to introduce a perspective that was suited to the context he was operating in—management consultancy work in the Indian market—and while doing so, he recognized the importance of combining cognitive understanding of the problem with relationship improvement between the client and the consultant. And given the constraints of lack of data and the high cost of computing in the 1980s, the Professor and Head of SCC largely focused on qualitative modelling methods as opposed to quantitative methods that are generally adopted by the top consulting firms. These principles of appreciating the client context, the interaction between client and consultant, and qualitative modelling got deeply etched in my mind.

All these views seemed to vibe very well with my own thinking, and research interests. I was extremely happy that I was getting to work in an environment that seemed truly knowledge-intensive. I felt that my decision to join SCC was spot on. It generated a lot of interest in me to work with SCC. However, there were a few areas where I was sensing some discomfort. First, I was keen to work on the public systems issues more than IT issues primarily because of my research interest in applying systems ideas to understand and improve public systems. Second, I felt that we did not dwell much on the issues of power, conflict and the process of interaction between the client and the consultant and within the consultant teams. While I had had some exposure to the issues of power while studying about Critical Systems Thinking and Critical Studies in management (Ulrich, 1993, Willmott and Alvesson, 1992) during my PhD, I was not sure how these methods could actually be applied in consulting engagements to trigger organizational change. Nobody would like to be challenged openly about their assumptions, and the challenger would be shunted out if he did not provide a credible alternative.[23] Third, I also noticed during the training that others who had joined along with me (mostly MBAs or Masters in Urban Planning) seemed to struggle more and did not seem to connect with the vision or the methodology. Some of them were questioning if they had made the right choice by joining this Centre. One of them left during the training, while others endeavoured to explore further. After the training, another colleague and I were assigned to a management consulting study (World Bank aided project) on the Indian Silk Industry. At the same time, we were also informed that SCC would now be relocated from Hyderabad to Pune and operate under a new leader, a PhD in mathematics who had worked with SCC for

---

23 The method of Critical Systems Heuristics was designed to help affected groups engage with experts on the normative goals of a project, and transfer the responsibility of justification to the experts who were proposing a solution (for more, please see Ulrich, 1993). However, in the organizational context, the change usually needs to happen in the dominant group and the innovator may be the weaker group.

about four years and emerged as a strong votary of the approach. In addition, another Professor was inducted in Pune to provide guidance to SCC. I relocated to Bangalore for the consulting project, while the rest of the team moved to Pune.

Interactions with management consultants

It was in the silk industry study that I first got to experience the challenges faced by Management Consulting (MC) teams and their expectations from the SCC team. The domain of study (Indian Silk Industry) was new to the entire project team. Some of the consultants had worked on similar engagements in the textile or agro-based industries, but not in the silk industry which had both elements of agro and textile. So, they had budgeted for an industry veteran to assist as an advisor to this project and he was helping us get a perspective on the industry and the key issues in the industry. The Project Manager was very mature and seemed to have some clear expectations from the SCC team. As per the initial discussions on project objectives and plan, it was suggested that the SCC team (two members) along with the remaining six from the MC team[24] and the industry expert would jointly get an understanding of the scope, and then branch out into smaller teams for data collection, and then converge for analysis and synthesis. The Project Manager wanted the SCC team to help with structuring the problem and synthesizing the recommendations.

During the study it became apparent that the relationship between the SCC team and the MC team was not very smooth. There was fundamental conflict around the method, the role of the team and the nature of contribution from the SCC team. It appeared that most management consultants were arriving at

---

24 Three of them were fresh MBAs who had joined a few months back.

conclusions about the client problem situation by talking to each other about their perceptions about the problem and generalizing the observations using well-known management models, all the while struggling to get a holistic view of the problem. At the same time they were reluctant to use any of the systems methods to model and get a holistic perspective of the problem. This is where they expected the SCC team to contribute. The SCC team was seen as a specialist team which could diagnose and give superior recommendations due to training in supposedly superior methods. The SCC team thus had to play a dual role—help in data collection and analysis of some parts of the problem, and then help synthesize views of other teams; in other words immerse in some parts and also abstract the whole. There was no explicit clarity on the latter role in the project structure. How would the SCC team get a holistic view without joint work with the rest of the team? Such a role, in most cases, had to emerge through the course of the project except in situations where SCC members were the project leaders.[25] It also meant that the SCC members had to put in more effort than other team members. And when this synthesis role did not come across clearly, management consultants would pass remarks about the ineffectiveness of the methods and the systems experts. Some SCC team members who struggled with this tension preferred to hold on to the relationships and downplay the methods.

Given my background and interest in Systems Engineering I informally started playing the dual role of collecting data in

---

25 Some of the seniors also experienced this challenge and in some projects took the lead role, especially where the Management Consulting team did not have senior resources to depute. Whenever the Professor was invited to participate in a project, his experience and seniority made him a natural leader and others accepted it without any difficulty. This was not the case for others.

a specific area and also synthesizing. I tried synthesizing the inputs by using the System Dynamics method. The value chain process seemed straightforward, starting with Mulberry Farmers -> Cocoon Rearers -> Silk Reelers -> Exchanges -> Weavers -> Marketing, sales and distribution (cooperatives or private). And there were supply-demand challenges in each part of the value chain. I attempted to build a system dynamics model, and then realized that the model would become too generic to account for the variety of issues that we observed in different states (22 states of the Indian Union). Also, since we did not have all the quantitative data and would have to make a number of assumptions, I gave it a pass. At the same time it was also clear that the team was finding it difficult to make sense of the vast amount of information that it had gathered from interactions with different stakeholders across the country. The various levels of granularity captured by different team members also resulted in some funny situations and jokes within the team. After some thought, I proposed that the Viable Systems model, with its idea of recursive levels, could help us summarize the issues afflicting the industry at multiple levels— district, state, and nation. I then summarized the issues of one of the largest silk-producing states using this framework. Once the Project Manager seemed comfortable, they agreed to replicate this template for other states. In parallel I drafted the report on the national level. In the end we managed to structure all our observations using this framework, and the Project Manager and the rest of the team seemed comfortable with the output. I ended up writing almost 40 per cent of the report. In the end I felt that I as part of the SCC team was able to demonstrate some value in applying systems ideas to synthesize vast amounts of information and also developing relations with other team members.

However, I was not sure if the work produced any new ideas

or change within the team. One or two ideas that emerged largely appeared to come from immersing in the problem more than application of the multi-laws method. For instance, while debating on the recommendations for the silk industry study I proposed that instead of seeing India as a boundary and looking at internal capability development, shouldn't we see the North East region that was getting smuggled inputs from China as integral to that market and legalize imports in such markets. In some ways this challenged the notion of systems boundary and the main purpose of the study, i.e., to improve the domestic industry. The team felt that recommending legalization of imports (even in one region) would not go well with the government body. So, this idea was not explored further. Another very important point that we did not explore was how advances in IT could align supply-demand more effectively and aid the several small players operating in the industry (an example of siloed thinking).[26]

Subsequently, I participated in a few other management consulting engagements. Every engagement seemed to pose similar challenges of first aligning with the people, then helping evolve an approach for that engagement, and then playing a role in synthesizing the findings and recommendations. It was becoming problematic if the project team viewed the systems approach as one person's problem and not something that had to be solved collectively. Most of them were aware, but not really convinced about applying the method. They might have tried once or twice and given up since this did not seem to automatically lead to superior results. Also, they did not see the value of doing this as a collective exercise and outsourced the activity to SCC

---

26 While researching for this book I came across an interesting piece of work that talked about how the silk industry in Kanchipuram had grown stronger through the use of ICT (Bowonder and Sailesh, 2005).

personnel. What I observed was that the method was providing a good, integrative framework to organize whatever points were emerging through the talk, but somehow people found it easier to talk about their perspectives rather than model them. Was it because the methods were not clearly specified in such a way that people could quickly learn and use? Or did applying the methods or making sense of the problems using some of the principles of the method actually demand a certain degree of expertise that was not easily attainable without guidance? I felt that there was a lot of interpretive element involved; this to me was dependent on collective experience, and not just the proficiency in the method.[27] My training and interest in the methods kept me focused on modelling the topics through the method. However, it was difficult to build consensus. Most management consultants dismissed multi-laws as an abstract theory produced by an academic, and did not see much relevance for it in their project work. The existing differences were exacerbated with the appointment of a new head of management consulting in the early 1990s. They seemed to carry a different view and started deriding SCC and its methods in conversations among themselves. It may be noted that the method emerged out of handling several consulting assignments and reflecting on the method. Since it was designed by a Professor and certainly involved a certain level of deep abstraction that most consultants struggled with, they found it convenient to brand it as too theoretical or academic. Within SCC there was a feeling that management consulting professionals were largely relying on their experience in doing projects and not really keen to explore methods that were outside mainstream managerial thought,

---

27 Stacey (2012) provides a detailed discussion on this issue in the techniques of leadership.

certainly not the high level of abstraction that systems models required. The reasoning within SCC was that if management models were second-order abstractions,[28] systems models were third-order abstractions. For example, we could show that popular management ideas like Management by Objectives, and Balanced Scorecard could be easily developed using the more abstract ISM. Therefore, systems models could enhance the ability to analyse and interpret situations more than management models. We did not realize that we were pushing people further away from reality and that such abstractions are of limited use when it comes to implementation and change.

While SCC was busy dealing with the management consulting challenges, the IT services division grew significantly in size and influence. It not only increased its presence in international markets significantly, but also spawned a new set of successful and confident leaders. They also managed to win and deliver some mega projects like the depository clearing system in Europe which significantly enhanced the visibility of the IT services business in the global market. While SCC was not involved in the rapid rise of the IT services business, the other R&D unit SEC emerged as a key contributor to the growth of the IT services business by developing several migration tools. Also, SCC didn't seem to figure in part of the other technology related investments made by the MD in the area of IT. Under his leadership DCTS had experimented with OCR/AI technologies, PC Lab, silicon graphics and several others.[29] It was only in early 1990s that attempts were made to align SCC with IT. There was

---

28 First-order abstractions are typically narratives or stories about one's experience.

29 Some of these were carved out as separate Joint Ventures. The MD believed that this would lead to more diversity and foster innovation.

no clarity why this alignment did not happen earlier. Most of the IT professionals had known about SCC and participated in the training programmes on Systems Engineering. They probably saw it as a specialized competency suited for management consultancy problems, and management consultancy itself seemed a different business altogether.

Interactions with IT professionals and leaders

The efforts to align SCC with IT, as envisaged by the MD, started in the early 1990s. One of the initial areas where some joint work was attempted was in developing a framework for Information Systems Planning called ISP. This was developed to tap into the consulting market that was opening up in India with governments and public sector institutions as they started their journey to leverage IT. Global firms like IBM had something similar at that point. Indian firms like NIIT had developed a similar approach in the 1980s (Sharma, 2009). Some of the initial institutions where ISP was applied include a public sector insurance firm and a national pension organization.

Another important work that SCC initiated in 1995 was to model the complexity in the software development process. Inputs were gathered from 50+ senior and middle managers and a cybernetic model comprising 80+ elements was constructed. While this was used to model project dynamics and help in estimations, this effort failed due to the lack of relevant data. Also, the qualitative information and insights in this model were not analysed and exploited. About five–six years later, in 2001, when I studied this model in great detail, I noticed that the collective mental model had patterns that could potentially explain the organizational evolution five years before and five years after, i.e., from 1990 to 2005. It also pointed to potential ways to group organizational elements and internal systems, for instance, the criticality of combining CRM systems with Knowledge Systems or the importance of coupling process with content of software development. The quality and CMM[30] initiatives tend to view these two in isolation, with the result that reconciling product quality with process quality continues to be an issue.

DCTS went through a leadership change in 1996. The MD, after spending about three decades in building DCTS, gave way to a new leader (hereafter referred to as CXO) who had been wedded with the IT services business since its inception. This also led to a leadership change in SCC. A younger leader from the SCC team was asked to head the centre. The Professor was requested to continue in the capacity of Advisor to DCTS. The SCC unit under the new leader was shifted from Hyderabad and co-located with the SEC unit in CRDD Pune. The idea was that the SCC unit should work closely with SEC and the IT services business to institutionalize systemic problem-solving capability. After the training, 10 newcomers who joined in 1996 and three seniors were asked to relocate to Pune. Two other senior colleagues who had been part of SCC preferred to stay back in Hyderabad. A couple of other people decided to quit DCTS and joined other firms that were launching ERP consulting practices. The team that landed in Pune was mostly made up of newcomers with two–three senior people who had been with SCC for a couple of years. However, the new head of the unit was also involved in another management consulting engagement, and had to divide his time between mentoring and guiding the new SCC team and his project commitments. The project commitments

---

30 CMM refers to the Capability Maturity Model popularized by Carnegie Mellon University.

invariably took precedence. The other seniors were not in a position to provide direction to the newcomers since they did not have the required level of expertise and also did not seem totally convinced about the approach. Some of the team members who were interested in exploring the software development process using System Dynamics started working on it.[31] They modelled the software development process using the system dynamics tool and tried to analyse the linkages between project size, workforce requirements, error rates and time and cost overruns. However, they were struggling to get real data from projects to validate the model and encouraging Project Leaders to experiment with these models. Others were exploring alternative options. The day-to-day talk seemed loaded with negative feelings about the method and the unit.

In April 1997, after completion of the silk study, I re-located to Pune. When I landed in Pune, I saw that the DCTS senior management was serious about reorienting SCC towards IT problems and there wouldn't be any management consultancy projects going forward. I was very disappointed. I had left my earlier IT job to do a PhD in public systems. And here I was being asked to go back and focus on IT issues. This situation may sound familiar to many people who have left IT to do an MBA and re-joined IT organizations hoping they would do more strategic or consulting work, but ended up in roles such as Business Analysts or Presales. I left my first job in software product development out of a feeling that while programming was engrossing,[32] the

---

31 It was also the time when the System Dynamics journal started publishing some works on the same area.

32 Once you get into designing an application it draws you into it until you complete it. The iterations to improve performance, look and feel can be never-ending. The change in user requirements or the tool can add to these iterations.

fundamentals of developing an application did not seem to change much. Everything somehow had to fit into the standard RDBMS data structure.[33] This seemed pretty constraining. The disappointment almost forced me to quit DCTS, but my interest in Systems Engineering and interactions with people like the Aeronautics Professor held me back. I was not sure if there was any other institution in India that was working with these methods and also how many had a strong vision about consulting and solution design. With great reluctance I started to revisit the IT issues. It seemed like I had acquired a higher qualification to tackle a much lower-end software development problem. There was an element of discontent.

However, when I started understanding the IT issues, after a gap of almost five years, I realized that IT solution design had changed significantly and seemed pretty complex. One had to understand and connect several elements—business context, user experience, software, hardware, economics, and there were very few rules to guide this process, unlike in manufacturing design. I felt that Systems Engineering could have a role to play in architecting and designing good solutions. I also wondered how IT professionals, who did not have exposure to inter-disciplinary methods or methodological issues in combining different methods, handled such complexity. Also, how did they understand the pros and cons and assumptions behind the plethora of methods that were emerging in software engineering while making design decisions? However, I was still reluctant since my interest was in learning about complexity and change in public systems more than technical complexity or software design. I think I carried a

---

33 While I was aware of the changes that were taking place on the user experience front, I couldn't visualize the transformations that were going on in the internet world or data.

strong belief that superior thinking can lead to an improvement of public systems. Most of my colleagues did not seem to have such constraints and found their way into software development projects or acquired skills in enterprise business solutions like ERP (SAP/Oracle) and Business Intelligence and moved into relevant projects/groups.[34] Also, I realized much later, that at that point I did not seem to understand the three elements of the idea of systems consulting—a holistic way of understanding problems, innovative use of IT, and efficiency and speed in software engineering. I started understanding more about the second point (innovative use of IT) only around 2001, i.e., three–four years after I first heard about systems consulting.

As I started to think how Multi-Laws could be applied to software issues (and noticed that professional bodies such as INCOSE were popularizing the use of Systems Engineering for Software Systems), a new problem emerged. Around the middle of June 1997, the new Head of SCC had decided to quit DCTS. Another Professor who was recruited in 1996 to mentor the team had quit in early 1997. The team was now asked to report to another manager at the Pune R&D centre. While the new manager had some exposure to Systems Engineering, he was not an expert in this area. In this scenario I had to take leave to attend a family ceremony in Hyderabad. Since I was in Hyderabad, I went to the office to meet the Professor. He was now advisor to DCTS. While speaking to the Professor, I shared with him my concerns about the way things were breaking down and the absence of a clear direction. He said that he was constrained to act in his present role, but suggested that if I was interested I could

---

34 The industry was facing a huge resource crunch leading to phrases such as "Trespassers will be recruited".

come and work with him in Hyderabad and we could jointly look at some problems around information and organization. He also indicated that a vacancy had been created since one colleague who was working him had decided to quit a couple of days ago. I couldn't believe my luck; I was not only getting to work with the Professor on systems thinking, but also stay in my hometown. I relocated to Hyderabad in August 1997 and started working with the Professor. We agreed to focus on two key aspects: (a) training on multi-Laws and (b) research to go beyond multi-Laws. We also planned to take up some internal consulting work on a need basis. In hindsight, I feel that the last one should have been a priority since there were no active projects or engagements in IT that used this approach at that point of time, but I couldn't think of taking that path.

Reorienting SCC to IT services and business challenges

One of the earliest tasks I had taken up was to structure the training programme for IT professionals—both for trainees and experienced professionals (Project Leaders and above). We prepared the new course material (one called Introduction to Systems for trainees and the other called Information Systems Planning for experienced professionals) and initiated pilot training programmes at the newly formed corporate training centre in Kerala to test the programme and also educate some trainers (Train the Trainer). The Corporate Head for Training, a senior leader hired by DCTS from a reputed government research centre, was a recent convert to systems thinking. Under the guidance of the Professor and the MD, he took the initiative to ensure that this concept got embedded in the training programme at multiple levels and locations. We conducted more than 50 training programmes between 1997 and 1999. I was a faculty for about 30 such programmes and covered 1,000–1,200 IT professionals in DCTS, about five per cent of the organization then. Participation in these training programmes as a faculty, gathering feedback from participants, and the need to ensure consistency across programmes handled by different trainers pushed me to develop more material to explain the methods/concepts in a consistent manner, and add more examples and FAQs to make it easier to understand. Teaching people about the concepts also helped improve my understanding of the concepts and its application. In 1998 I put together a very elaborate explanation of the concepts and called it "Discourse on Multi-Laws" and showed how SCC methods could be used for requirements definition in the software development process.

To complement the work we had done to model the business requirements, we also felt that it was important to apply the Systems Engineering discipline to another important and related area, i.e., project management. It seemed timely because this coincided with the publication of reports on the poor success rates of software projects and the criticality of project management, notable ones being Standish Group's CHAOS reports (Rahman & Kurien, 2007). The hypothesis that guided us was that the problem complexity should have a bearing on the project strategy and process. Further, by combining principles of Systems Engineering and Concurrent Engineering we could address software quality and process quality simultaneously. In order to validate this hypothesis we initiated a project in 1999 to unearth the patterns in project management in ongoing projects. I conducted about 10 workshops between 1999 and 2000 to elicit key practices adopted by different types of projects—Y2K projects where the requirement was very clear both in terms of scope and time; custom software development projects which had challenges in requirements; product implementation projects where the focus was on controlling customization and time to market; and in-house product development where the requirement was fuzzy and constantly evolving. I used the in-house developed ISM tool to capture the mental models of 50–60 project leaders and senior project managers cutting across different locations.

One of the findings from this exercise was that even though projects seemed to pursue similar higher level objectives, the pattern of relationships among objectives was different. This pattern varied by the type of project—Y2K, software development, software maintenance, software implementation and product development. This insight validated our hypothesis that content and process are tightly inter-related. The project management patterns also revealed a number of feedback cycles, reinforcing the point that software development and maintenance involved more iterative work and cannot be treated as a linear process. Both these insights challenged the core assumptions behind quality processes that tried to enforce a linear discipline on the software process. The pattern of relationships in the specific case of Y2K projects also revealed how project teams could build relationships and mine the client base to deliver more complex software projects in future—in other words, Y2K could be a watershed for Indian IT services. Based on these insights, I put together a report on patterns in software project management and how these could be used to improve the understanding of project leaders and managers. I also saw an opportunity to integrate this idea with the quality process. The quality manual at that time did not have any explicit guidance on how to gather requirements. It only had one sentence "develop requirements document", suggesting that the process was seen as independent of the content. I used this observation to seek time from the Head of Quality to discuss the importance of integrating content and process and suggest ways to bring Systems Engineering into mainstream. We even did a workshop with their team to help them see the connections. But, the quality team did not seem keen to bring this into the fold and there was no management push either. It was also the time when CMM was gaining in importance and the quality team and the new DCTS management were keen to embrace that since it had direct visibility in the US market and could possibly attract more business. On the other hand institutionalizing Systems Engineering in the quality process seemed like an internal exercise with no visible or immediate business impact. There was potential in developing some unique ways of handling project complexity, perhaps something like the agile methodology or the grounded approach to software development, but that was not explored. Much later, in 2006, DCTS started a practice for programme management services and developed training programmes to convert project managers into programme managers, with the resultant difficulties. The easiest thing they found was to get the Project Management Institute (PMI) certifications and encouraged more people to get these. It helped in signalling the project or programme management talent in the company, whether such skills were ingrained or not.

One of the offshoots of the ISP training programmes that we conducted in mid-1997 for senior professionals was that some participants sought our help in their projects. One of them was the Head of a branch banking product implementation team. He had approached the Professor for assistance in designing processes for the product implementation. Consequently, a workshop was organized in the first week of October 1997 in Hyderabad. This branch banking product was abstracted by DCTS from its experience in implementing similar projects for banks in the late

1980s. This was prior to the core banking revolution that swept the Indian banking sector between 2000 and 2010. Participants were apprised of the need to see the problem in a wider context with a view to raising relevant questions. An overview of the operations within a bank and their interrelationship with the wider financial system was provided. The discussion touched on issues pertaining to changes in the banking sector (bank versus branch automation), functionality of banking products, marketing and implementation. Participants were then asked to present the process model currently in operation along with the expected (and pessimistic) time frame for completion of the project. The group was then asked to estimate the probability of completing the implementation process within the expected time. The group found to its surprise that the probability was quite low. Participants were then asked to identify various factors affecting the implementation process at various stages. These were classified into three categories: implementation related, product related and client related. These factors and their interdependence were then captured in the form of a Cybernetic Model (CM). Analysis of the CM showed that there were some feedback loops operating within the implementation process. But, a majority of the loops flowed through factors relating to marketing, product development, training, DCTS policy and client that were outside the domain of implementation. The effect of these loops was, however, felt in the implementation process thereby affecting ease of implementation and resulting in time and cost overruns. In essence, there were basic limitations to the extent of improvement that the product implementation team could achieve on its own. Another gap that was identified was the absence of strong mechanisms for control and co-ordination among implementation teams across branches, and the development and marketing groups. As a result, consolidation of learning and training specific to this product implementation was poor. One of the suggestions we made was to restructure the product team as a strategic business unit instead of seeing it as a bunch of projects. We also highlighted some factors that needed attention within the implementation process, for instance, project management, requirement analysis at pilot and branch levels, client-consultant interaction, and technical aspects. We also proposed that the time estimates in the process model will have to be refined taking into consideration the above factors. An interesting outcome of the workshop was a possible approach to market the product. We observed that the Cybernetic Model of a generic bank could be used to demonstrate the value of the software product for branch operations. However, this exercise failed to predict that the product itself could become irrelevant in the near future due to RBI's mandate to Indian banks to shift to core banking solutions.

I understood more about the core banking wave in particular and banking in general when I got to participate in another assignment in December 1997. It involved designing an Information Systems Strategy for one of the public sector banks in India. This study was carried out by the Management Consulting unit based out of the capital region. The Project Manager, a banker turned management consultant, had undergone the ISP training and wanted to use these methods in this engagement. One of my colleagues was asked to work on this project. However, midway through the project, he had fallen sick and I was sent in as a replacement. When I joined the team I noticed that my colleague had attempted to model the requirements using a Cybernetic Model (CM) with support from the rest of the team. But, they did not seem to get any real value from the exercise. And this had resulted in a lot of arguments about the relevance of this technique for the engagement. I had a discussion with the Project Manager to understand his concern and then analysed the model to tease out a few patterns about the growth strategy of the firm, and other factors that could give the business context for the IT planning exercise. One of the key learnings for me from this project was the idea of critical success loops as opposed to critical success factors[35] that need to be factored into Information Systems Strategy. A couple of years later, in 2000, the same Project Manager sought my help again when DCTS was planning to pitch to the Chairman of a large public sector bank about its capabilities in large-scale systems change. This was a precursor to the core banking deal that DCTS eventually won from the bank. The head of marketing of DCTS had organized a meeting with the Chairman of the bank to apprise him about the large-scale consulting experience that SCC had. Three of us (Professor and Advisor, Professor of Computer Science who was now the sponsor of SCC and I) made the presentation to the Chairman of the bank. We provided an overview of the large consulting projects that SCC had delivered and then presented the idea of aligning IT with the bank's strategy and organization using the idea of critical success loops. The presentation appeared to serve the purpose of keeping the client interested in DCTS. However, these activities did not lead us to recognize the potential opportunity in combining Information Systems Strategy with core banking implementation. Each individual, including myself, seemed to be preoccupied with their own world.

The possibility of combining consulting and implementation came up in another interesting project in mid-1998 that I

---

35 The idea of critical success factors was popularized by the Centre for Information Systems Research at the MIT Sloan School of Management.

participated in. It involved evaluation of ERP[36] for a large defence organization that was into maintenance and repair of large defence equipment. DCTS, like other competing firms, had set up a new group to look at such emerging opportunities. A business consultant from one of the five big consulting firms was hired to head this unit. He then went about recruiting a number of techno-functional consultants. He announced himself as the Project Director and wanted to know how each team member would add value to the project. This was the first time I was witnessing the jargon of the big five firms. When I said I had a background in systems thinking, he immediately said, "Ok, you can then look at HR/learning."[37] About four people from SCC (two of them from Pune) participated in this engagement. One of my seniors in SCC in Hyderabad was the Project Manager. The team was a large one with about 20+ people including several functional consultants and MBAs. We went through the process of collecting data on different functional areas—HR, Finance, Maintenance, Inventory and others. I was assigned to HR along with two others. We gathered the information. After that my SCC colleagues and I tried to model the whole system. The idea was to extract critical patterns that could influence the weightages being assigned for ERP evaluation. Our analysis suggested that this particular organization may have inherent constraints in terms of time to repair since it depended on other countries for its imports, but could improve responsiveness by maintaining

---

36 The ERP wave started in 1997 with a number of Indian IT firms creating competency units for products such as SAP, Oracle, JD Edwards and BaaN. Some firms felt that this kind of technology required consultative selling and there was an opportunity to combine consulting and technology capabilities to drive enterprise transformation.

37 Systems thinking was popularized by Peter Senge through the work on Learning Organization, Senge (1990).

high morale and people engagement. Therefore HR systems will not only need to capture relevant data about employees that is critical for the core processes, but also be assigned slightly higher weightage than would normally be given. When I presented this view, it did not seem to make sense to the key leaders. They went ahead with the approach of assigning higher weightage to core processes and lower weightage to non-core processes, based on the advice of BPR methods. Also, they seemed more concerned about getting the job done, there was time pressure to evaluate different vendor products and finalize the report. I was not part of that process and also did not see much point in participating in that aspect. The final report was eventually prepared and submitted. The whole study became meaningless when one of the India-based ERP vendors offered the software at a subsidized cost and got the buy-in of different stakeholders to win the order. The only gains for DCTS were that some people hired under the ERP group got some project exposure, and the HR head of the defence organization later became a senior leader in the HR division of DCTS. However, there was no collective conversation or deeper inquiry into what we learnt from one of the earliest ERP consulting projects. This particular study did point to the challenges in combining consulting and implementation. The team was largely staffed with management or tech(no)-functional consultants[38] (who really did not have implementation experience) and a few with pure technical experience (but no understanding of the functional aspects). SCC methods seemed to be a good bridge, but both sides resisted another new method. Thus, while we did these studies to embed systems ideas into software projects,

---

38 They were mostly tech-*no* functional consultants, i.e., consultants with functional experience and exposure to configuration of ERP tools. But, they did not have deep technical knowledge.

they did not make any strong impact on the new management or IT leaders at DCTS.

In addition to participation in the enterprise IT strategy projects, under the guidance of the Professor I embarked on a research programme to improve the firm's understanding of IT and organizational change. Some of the topics we researched in detail were Information, Organization, People and Business Ethics. We wrote some joint reports on "Criteria for Information Systems Design", "Human Resource Management", and "Qualitative Modelling". These activities started shifting my attention from public systems management to understanding organizational and managerial issues in businesses and enterprises. Another important shift happened while we were developing a paper on business ethics. When we analysed what was going on in the world of business ethics, we came to the conclusion that ethics is highly context-specific and it cannot be reduced to a set of rules that can be consistently followed. It appeared that the rise of interest in ethics in business was a reflection of the growing interdependence among people in the workplace, and such interdependence would push people to become more integrated personalities. At that time I was not aware of Norbert Elias' work on the process of civilizing. The Professor, while not being exposed to the literature of Norbert Elias, Ralph Stacey and John Shotter, seemed to relate to the notion of I-We balance in some ways. In his view,

> A manager should be a seeker and should develop a sense of detachment as the scale expands so that he can still feel the spirit of the problem that the organization is facing and articulate this for others.[39] This can happen only when the manager's personality is merged in the totality. A true leader recognizes this relationship.

---

39 Personal notes captured from interactions with the Professor.

While I was trying to combine research, training and consulting interventions, my colleagues in Pune were getting frustrated with the lack of clear direction and mentoring. In 1998 there was a meeting between the SCC associates in Pune and the Professor and Advisor. The Computer Science Professor who had taken over the responsibility of SCC in Pune invited the former Head and Professor to speak to the team and plan for the future. A majority of people apparently complained that they did not have enough project experience and without that found it difficult to either get a deeper understanding or influence others. In response the Professor and former Head of SCC evidently asked them whether they looked for experience before they got married. While this may sound like a logical statement urging them to think more deeply, it probably ended further conversation. People withdrew and started looking for alternatives. It is possible that they missed the handholding and mentoring that is critical for understanding complex concepts and developing expertise. Project experience is one way of gathering that, but it can also come through a richer quality of interaction. However, such facilitation was not available since there were no people with such expertise to engage or guide them. Transferring the unit to Pune had not really helped. It had in fact weakened the fabric of conversations that was holding the unit together. People still came to the Professor and former Head for advice on complex problems.

Attempt to revive SCC in Pune
Around April 1999 I got a call from the former MD's office stating that he wanted to see me. I did not know the reason. I wondered if it had something to do with an article that I had written earlier in the year on moving up the value chain from product implementation to product development to which he

had responded positively. So, I went to my manager, the Professor, and inquired if he knew about this. The Professor was surprised as he did not. He asked me to put in a travel request and approved it. Soon after that I received another call, this time from the Delivery Centre Head. When I met him I found that he was curious to know who I was and why I was trying to meet the former MD. I told him that I did not know much about the background of the organization, and that I intended to discuss Systems Engineering and what I had been doing. The Delivery Centre Head seemed worried that I might say something about the local delivery centre issues to the former MD. I calmed his fears. Then I prepared for the meeting and went to Mumbai to meet the former MD. The meeting was scheduled for 4 pm in the evening. I reached before time and his secretary asked me to wait in the lobby. After some delay I was asked to meet him. This was the first time I was meeting him and I was nervous. He asked me to sit down and inquired about my work. I told him about the activities that I was handling in terms of training, consulting and research under the guidance of the Professor and former head of SCC. After about two sentences, he said "you people have made it very complicated … most IT professionals would be keen to learn and improve their problem-solving capability. However, the method was too complicated for them to learn." Saying that he turned his gaze away from me and towards a document he had in his hand. I did not know what to do. He then said "You can go". I stood up, thanked him and came out wondering what had just happened. Perhaps he felt that consultants have a role to play in simplifying complexity for clients and there was business value in doing this. In other words, consultants should not only grapple with complexity, but also articulate the outcomes in simple terms so that their clients can understand and implement more effectively, and he expected SCC to develop this skill among consultants.

However, this was a paradoxical situation for us in SCC—how do you teach complexity management in a simple way when we ourselves were trying to develop the expertise? I was lucky that I had prior research experience, and got an opportunity to understand these ideas better through research, teaching and practising it under the guidance of the Professor. I believe such a process was helping accelerate my expertise, but the same cannot be said of others. They were operating in different contexts, and a training programme by itself could not generate the desired skill and motivation to develop the expertise.

In August 1999 I got to meet the new Head of SCC (the Professor of computer science who had shaped the SEC unit in CRDD). He had come over to meet the former Head of SCC in Hyderabad as part of their joint work on a social project. I came to know during the meeting that the SCC team in Pune was now formally reporting to him and he along with the Professor and Advisor had recruited another seven or eight people to strengthen the team. The Professor of computer science wanted me to train the team and also move to Pune to help re-build it. I agreed and moved to Pune. By October 1999 we completed the training for the newly joined associates. During this period I also had discussions with other senior colleagues in the team about what could be done moving forward. Most of them didn't seem very positive about any turnaround. Some of them decided to move into the Business Intelligence team, while others continued exploring alternatives in ERP or project management.

After the Y2K wave passed, in January 2000, we were left with a bunch of newcomers who had just completed the training. We tried to structure our work into three parts—one focused on developing tools and exploring synergies with IT R&D; the other focused on working on projects from internal clients; and the third focused on training. In relation to the first, we did some work to combine systems output with Object Oriented Method and Formal Methods. It was difficult to sustain these interactions, as there didn't seem to be any explicit demand for such work. If we had explored further, we might have made some inroads into the area of semantic technology and ontologies that are now gaining currency. We also worked with the newly formed domain practices (Banking and Government) to help structure their unit. Some of us also continued to support training programmes for entry level trainees and for experienced professionals (Continuous Learning Programme—CLP). I did a few CLP programmes in Mumbai and Pune. During one such session in Pune, in May 2000, I met a seasoned IT professional who had just returned to India after finishing his stint as a Regional Manager (RM) for New Zealand. He had some exposure to systems thinking (he had read Peter Senge's book on Fifth Discipline, 1990), the ideas of Winograd & Flores (1986), and was interested in understanding better the Multi-Laws approach, particularly the Viable Systems Model (VSM) and past projects of SCC. His experience in New Zealand had also taught him the importance of being innovative in penetrating a market that was relatively small, and he wanted to do something around this. I had some discussions subsequently with him and he suggested that there might be a case to start something like a centre for research in enterprise innovation.

Search for a mission critical project—supply chain development

In April 2000 the Head of SCC (Professor of Computer Science) suggested that we should consider designing a software product for academic institutions, and stated that his alma mater (one of the Regional Engineering Colleges (REC)) had agreed for a requirements gathering study. His idea was that we could use this opportunity to design a component-based solution for academic institutions, and this could also contribute to the larger goal of developing the supply chain of DCTS. I felt that this could be a good project through which we could align SCC and SEC efforts and set a platform for future work. I also saw this as an opportunity to document a detailed case study of the entire Multi-Laws methodology right from analysing the organization to defining the detailed requirements. With great eagerness, I along with a small team of two people from the newly trained team carried out the requirements gathering at the REC, and then modelled all the information to come up with a very detailed report (IS for Engineering Colleges—ISEC). It had four volumes in all: volume one discussed the client-specific requirement and business case for automation; volume two discussed the bigger picture for IT-enabled transformation in engineering education and a business case for product development; volume three discussed the step-by-step details of the methodology; and volume four contained all the client artefacts and appendices. I felt we had done a very thorough job of not only defining the specific requirement of the client, but also creating a generic model for a product and detailing out the methodology at a very granular level.

We submitted one of the volumes covering the high-level business case and requirements to the client (REC) so that they could use the report to seek budget approval. I then sent across the four volumes to the Professor and former Head of SCC for his feedback. His feedback was that it seemed far too detailed. In the meanwhile, the Professor of computer science sent the final report to the former MD. His response apparently was "you guys have complicated the whole thing". That left me wondering what more could be done. How could we develop expertise of consultants without taking them through the details? Should we look at first understanding their expertise and then help them explore the new methods, something like my earlier attempt to tease out project management patterns? I realized that such an approach would require me to immerse myself in ongoing projects.

Between May and July 2000 a couple of senior colleagues in the team decided to leave SCC. One of them moved to the Artificial Intelligence R&D unit, while the other quit the organization since he felt that his four-year effort was not recognized and he had not been promoted, while others who had migrated to the Business Intelligence or the SAP practice had got promoted. It seemed that organizational incentives were aligned with billability; the complexity of skill did not matter. The newcomers in the team were also becoming restless since there were no real client projects where they could get involved. They also did not seem to see any value in participating in internal projects, developing the methodology or training people. And in their interactions with others in the same location they were possibly getting pointers that quicker growth was feasible by learning simpler programming skills. I felt that there seemed to be no belief or affinity within the SCC team to work through the challenges. The Professor of computer science was also aware of the situation, and he felt it might be a good idea to allow everyone to find their way.[40] The newcomers were therefore given an option to undergo IT training and then get deployed

---

40 He was also of the view that the SCC team should be like sugar which should infiltrate and change the culture of DCTS.

into IT projects. In August 2000, the Professor of computer science announced that he would be moving to Mumbai to take over the role of the CIO of DCTS. His original intent was to understand what kind of systems DCTS was building for its clients. The market was shifting from migration business to business solutions and software maintenance and he felt that it was important for him and the software engineering centre to go beyond the migration tool-sets and reorient themselves to the new realities. However, his discussions with the CXO had led him to take up DCTS' internal systems as the area of focus. It was also the time when the CXO was getting key IT leaders to manage different corporate functions, and the Professor of computer science, although from R&D, had proven himself by supporting DCTS, IT business with software tools in some large and technically challenging projects.

It was during this fluid phase (in October 2000) that the former MD visited CRDD for a meeting of the research board. He wanted to meet the SCC team. Two of us who were left with SCC went to see him. He and the former Head of CRDD were in the room. The former MD stated that he wanted us to do some research on the state of engineering education in the country and ways to improve it, and while doing so, take guidance from the former Head of CRDD. The background was that one of the state governments in India wanted to set up an Indian Institute for Information Technology (IIIT) and had asked the former MD for his views. He had proposed that instead of setting up a new institute to produce professionals for the IT industry, they should look at enhancing the quality of engineering education in the existing institutions. He felt that there were a number of engineering colleges that attracted students of similar calibre as the top institutes such as IITs, but the quality of output was lower than that of IITs. The state government agreed to this view and set up a committee under the leadership of the former MD to come up with a detailed proposal. The MD wanted us to help develop that proposal. However, we did not get this background during that initial meeting, and I did not understand why the SCC team was being asked to do this study, and particularly why me. The only connection I could see was that the former MD probably remembered that I had worked on the IS for Engineering Colleges study. We agreed to analyse this. My colleague was not involved in the IS study, but I had researched the state of engineering institutions as part of the study on IS for Engineering Colleges. I used some of that analysis and then handed it over to my colleague to add data about the top 30 institutions and share it with the former Head of CRDD. I was at that time in the process of relocating to Mumbai as per the advice of the Professor and Head of SCC who had now taken over the role of CIO of DCTS. I moved to Mumbai in November 2000. Within a few days of arriving in Mumbai, I received a call from the former MD's office asking me to meet him. When I went into his office, I found my manager (CIO) was also there. The former MD then asked me about the status of the engineering education report that he had asked us to prepare. I told him that when I transitioned from Pune to Mumbai, I had handed it over to my colleague to complete and submit to the former Head of CRDD. He looked at my manager and said, "Is this the kind of people you have?" I told him that I would check the status and send him the completed version and came out of the room. I went back to my table and couldn't hold back my tears. Was I being irresponsible? Possibly yes; since I had a deeper understanding of the issue compared to my colleague, I should have probably completed it. Why didn't I do that? The transition seemed to have played a role. I had seen this as a task given to SCC in Pune and when I transitioned to Mumbai under the CIO office, I did not feel it belonged to me. Maybe I also did not fully understand the importance of the study. Later I caught up with my colleague and found that he had not made much progress and he had also left Pune to undergo an IT training programme. I then prepared the entire report on the current state of engineering education, the gap between premier institutes and the next 30 institutions, a roadmap to close the gaps while identifying potential colleges in the state where this could be piloted. The idea was to improve the quality of education in the next-level institutions so that India could produce 30,000 high quality engineering graduates compared to the 3,000 produced by IITs (of which 2,000 went abroad and 500 went into MBA programmes). The former MD liked the report, and that also seemed to change his perception of me.[41] He then asked me to speak to the concerned colleges and facilitate other discussions. It was during one of these discussions that I got to meet another renowned personality, the former Head of a government institution that was responsible for science and technology. These associations took me into a few other avenues and possibly whetted my appetite and interest in public systems improvement. For instance, (a) seeking approval from the state government for granting autonomy to the three selected institutions; this was granted around 2002; (b) preparing a report for an independent trust for driving excellence in higher education in India—we had presented this report to a very senior person at Reserve Bank of India (RBI) and were told later that

---

41 In fact this seemed like a major turnaround from my earlier interaction, where he had mentioned "you guys are complicating things". I wondered if my proposal writing skill had improved in a year or was he being polite?

while it was a good move, RBI could not fund such initiatives and it was dropped; (c) making a proposal to the chairmen of leading banks to subsidize student loans for selected engineering colleges (they were not convinced and it was dropped); and, (d) taking the idea to the Chief Minister of a neighbouring state that had heard about this initiative and wanted to replicate it in their state as well. In 2002, the former Head of the government department also requested my help in preparing the "Review of Premier Institutes of Technology" report. These studies created possibilities for engaging the supply chain in much deeper ways, i.e., not only seeing academic institutions as suppliers of trained engineers, but also help in developing the quality of academic education and research, and also evolve a product for engineering institutions. However, these were in no way aligned with the supply chain initiatives of the DCTS mainstream organization. DCTS management seemed to treat these like pro bono social initiatives of the former MD.

In early 2001, the Professor and Head of SCC (also the CIO) felt that there was an opportunity to translate these supply chain studies into a strategic initiative for DCTS when one of the IITs expressed an interest to develop an MIS solution, and was willing to sign an MoU with DCTS. The Professor also felt that it was an opportunity to build a componentized solution and possibly seed some joint research with the Department of Computer Science in this area. The Professor thought that this could help push DCTS into componentization and reuse from an industry perspective, a strategy that might not only accelerate custom development, but also aid in potential product development (in other words, industrialization of software development). I further developed this idea using my understanding of the challenges in engineering education and articulated a strategy that could benefit engineering colleges as well as DTCS (illustrated in Figure 3 below).

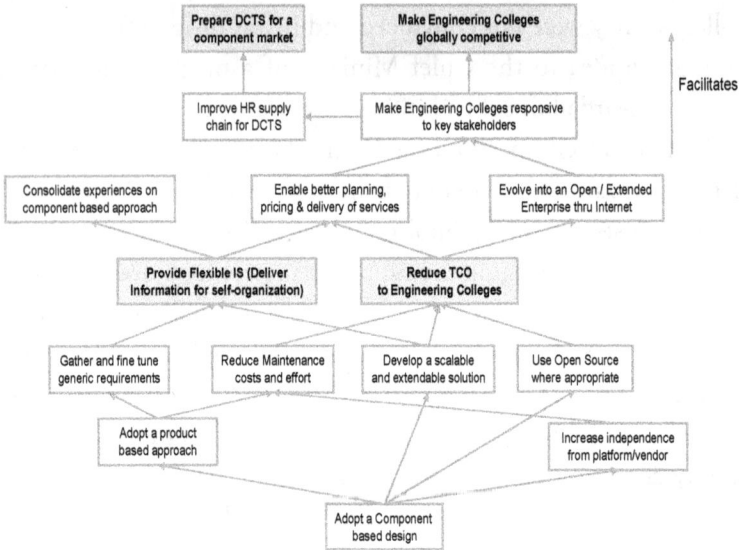

**Figure 3: Strategy to connect SCC and SEC with
supply chain development**

We started working on this strategy in early 2001 with one of the IITs as the seed client. We gathered the requirements and defined a componentized model of common and distinct processes. Here we went beyond defining the process models and metrics, to actually identifying potential business components that could be used in a standardized way to service different needs.

My manager then asked the Head of the newly formed Architecture Consulting to validate our design. They came back with some suggestions, but seemed comfortable with the core ideas proposed. We also got the report reviewed by the internal Finance & MIS team. They came back and said that they did not see any report templates in the report. We made the relevant additions. My manager then got an approval to develop the software product and identified one of the newly formed delivery centres as the place from which it would be developed. In consultation with the Head of the Delivery Centre, they also identified a senior project manager. The Project Manager had been with DCTS for more than 15 years. After he came on board and went through the concept and requirements document, he gave a simple feedback—the requirement was only 20 per cent complete. I was a bit shocked. I thought we had done a good job of taking a comprehensive view of the requirement and developing a component-based design. Through further discussion with the Project Manager I understood that a requirement specification for him (based on his experience in global software projects) had to be specified at the level of field size, character type, screen layout, application logic, and so on. What we had provided were the variety of stakeholders and their needs, the different business processes that met these needs, the key decision points and information needs at each of the process steps, and how this could be structured into standardized components. We expected that details such as field sizes, attributes, screen formats could be inferred by the project team from the forms and templates. This is an example of the divide that existed between the reality of the project teams and what I thought as part of SCC. Software teams were used to clients specifying the requirements at a fairly granular level. Their job was to translate those requirements in the chosen programming language into an efficient piece of code and test the application. Since the Project Manager was reluctant to take any step forward, we had to develop more detailed templates and add additional information so that the project team could get into detailing the User Requirement

Specifications (URS). I transferred my colleague to this project team to help with detailing the URS. These were some of the early attempts to bring systems ideas into the mainstream in IT. At that time my manager also hinted that I should possibly take up the role of a Product Manager and oversee the development and marketing of the product. I was not keen to go down that path and become a full-time software product manager. I was still hanging on to the issue of institutionalizing systems thinking, and had a strong inclination towards research & consulting. The person identified as the Project Manager might have also seen it as an one-off engagement. A product for academic institutions in India was untested market, a new territory. We had done some estimation of the market and felt that we could recover the costs by targeting a few institutions in India. DCTS eventually completed the product (about 20 person-years of effort) and did a few implementations. However, the universities in the US started using some of the ERP systems like Peoplesoft, and these vendors later customized their solution for academic institutions. DCTS, around 2011, launched a platform service for academic institutions leveraging the advancement in cloud and one of the ERP products. I am not sure if they leveraged the initial work done in this direction. I feel that an opportunity to bring SCC and SEC together through a strategic or mission critical project was lost. DCTS management did not seem to see this as a strategic assignment that could enhance the capability of the organization or its domestic market strategy. Perhaps they were expecting the CIO to show the way. And the CIO in turn was expecting someone like me to play the role of a product manager, and I didn't seem to view myself in that role—a complex interplay of intentions.

Moving out of SCC

Around August 2001, the former MD suggested to me that I should try and revive SCC. He said he would speak to the CXO to sponsor the initiative. I was not sure if it would work. I suggested that I would first put down my observations on the challenges and possible directions and then we could discuss with the CXO to arrive at some decisions. I gave a lot of thought based on what I had observed in projects, in training, in designing a component-based solution, and in exploring interactions with IT R&D teams. Based on this I drafted a report showing how Systems Engineering had evolved over two decades, contributed to over 40–50 management consulting projects covering six–eight industry verticals and five–six types of engagements (strategy, organization, ISP), and trained about 5000+ IT people since 1997, but was left with practically one–two people in SCC. About 50-odd people had joined the group over time, some had moved to other parts of the organization, while others had left. I also indicated the issues at three levels—technical (how people perceived the method), managerial (organizational incentives, resource allocation) and strategic (lack of mission critical projects that could unify efforts). I then suggested that if we have to institutionalize this, then we will have to look at it as a three-year change programme. It should start with creating some internal demand by focusing its application to strategic areas of interest to the company such as consulting, componentized solutions, internal strategy, and quality. This should be supported by creating structures and incentives that aligned a critical mass of people to these initiatives. I indicated that such an initiative might cost the organization about $2–3 million. We could influence 30 per cent of the projects and people out of an estimated 20,000 people. I then discussed it with my manager and he suggested that we should discuss this with the CXO. When my manager and I started the discussion with the CXO, he interrupted and asked me what I thought was the problem and also inquired if the method wasn't too academic. It appeared that he carried the perception that many others had. I then explained to him that we will need to see this as a strategic change issue, and it will require multi-level interventions to make it work. He then said he would think over. Nothing happened after that. In the absence of any further dialogue I was left to making my own guesses. I felt that the CXO was not convinced about such a change initiative. Or he was not convinced about the type of problems we wanted to focus on. I also wondered if he saw Systems Engineering as a specialized competency to deal with complex management problems that should create its own revenue stream. Perhaps he was expecting me to put my hand up and say I would do it and show him some business case in terms of possible revenue, target clients, sales buy-in and so on, typical of any new competency development efforts.

Also, in 2001 the Quality team wanted to internalize the new CMMI initiative (Capability Maturity Model Integrated). CMMI emerged out of a realization that there were different CMM models and these needed to be integrated into one unified model and also incorporate the CMM for Systems Engineering or system integrators. I attended the first session and realized that some of the concepts that were being promoted under SCC were now integral to CMMI. In any case, we were arguing for the incorporation of Systems Engineering into the Quality Process, but that was sidestepped in 1997 when CMM became popular and everyone wanted to be on bandwagon. I noticed that the quality teams who were riding high on the success of CMM initiatives such as Software-CMM were immediately trying to do a gap analysis without understanding the thinking behind it. I felt that they were treating it as an exercise in getting certified. After the training programme I wrote to the CIO that if DCTS internalizes the CMMI programme in principle, then much of the systems rigour would come into the organization. There wouldn't be a need for duplication of effort from Systems Engineering.

My belief at that time was that such a large-scale change would need significant focus from the top and strong leadership involvement. By 2001, a lot of cynicism had set in within the organization and it was difficult to change the perception in the face of steep power differences. I personally felt that I couldn't drive such an initiative as I lacked credibility to influence the senior leadership of the organization. I also did not have sufficient experience in challenging the prevalent pattern in an industry where anyone who had not demonstrated success in acquiring clients or generating revenue would be treated with scant respect.[42] And building a team to influence the rest did not seem the right way. This conclusion was highly disappointing. My whole world seemed to crumble. I found it difficult to introduce myself as a PhD in Systems Engineering in an environment where a PhD was equated to academic and impractical, and systems view was seen as idealistic or elitist. This was the time when I had my first identity crisis. But, I did not seem ready to give up the intent. I felt that the only way I could persist with the intent was to build experience in addressing key issues faced by the IT services business.

In September 2001 I reached out to the former RM of New Zealand to inquire how he was doing on the business research front. He indicated that he had done a consulting engagement in Australia and applied some of the ideas of VSM along with other

---

42 Similar views about the thinking in the industry are made in Rahman & Kurien (2007), p.219.

methods and felt very positive about the whole thing and was seeing some demand for such services. He indicated that he was now getting more clarity on what he wanted to do—something like research on enterprise innovation, but as a self-sustaining unit. He indicated that he was trying to give formal shape to his unit and suggested that I could join it if it was of interest. Since I had been trying to understand how to institutionalize systems thinking, I felt that it might provide an opportunity to demonstrate the relevance of systems ideas to client projects in global markets, and also understand better the patterns of innovation. I decided to take the plunge. I discussed the matter with my manager and later drafted a note to the CXO and the former MD. It was on the following lines:

> My sincere submission is that lack of demonstrable business results and success stories in today's environment is impeding both SCC's and my ability to influence people or groups in DCTS. Systems engineering today requires a different structure. If DCTS has to internalize Systems Engineering, it has to adopt a strong top-down pull and push strategy through changes in HR policy, Training, Quality and Sales. This has to be combined with a bottom-up strategy that relies on demonstrable business results. I sincerely think that I can serve DCTS best by being part of this bottom-up strategy.

The request was approved and I was possibly the last one to exit SCC. It ceased to be a formal unit in late 2000.[43] In October 2001 I joined the quasi R&D/business unit—a small centre for research in enterprise innovation, later called the Enterprise Innovation Lab (EIL). My intent was to help build management frameworks and assets using systems ideas. In other words I was moving from

---

43 I worked under the CIO budget for about six months.

process innovation to service innovation. This was also the first step I had taken to move out of a formal R&D unit and closer to the mainstream IT services business and leaders. I did not foresee that this step would take me into an entirely different direction, almost counter-intuitive, four years later.

In 2004 the Professor of Computer Science & CIO, persuaded by the former head of SCC and Advisor to DCTS, decided to restart SCC in Hyderabad and rechristened it the "Business Systems Centre" (BSC). The turnaround of the Professor of Computer Science itself is of interest. He had been with DCTS almost since 1982 as the Head of the Software Engineering Centre (SEC). The focus of this centre, in early days, was to build tools for migration. This was a huge market targeted by DCTS in those days. And they were pretty successful in delivering clear efficiency and productivity improvements to projects. Over time they tried to productize this experience and consolidated all the tools under a brand called SuperCraft, an equivalent of IBM's Rational Rose. And in doing this the Professor of Computer Science intuitively adopted systems ideas such as parts, relationships, sub-systems and the whole. One of the members of the Research Advisory Board of CRDD had apparently indicated this to the Professor during one of the reviews. In 1998 when SCC in Pune went into a flux, the member of the Research Advisory Board suggested that the Professor of Computer Science would be the right person to provide leadership to SCC since he had an intuitive appreciation of systems ideas and had used it in building SuperCraft. It was also around this time that the former MD had involved the former head of SCC and Advisor to DCTS and the Professor of Computer Science to design a solution for accelerating the adult literacy campaign using the rising pile of computer hardware that was fast becoming obsolete. Interactions with the former head of SCC started influencing the thinking of the Professor of Computer Science. However, he was not very conversant with the concept of Cybernetics and the Multi-Laws qualitative modelling approach used by SCC and was not clear how it related to his ideas on software systems. It was around 2002 when he decided to move out of the CIO role;[44] he started taking more interest in the systems and cybernetics concepts. Another senior person who had returned to India from a Regional Manager role in the US also wanted to be part of this initiative. This led to the creation of the BSC with a focus on using Multi-laws to design Business Systems. That is how the group got revived and a few more people were recruited to pursue different research topics. In late 2004 I transferred all the assets, case studies and tools that I had maintained as part of SCC to the new team. I did not go back to the team, however, since my thinking seemed to be moving in a different direction. Today BSC has become more visible as one of the innovation labs in DCTS[45] and is actively meeting the targets for innovation in terms of the number of papers published in DCTS Journals and the number of patents applied for. They are making their presence felt in the professional bodies of cybernetics and are being invited to make presentations to IT clients. But, is it making a difference in terms of improved capability? Only time can tell. In 2015 the leader of a competing firm declared that his firm would adopt Design Thinking and announced that they had launched initiatives to institutionalize the same.

---

44 In the two years as CIO he had proposed a certain way to architect DCTS' internal systems, but this did not seem to gel with the DCTS leadership and their sense of urgency.

45 EIL was the first innovation lab in DCTS. It was different from a traditional R&D unit. It was more like SCC in its earlier days, closely tied with consulting practice. Around 2005, DCTS created several innovation labs and reduced CRDD to another lab in the ecosystem. The idea of Design Thinking was possibly lost after this change.

Reflecting on the experience

Much of what I have narrated thus far may seem very obvious to anyone associated with large change programmes, a case where a powerful vision failed to either generate an external demand or mobilize internal resources to rise above routine work since it was not supported by changes in organizational processes, incentives, quality of resources, and acceptance at middle management level. That is how I diagnosed the problem in 2001. SCC emerged out of the MD's view that DCTS could leverage the Systems Engineering discipline to understand and deliver holistic solutions to complex client problems. The initiative of the Professor of Aeronautics and his colleagues to approach management consulting projects from an action-research perspective helped define a methodology that seemed very logical, theoretically grounded and practical—probably one of the few experiments in the practical application of systems theories to real-world problems. Apparently one of the largest global technology firms expressed an interest to partner with SCC at one point. The projects done with the management consulting unit might have even led to a powerful positioning in the domestic market. However, it did not lead to a similar positioning or demand creation in the export markets for IT services. The relatively aggressive growth of the IT services business, emergence of leaders in the IT business who had tasted success in developing the international business without any help from such methods, changes in leadership in the mid-1990s and dissolution of the management consulting practice in 1998 resulted in a breakdown of several relationships and several areas of misalignment. Some of obvious areas of misalignment with IT services business included:

(a) Absence of clear demand—there didn't seem to be any

explicit demand for Systems Thinking skills from the export market, unlike other IT skills. A large part of the organization was still working on meeting demand for IT skills. It was only in the late 1990s that the organization started targeting the demand for Business Analysts or Functional Consultants.

(b) Absence of sufficient ongoing projects (even in the domestic market) where such ideas were being used and could help IT professionals gain practical skills post their training.

(c) Absence of any focused investment in mission critical projects that could possibly align the efforts of R&D and Quality units.

Attempts to bridge these gaps by a new set of people were not fruitful as they struggled to develop the expertise quickly and did not have the experience in grappling with the change problem. In 2001 the group lost its identity. One could argue that SCC should have tried to become a viable competency unit by generating its own business, and should have aligned with IT services much earlier. It should have hired the right people with IT background, and the management should have embedded this in the quality process. While these may sound like valid arguments, they still do not explain the situation completely. Why did people who had the vision and power struggle to bring about the desired culture change in the growing part of the business?[46] Or, is it a

---

46 A very strong view in management thinking is that leaders can create new cultures. For instance, MacDonald (2013) throws some light on how Marvin Bower developed the core culture of McKinsey in its initial days. In the same book MacDonald argues that the core cultural values went through changes as new leaders came to the helm, for example during the tenure of Rajat Gupta. What about other employees and how they respond to the leaders? Don't they influence the process of culture?

reflection of the nature of complexity in Indian IT services that calls for a different way of participating and managing? I think it will be useful to look at the narrative themes and how some small differences in interpretations by people in their interactions amplified the differences, even though at a high level most of them seemed to agree that a holistic approach to problem-solving is a good capability to develop.

One of the areas where we see differences in meaning is in the way the MD's idea of using IT to solve complex societal problems was shaped by SCC. The MD gave a lot of freedom to the Professor to develop the Systems Engineering programme. The Professor of Aeronautics also responded appropriately by focusing on defining the approach to complex societal problems, and Multi-Laws seemed to be a good way to understand the nature of challenges that the management consulting unit was handling. Intellectually, he may have even pushed the barriers by linking this with Indian philosophical views and articulating the idea of a conscious organization.[47] However, linking this to software development seemed a bit hazy. Initial attempts were made with ISP, but these were not sustained in the same spirit of action research to tease out the gaps and relevance from a CIO's perspective. It mostly stopped with a view of the core issues, but did not go into details on what it meant in terms of architectures or software solution design and development of sufficient case studies in the context of IT. Some of the people who joined SCC in the earlier days also did not have IT backgrounds and possibly could not help in translation. When I joined and was asked to look at aligning with IT, it took some time for me to shift my

---

47 Just like Peter Senge positioned Systems Thinking as the Fifth Discipline of a Learning Organization, the Professor viewed Multi-Laws as a way to build a Conscious Organization.

focus from public systems management to IT systems. I did make an attempt to bring more consistency into the method (that was critical for software developers), building a very detailed example of translating the strategic priorities of the firm into detailed process models, metrics and a set of high-level business requirements (not the screen layouts or data structures). I had the background to do this since I had done software application design prior to my PhD. However, there was possibly a resistance to go into known areas since I was keen to explore the unknown more. I did not want to go down the route of Structured Systems Analysis and Design (SSAD) and similar methods that I had left behind in the early 1990s. Also, we did not see cases where IT R&D teams made efforts to use SCC methods. A typical view that emerged was that SCC methods lacked the consistency that software development demanded (the world of 0/1). Yes, these methods were meant to deal with ambiguity and interpretive in nature, but I sincerely believe that something like semantic technology could have logically emerged out of such an exploration.

A second area where subtle differences in meaning can be seen is in the purpose of the group. What was the role of SCC? Was its job to change the organization, or develop a specific expertise that could be applied to complex problems, or build a viable practice like most IT competency units? The group was set up as an R&D unit. The MD wanted SCC to help change the way DCTS consultants conceptualized problems. One of the arguments that I heard was that the management would not be interested in SCC earning $10 million on its own; instead it would be interested in whether SCC can help DCTS earn $100 million more through improved quality of solutions (a non-linear 10X growth). Did all the leaders carry the same view? Even though many of the senior IT leaders had some exposure to SCC through training, they did not seem too interested in SCC methods, and the success with management consultancy did not matter to them. Management consultancy itself was an outsider to the IT business. The IT leaders were possibly dealing with entirely different issues and in their own ways. And the new CXO probably felt that while there was something useful in SCC, he was not sure how to leverage it. He possibly treated it as a specialized competency, like other IT skills, and would have taken notice if it generated some revenues on its own or had made some significant impact on customers. He did not seem to carry the same vision as the MD. This may be because he was not deeply involved in the regular discussions around SCC. The Professor and Head of SCC reported directly to the MD. Also, the new CXO seemed to view the definition of DCTS itself in a different way. For him, it represented two types of services that DCTS offered to clients: (a) IT services which was the core business, and (b) Consultancy, an aspirational capability. He did not view DCTS as offering a systems consulting capability or holistic problem-solving in whatever it did. I am not sure if there had been enough debate on this among the senior leaders. I think there was a gap here right from the beginning which became more obvious during 1996–2004. Relationships among senior leaders like the MD, Advisor to DCTS, CXO and the Professor of Computer Science kept SCC alive. Since the firm was growing, it was easier to sponsor a 10-member SCC team under the corporate R&D agenda without disturbing the relationships among senior leaders. But, integrating it into the core capability of the organization would call for more energy, involvement of managers at different levels and possibly conflicts. The next level of mapping and influencing was not happening.

A third problem was in the way these methods (third-order abstractions) were communicated to the IT professionals and how they responded to it. The MD was a professional in the true sense. He believed that most engineers in DCTS were also professional like him and would be keen to learn and improve their problem solving capability, but the method was too complicated to learn. Assuming this to be true, we look at what happened in training programmes. Most of the training was targeted at people and projects at offshore. Usually people who were relatively new or who were on the bench attended these programmes. Some programmes like ISP did attract senior project managers. The typical feedback from the sessions was that this is the best programme they had attended and more people should be put through this programme. But, the moment they got back to their work, they did not feel they could apply it. Some did make attempts and only ended up with more confusion. They also felt that people needed lot of support while applying it in practice—perhaps this approach should be made mandatory, may be some of the techniques should be automated and so on. Also, there was no explicit demand from IT projects for this need largely because they did not understand how to use this and also did not incorporate it in the estimation process. These methods just did not seem to gel in the context in which IT professionals were operating. Most of them were either placed as bodies or doing projects where there was limited scope for requirements definition and so on. Informal accounts also suggested that IT professionals in general felt that there was no market value for these conceptual skills, whereas there was clear demand for IT skills with opportunities to go abroad and earn more, hence more value for effort put in.[48] One of the sales directors once asked me, if Multi-Laws is a superior methodology, then why

---

48 It seemed a lot like the language problem where people prefer to learn a global language like English compared to a national language.

are other consulting firms not using it? Also, since cybernetics as a discipline did not gain sufficient visibility in the US,[49] and the words cyber/systems were being loosely used to refer to IT, most IT professionals were not able to understand the significance of the concept. As a consequence, when the MD introduced the view that DCTS would in future look at delivering "Systems Consulting" not many really understood the message. Instead of viewing it as bringing systemic problem-solving capability to consulting, many saw it as a better name for IT services (wider meaning of "Systems=>Information Systems"). In other words, while extending the programme to IT, the entire social milieu was missing. People needed a certain level of expertise that would only come out of practice and mentoring. Also, since there were not many ongoing projects applying these, there were not sufficient case studies of successful application of these methods to IT projects. Whatever case studies that were typically used were still relevant (examples like Pensions organization computerization, or Insurance organization computerization), but these were not projects where DCTS ended up delivering the software (this happened much later and possibly had no connection to these studies). As a result, IT professionals did not see the credibility in the presenters or the stories to take them seriously. Interventions during projects also did not show any potential for amplification. Some of us were still invited to participate in some projects/discussions mainly as a resource who could possibly think better. But, there was no change in the pattern of relating. SCC was not part of the logic of acquiring clients or winning business or delivering IT projects. Real change

---

49 Conway & Siegelman (2005) provide some insights into the way Cybernetics as an academic field suffered due to its association with the military.

was not coming through. But, why was there no debate on this issue? Maybe there was. But, I can sense that it might have been very difficult to argue against the MD's views or the Professor's views. They could always muster a more powerful logic than what you could put across. Perhaps this was one of the sources of the problem. People who had to implement struggled to counter this challenge with their view of reality, as they would be seen as incompetent or not trying hard enough. They eventually rejected this challenge when the leadership changed and the new leader did not seem to carry the same conviction. This is what forced me to think seriously about searching for a place in the network. You need to be part of the network to be able to feel the constraints and explore the potential for change. You cannot do that being outside the network—the core IT services network. When management consultancy was also dissolved there was no specific network that we were plugged into, and aligning with training was not going to help us in accessing the network. Training was only feeding people into the network and there was no explicit demand that called for these skills or techniques. Based on the nature of interactions that I had with people and what I saw happening I came to a conclusion that Systems Thinking can only be learnt. It has to make sense to people for them to seek more information and develop the capability. The only way seemed to be to make it a forced discipline. Some suggested that we should make it part of the quality process or build tools or integrate it with DCTS tools. In other words, constrain and use disciplinary power. However, there were no management buy-ins and the quality teams also were not keen to enforce this. They probably had challenges enforcing their own quality process, and adding another layer to it would only complicate matters. They might have used CMM as a way to push their own ideas. But, studies show that even such initiatives have been used in superficial ways. I think such disciplinary power wouldn't have succeeded and the MD realized this. One key issue was to treat Systems Engineering as a technique that can be taught. What people look for in dealing with ambiguity and uncertainty is experience or practical judgement. However, learning the techniques alone is not enough to improve practical judgement. And as Stacey (2012) suggests, practical judgement depends on four elements: (a) ongoing reflection on judgements made and consequences which takes the form of narrative and reflexive thinking, (b) continuous participation in conversations to widen and deepen communication, (c) spontaneity and improvisation, and (d) rhetoric and ethics. And some of these elements could not be sustained in this process. The problem got exacerbated by targeting this in the entire organization (intent of scalability). The focus probably should have been on finding ways to participate in IT projects and contribute to the way they dealt with ambiguity or uncertainty. I followed this path subsequently (from 2003 onwards), but was reluctant to do this in the earlier period.

Another major reason for failure, something I started realizing in 2005 after reading about Ralph Stacey's views on complexity and management, is that we were definitely complicating the space by adding more complex models to already problematic management concepts. Building more complex models on the same scientific paradigm was probably a key issue. Practitioners invariably recognize this once they step into work and find their own ways of using concepts to navigate their work and getting things done. People with some grounding or deeper association with concepts tend to look at the world using these concepts (as specialists or experts) and find it more difficult to connect.

And I was possibly in this boat. What I have realized is that both ways are problematic. Those who are so-called practitioners carry with them a number of problematic assumptions which become manifest in their engagement and in turn sustain different kinds of power relationships. On the other hand, experts tend to get trapped within their concepts and struggle to see what is emerging in front of them. In between there are a number of people who feel it is economically safer to go with the practitioner or whoever is powerful in terms of access to resources. Was putting too much cognitive focus on the problem-solving approach one of the problems, and did we downplay the interaction process in which these problems were analysed? Yes. There was certainly no explicit focus on the process of interaction. I think the Professor and former Head of SCC understood the subtle aspects of language and interactions. He had indicated several times that he wanted to have a linguist in the team. One of my seniors during his stint at a UK university introduced the notion of languaging, using the models as a way to converse about the problem. But, these did not really influence the way we interacted either within the SCC team or with the internal clients. While ideas such as "triadic approach client-consultant-problem", and the "problem changing as we speak", and "there can be no objective representation" are extremely insightful, I think we downplayed the client-consultant interaction process. Over the years I have realized that whatever you produce has to be within this nature of interaction and cannot be entirely outside this. This is extremely critical from a change perspective. But, the focus was still evidently an intellectual exercise of shaping the problem structure.

The conclusions that emerged from the failure of diffusion (in 2001) did not seem to help much. The real issue that was in front of me was how do I re-build relationships with people or alter the nature of relationships between teams and their clients. This breakdown of relationships and difficulty in forming new relationships was the real issue. Nothing could be done about this. Systems thinking as a skill did not seem to help create the initiative or capacity for creative intervention nor deal with the power imbalance in the system.[50] I did not take the route to restart the group since I felt I did not have the kind of connects that would be required to run such an initiative. My managers at that time may have viewed this as a situation where I was not showing leadership to take the challenge and show the way. To me, however, this seemed too big a problem to tackle on my own with no sign of any like-minded individuals to work with. I had to build from scratch and I felt that it might be better to network and engage with people who were interested in this topic rather than build another team.

Conclusion

In this chapter I discussed the challenges that an R&D group in DCTS faced in institutionalizing integrative thinking. While it was able to demonstrate the relevance of such a perspective through action research work with the management consulting unit, the same strategy could not be used with the IT services unit that grew at a much faster rate. The work done with the management consulting unit was perceived to be of least relevance by the IT services unit. Efforts to influence the IT services unit through training and other interventions did not seem to yield results. These gaps were arising out of different

---

50 Reflecting on it now, I feel that interpreting the scenario as a failure of diffusion is problematic. It does reduce the capacity to act. Instead, if one sees failure also as a potential social construction, then one could pay more attention to the positives in that experience and move ahead more confidently.

assumptions about customer needs. The IT services unit saw software skills and software projects as the main area of demand, while the former MD and SCC saw it in terms of holistic problem solving and consultative skills. It is possible that the IT services unit was realistic and took a view that was easier for the majority of the workforce to align with. In the process they may have lost an early mover advantage to develop a higher-level capability. To me this experience also raised questions about the way R&D should operate in services organizations, and the way we conceptualized services organizations or the unit of analysis/ intervention. Individuals or projects seemed to be very fluid entities to focus on.

Chapter 4

Differently Abled: Evolution of Consulting and Domain Practices in Indian IT Services

In this chapter I discuss the evolution of consulting and domain practices in Indian IT firms, two higher-level capabilities that had explicit market demand (unlike integrative thinking). I will primarily narrate the turbulent transition that I observed in DCTS. I will show how an independent and profitable management consultancy practice that had been in operation for more than two decades was dissolved in 1998 as part of the organizational realignment; how some small groups of IT professionals emerged to address this gap; and how consulting was re-discovered as a strategic growth area in 2003 and launched as a formal practice in 2005. Industry analysts commenting on the state of the consulting practice in 2004 suggested that the practice had the vision but lacked execution capability, and was relatively weaker compared to other Indian IT firms that had started their consulting practice much later in the late 1990s. The former MD, in a recent interview, lamented that DCTS missed an opportunity to build one of the largest management consultancies in the world. What happened? Why did leaders struggle to develop consulting capability and continue to do so, even though everyone was in agreement about the importance of consulting and there has been a clear demand for such high-value service?

Dissolving management consultancy: Creative destruction?
Let me start with some historical background about the origin of consulting in DCTS. DCTS emerged out of the need of a large industrial group to have an in-house shared services division to take care of the data processing requirements of the group companies. Once the visionary MD took over as the head of the division and understood the nature and potential of the IT business, he sensed an opportunity to turn the division into a viable unit by seeking business outside the group companies. However, selling IT directly to the industry or government in the domestic market was a challenge. There were major concerns that IT might replace labour, and technology was also expensive. Here then was an opportunity to advise clients on making effective use of IT and the choice of technologies. The MD also had a first-hand experience of this possibility while improving load balancing using IT at one of the group companies. Also, large auditing/accounting firms in US and Europe were already offering such services to clients since the 1960s.[51] Given this situation, the MD started positioning DCTS as an organization that would solve industry/government problems using IT, which means a holistic assessment of the situation followed by innovative use of IT.

---

51 Rahman and Kurien (2007) discuss the transition of auditing and accounting firms into IT consulting. One of the reasons for this is that auditing/accounting is a lot more similar to IT in the nature of rule driven work (Armbuster, 2009).

Management consultants used to front-end the client discussions with governments and industrial establishments, mainly in the domestic market, to help them identify ways to leverage IT. In the early 1970s DCTS had about 25 consultants/engineers who were involved in consultancy work for group companies/managing the computers, and about 250 in the data processing group (card punching).

However, by the mid-1970s when the MD realized that while there were very few opportunities for growth in the Indian market, the demand for IT services in US and UK was exploding due to proliferation of different standards in hardware and software, he decided to target the global market. He positioned one of his trusted IT leaders in the US market. Even though there was scepticism initially, it soon started yielding results, and in a big way. It was a phase when clients were launching several IT projects based on the advice of consulting firms, but were struggling to deliver projects on time and within budgets. They were also struggling to cope with constant change in technology where they had to rewrite/port applications from one technology to another. The proliferation was also aided by the anti-competitive suit against IBM (Sharma, 2009). These trends created a new space for providers who could just translate given requirements into software at a defined price and time. And when Indian offshoring emerged as a cheaper alternative to this problem due to the availability of better skilled resources who could handle this problem in an efficient way (often slogging for hours), it became feasible to delink conceptualization from implementation. This aligned very well with the interests of employees of Indian IT firms (who found an alternative route to go abroad), and managers (who could quickly scale up a profitable business). Such circumstances had put DCTS on a global journey. That is when the IT leaders realized that they could generate business on their own by engaging with the IT leaders of the client organizations and did not have to piggyback on management consulting. This unfortunate interpretation led to a redefinition of boundaries and widening of the gap between the two divisions, Management Consultancy (MC) and IT Services (ITS), and seeded fault-lines within the organization. The IT leaders possibly failed to see the situation on the client side. Technology proliferation was in some ways not only increasing the divide between business and IT in client organizations, but also challenging their ability to quickly develop internal IT capability.[52] Clients absolving control over their IT capability only extended the problem to a wider group of providers.[53] This seems to continue till date with job losses in the mature markets. This divide is sustained even within the IT services firms; very few people can grapple with business, technology and process complexity. By making the client organization (or their consultants) responsible for the requirement, the IT service firms restricted themselves to technology and process complexity. The MD perhaps understood this issue.[54] He tried to maintain the balance between the two lines of business (MC and IT services) by having both groups directly report to him and therefore treated at par in terms of strategic importance.

---

52 The client organizations preferred to outsource it to consultants as explained in Rahman & Kurien (2007, p.159).

53 This problem is now being recognized by some clients, especially in the wake of a digital revolution. Some firms whether in banking or telecom are now calling themselves technology firms to attract talent and rebuild their capabilities.

54 In a recent interview, the former MD makes an important point that clients should seriously look at building their internal capability.

In the 1980s, aided by the MD's vision[55] and help from the Systems and Cybernetics Centre (SCC), the management consulting unit did some high profile engagements with the government and the public sector. One of the earliest organizations that this combine worked for was the Urban Development Authority, helping it in corporatization with a focus on societal benefit. DCTS also worked with state governments to try and figure out why the central government aid was not reaching the people. About 40 such high-end engagements were done apart from several other projects. This management consulting work helped position DCTS as a thought leader in the domestic market.

However, as years passed by, the two organizational units (MC and ITS) kept moving apart. In the 1990s the IT services unit started growing at a much faster pace compared to the MC. The markets they operated, the type of people they recruited, and the processes they adopted also became distinctively different. The IT services unit was largely addressing the global demand for IT skills, hiring engineers and relying on strong recruitment, training and certification of associates, and rigorous quality management systems. MC was focused on the domestic market, targeting the government, public and private sectors, and mostly hired MBAs. Since each had to be a viable unit, they also tried to get business that would contribute to their growth. Whether it aided the other unit did not seem to be a constraint. As a result, there were

---

55 According to the MD, management consultancy is one of the best professions and there was a clear market for consultants who could help reduce complexity for clients. While complexity is predominantly a characteristic of social phenomena, people in general want things to be simple. There is hardly any limit to the price that people are willing to pay to keep things simple. Consultants should not run away from complexity. Rather, they must grapple with change head on, understand the intrinsic nature of change and learn more effective ways to cope with it. Herein, there is an implicit view that one can build better models to understand complexity.

pure management consulting projects that did not result in any IT work and there was pure IT work that did not require any management consultants.

By 1997 management consulting work was contributing to about 10 per cent of the company's revenue,[56] with a higher revenue realization (three times more) than the IT services division. However, the power relationships between the management consultants and the IT leaders started changing after the MD retired and one of the IT leaders became the new CXO. Organizational boundaries also promoted boundary judgements—where what lay inside became sacred and what was perceived as being on the outside became profane—which manifested in the interactions between individuals from the two groups. Some of the interactions revealed the nature of undercurrents. While management consultants would take pride in their superior revenue realization, IT leaders would counter this with scale and global exposure. IT leaders managed 10 times more in revenues, had a large number of people reporting to them, and international exposure. At this point it may be useful to throw some light on the linkage between scale and power. It is a typical practice to see a manager in IT firms having a large number of direct reports, much higher than the suggested norm in management, which happens to be six–eight. The span sometimes is as large as 25–30 people. This large number is an outcome of the nature of work—a majority of the IT professionals are provided to clients on a T&M basis, and the clients take care of allocating work and monitoring the work. This means there is less day-to-day monitoring for DCTS managers and only periodic checking

---

56 This is higher than the proportion of consulting revenues reported by leading Indian IT firms as of 2014.

with the clients for customer satisfaction and billing purposes. This means they could take on more people. And when a manager gets measured by the size of revenue he is controlling and when revenue is proportional to the number of people, then scale is a key source of power. Management consulting, by its nature, doesn't follow this logic. It requires regular mentoring and joint problem-solving. The logic of scale and profitability was more attractive to senior management when compared to work that required active supervision.

Other ways in which differences were expressed were in terms of the nature of work—thinking versus doing. Management consultants typically felt that their work involved complex thinking and viewed software work as low skill and low value.[57] On the other hand, IT professionals would consider management consultants as only producing abstract concepts, reports or presentations (PPTs), while they delivered actual software code that worked and made a difference. In other words, IT professionals balanced low value with tangible nature of output and belittled the intangible nature of output of management consultants, however strategic it may be. This debate on intangibles also went a bit further. The pre-sales teams that prepared proposals for IT services would challenge the management consultants on the lack of difference between their own work and that of a consultant. One of the management consultants apparently used

---

57 While task fragmentation theory argues that software work can also be divided into conception and execution, Ilavarasan (2008) shows that there is no such distinction in software work. This is because most of the workforce in IT services is homogenous. I would add that it may be a situation where their qualification is irrelevant for the task on hand. So, practically the task is challenging for all alike and they allocate work based on discussions amongst themselves and relative power differences. But, management consulting was seen as distinctive from software work possibly due to the MBA-engineering divide.

the following analogy to point to a distinction. He said that "there is a very thin line which separates a barber from a neurosurgeon, one operates above and the other operates below."[58] Another way the IT leadership challenged the management consultants was by saying that they were not in the same league as McKinsey. And if they were not at that level, then it was not worth persisting with this business[59], even though management consulting had a niche space in the Indian domestic market and was a profitable venture. These problematic interpretations closed possibilities for exploring alternatives, i.e., types of advisory work that could be relevant in an IT services context.

Efforts to align the management consultants and IT leaders seemed to prove counter-productive. Insiders[60] recounted an incident that happened in early 1998. During one of the meetings in Chennai the former MD had invited management consultants and IT services leaders for a meeting to discuss potential areas for collaboration. During the meeting, the management consultants apparently indicated that they saw little connection between what they did and what the IT services team did. They indicated that they were focusing on advising CXOs, while IT services business focused on a different problem. The MD then intervened and suggested that perhaps the management consultants were referring to themselves as "Brahmans" (higher caste) and treating the computer consultants as "Shudras" (lower caste). This way of categorizing the class difference between the two groups could have further added to the perceived difference between the two.

---

58 An anecdote shared by a former management consultant in DCTS.
59 Some of the key IT leaders seemed to be in awe of Jack Welsh and his principles for General Electric—"we should be in the top two or three businesses that we operate in".
60 An anecdote shared by a former management consultant in DCTS.

These differences became stronger, and in later days one could see people excluded on the pretext that one was a strategist, which means he/she was not practical.

While there are different ways to engage with the difference, unfortunately, in this case these conflicts did not lead to any fresh perspectives or deeper engagement. For instance, an attempt was made to bridge the gaps between MC and IT services with a common language of systems thinking that was developed by SCC (Systems Cybernetics Centre). This failed because both the management consultants and IT professionals struggled to relate to the method (discussed in Chapter 3). It also appeared that the IT leadership did not really internalize the culture of its former leader who put in a lot of effort to understand the IT business and engage the workforce. The IT leaders didn't seem too keen to engage with the difference and possibly saw it as a distraction from their pursuit of scale. For instance, the IT leadership did not seem comfortable with the pricing models used in management consulting proposals. The management consulting proposals followed different pricing models and allowance structures. Once the IT leaders moved into managing delivery centres (in 1996–97), they started taking a closer look at the management consulting proposals and began pushing them to adopt the guidelines of IT services business. Examples included staying in guest houses and using shared accommodation, even though management consultants could stay in hotels and charge the costs to clients.[61]

---

61 Management consultants see these as important factors in developing and sustaining their image with their clients who usually happen to be senior managers. I can recount a conversation that took place between one of my colleagues and the CXO of a client. While exchanging pleasantries at the beginning of a meeting the client asked the consultant when he had arrived in the city and where he was staying. The consultant felt that revealing the place where he was actually staying might not create a good impact. He therefore named a four-star hotel. The client, in turn, suggested that he stay in a different (i.e. a five-star) hotel next time.

The IT leadership felt that the best way they could use the management consultants was by positioning them as functional subject matter experts (SMEs) in ERP projects, as Business Analysts (BAs)/Project Managers (PMs) for ADMS projects. Such placements were attracting higher billing compared to the IT services. However, this couldn't alter the average billing rate of the firm since it was a relatively small number. Finally, in 1998 the leadership decided that it was time for the organization to dissolve its prevalent structure (MC and IT services) and instead move into a model of Business Lines (BLs) and Technology Lines (TLs). The MC team was told that they would not exist as a separate horizontal practice, but will have to become part of a Domain Practice or Service Line or a Delivery Centre. Recruitment in MC was stopped. Some people who did not like the idea left the organization (they either went into the industry or capitalized on the emerging ERP demand). Others who had some domain background moved into practices of interest like Government / Banking / Manufacturing or service lines such as ERP or Business Intelligence. Others tried to align with the Delivery Centre Heads and took up BA/PM, sales roles. How did this shape up? Did it help the firm deliver more domain consulting? Did it help extract domain models from projects and create accelerators? Did it improve revenue realization per consultant?

When the management consulting unit was dissolved in 1998 and people were assigned to different technology groups (Domain Practice or Service Line or Delivery Centres), they had to go through different kinds of struggles. Here is a sample of the struggles that management consultants went through in different roles in practices, PM, BA and sales. One of the expectations from management consultants was that they would help in the process of asset creation (practices were mostly run by people who came from the IT side). Many seemed to struggle with this perception, since a majority of them were either functional specialists or generalists who worked on different industry segments. The tendency to prefer status quo was rampant. Those who joined the practices did continue to do some work in specialized areas or in helping build the value chain and process models of a typical industry, but they found relating to the IT side of things challenging. The work done by the offshore delivery centres did not require deep domain understanding. As a result, they were invited only if there was a specialized need that the delivery centres could not address, for client proposals to provide relevant case studies in a domain, and to train delivery teams on domain concepts.

The IT teams also had some concerns about the effectiveness of management consultants in helping projects as BAs. Management consultants were not aware of the requirements specification methods like Unified Modelling Language (UML). The business process modelling skills that they typically possessed did not help document requirements at a level that programmers could relate to. IT people felt that having a good programmer who could think and define/understand requirements was much more useful that having an MBA who could talk at the level of process maps or strategy. Management consultants may not have understood the complexity in IT projects, but did IT people understand the problems of the MC? They tried to force domain consultants to learn IT so that they could understand what the domain guys were saying. An example of this was what happened with the discussion on operating models and IT & BPO possibilities. DCTS hired some good domain experts who could engage clients on their operating models and come up with ideas on driving more efficiency in the IT & Operations models through integrated IT & BPO services. However, DCTS at that point did not seem ready to implement such models. It was also at this point enjoying growth without doing the tough stuff. A majority of the IT leaders therefore felt it was not worth entering a terrain that was untested and risky, and transferred the responsibility or justification to those who came up with ideas. The IT team would thus challenge domain experts saying they needed to detail out the solution design to a level that they could understand it. Needless to say this was frustrating for the domain experts. They couldn't do everything on their own and needed people who understood the technology to work with them. As a result, some domain experts left the organization. This perspective also had implications for product development or development of any accelerators. IT personnel were comfortable with taking a piece of code and asking if it could be converted into a product, but the other way of taking knowledge across projects and codifying that into a product seemed problematic. Good domain architects or solution architects were also absent at that time. A senior IT manager made an interesting remark about the irony of the situation: "we need domain guys to understand the client requirements, not to talk to us."

Some management consultants did begin to appreciate the complexity on the IT side and the limitations of management consulting approaches to advise on technology choices.[62] For instance, there was an engagement to evaluate the business case for a B2B reverse auction business. The management consultant surveyed a few prospective customers and came to the conclusion that there was no market for such a venture at that point. Later he started his own venture—Software as a Service (SaaS) offering for Small and Medium Businesses (SMBs) that turned out to be successful. And after going through the struggles of creating

---

62 Views shared by a friend and former colleague.

such a business he feels that it is extremely difficult to predict how technology is shaping up and what might succeed or fail. Technology companies that were written off in their early stages turned out to be great successes later.

A key point that is worth mentioning at this stage is that in terms of power and social complexity there was no real advantage of being either MC or IT services. Mastery of MC tools by itself does not assure dealing with power difference. If the reverse had been true, they would have engaged with the power difference in creative ways instead of leaving or getting aligned. Reduced to a technical skill, the skill itself was not useful since IT professionals developed their own ways of representing problems and management consultants did not have any specific contributions here. The management consultant tools could at the most help with ERP evaluation or financial analysis. These two were easily grasped by IT people. Power differences and technical gaps added to the conflict. In a way moving up the chain seemed to be motivating and feasible from the IT people's point of view, but for the MC it was moving down the chain. Moving from a management consultant to a business analyst was seen as a demotivating activity. The possibility of creative destruction was wasted. Instead of blending management consulting with IT services, DCTS ended up losing management consulting. The change also destroyed identities of some consultants.

Incubating a differentiated service: Enterprise innovation

Let me now turn to the situation from 2000 to 2004 when there was no explicit management consulting practice. There were small groups in different parts of the organization claiming to fill this gap, for example, Strategy Consulting Practice, Architecture Consulting Group, Performance Engineering Consulting, and

Domain Consulting Group. The emergence of these groups also signalled the increasing expectations and needs of clients.

In late 2000, an enterprising young leader who was the RM of the New Zealand market returned to India and wanted to settle in Pune. He had plans to start a centre for research in enterprise innovation, possibly influenced by what he saw in the ANZ market and also as a result of the dot com era where there was a lot of focus on technology-enabled business models. He attended one of the training programmes that I was conducting on systems approach and later seemed to be interested in the ideas of viable systems. He seemed different from the RMs/ project managers/other leaders that I got to interact with. He came across as a more strategic thinker with strong business acumen, ambitious and entrepreneurial. I also understood that he had spent a lot of time with the Hewlett Packard relationship in Bangalore and seemed to have internalized the client's working culture. He also had a good working relationship with some of the IT leaders in Bangalore and in the Insurance domain, since some of the projects in New Zealand were based out of these centres and practices. He was also connected with the CXO's office due to the same reason and had the blessings of the CXO in giving shape to the idea he had in mind. We had some discussions on the topic of enterprise innovation, but nothing emerged immediately and then I had to move to Mumbai in late 2000 when the Professor of Computer Science took up the CIO role and gave me the option of joining him.

I reached out to the former RM of New Zealand again in mid-2001 when I was keen to move into the reality of the DCTS IT world. I eventually joined him in October 2001 and by that time he had also got a formal approval from the CXO to start a small Enterprise Innovation Lab (EIL).[63] I understood that in the early part of 2001 he had managed to sell and deliver a consulting engagement in the Australian market. That gave him a lot of confidence that there was potential to create a new practice around business consulting. His idea (coming from the IT background) was to do it differently, however, and not like traditional management consulting. He was keen to look at ways to create new revenue streams for the organization, either in the form of innovative business models or mobilizing new business with technology. His experience with using systems models like the Viable Systems Model in the Australian engagement had given him confidence that we could potentially use these ideas as a differentiator in developing this practice. That is where he also saw value in partnering with me, given my background in systems. The idea of creating new business opportunities that leveraged technology was also of mutual interest to us.

Once I joined, we tried to expand the team. I reached out to the training centre to seek an option to select a few candidates for the lab. We did a presentation on the lab, conducted a test with technical and ethical questions, followed by an interview. Then we inducted three more candidates into the lab and another six people from the local institute and had about 10–12 people after 8–10 months. During this period we also developed a few frameworks for business model design, process design, accelerated learning, production support and maintenance, and analysis of trends in insurance, financial services and utilities markets. I spent a lot of time understanding the literature on innovation and in services. I also reflected upon the SCC experience and tried to tease out a

---

63 The term "Lab" was chosen instead of two other terms that were widely used ("Centre" or "Group") to avoid being branded as elitist or ordinary.

framework to explain the failure of a methodological innovation. I narrowed it down to four dimensions that need to be aligned for innovations to take off. It was in line with the key principles of management – Vision & Values, Intellectual Assets, Pattern of Organization, Stakeholder relationships (VIPS).[64] I had put assets as a central factor and thought that any innovation (new asset or Intellectual Property) had to align with these factors. I also now understood the attempt to diffuse Systems Engineering as a failure to recognize it as a systemic innovation, and create complementary elements to enable the same. However, the question remained whether we could orchestrate the organizational elements and achieve desired outcomes?

Once the team size increased to about 10, we were under pressure to generate revenues and make the lab self-sustaining. My colleague and I were actively searching for consulting opportunities. We reached out to leaders of practices to see if they might introduce us to their clients. We knew that engaging internal stakeholders was going to be problematic. For instance, we shared our perspective on insurance business models and potential ways to simulate such models with the Head of the insurance practice. After a couple of slides he stopped our presentation and indicated that our thinking was very woolly. Instead of developing such

---

64   This was also inspired by David Teece's work on Intellectual Capital (Teece, 2000). In diagnosing the issues affecting rate and direction of innovation, Teece observed that "economic and organization research needs a richer framework if the innovation process is to be better understood. Economic research needs to pay greater attention to organization structure, both formal and informal, and organization research needs to understand the importance of market structure, internal structure and the business environment." He identified a set of factors that contributed to the rate and direction of innovation. For example, business environment, strategy/history, organizational structure and incentives, internal culture and values, sources of finance/external linkages, human resources, competencies and decision-making quality.

models, he felt it would be far more useful to work on problems like predictive modelling. This was again an indication of the gap between what people at the field saw and what we visualized as part of an R&D unit. We were willing to work on bridging the gap, but needed support from the field in terms of key parameters of the model and datasets, which they did not have access to. Such discussions normally failed to develop therefore. It was also a signal that traditional forms of R&D in services may have some limitations. We also realized the importance of engaging external customers.

We thus took different routes to reach out to customers. For instance, proposing a training programme for senior leaders of the group companies through the group training centre in Pune, reaching out to the group companies that were based in Mumbai and Pune, or networking with some sales leaders to get opportunities to showcase our capabilities to clients who were visiting Pune. One such opportunity emerged in early 2002. We got a chance to present our ideas to the CIO of a leisure exchange business in the US. It was a client of the powerful e-business group in DCTS, which housed all the non-ADMS technologies like ERP, CRM and Business Intelligence. We got the chance primarily because the client had expressed an interest to know about DCTS initiatives in terms of innovation. The sales team had, therefore, planned a visit to the R&D centre and also an introduction to our group and ideas. The company had an ongoing relationship with this client that involved managing their legacy systems, CRM implementation and some customer analytics leveraging a partner company. Prior to the visit the client partner had a few discussions with us to understand what we would be presenting. But, there was some friction in the discussion. It looked more like he wanted to understand what frameworks we had and what ideas we would be presenting by constantly indicating that it did not make sense, there was nothing innovative, or that it did not have sufficient granularity/clarity and so on. This was my first brush with proposal making and the typical ways sales teams used the implicit power difference to extract more information. Then the day of the customer visit arrived. We were surprised to find that in addition to the client and the client partner, the head of the e-business unit also visited Pune. And when we presented our ideas around how their business model operated and what were the alternative ways one could enhance the business model, we managed to engage the attention of the client. He seemed to see some value in what we were saying and after the discussion suggested that we should send him a proposal on how we could help. I could see that interacting with the clients seemed easier and valuable compared to doing so with our sales teams or managers (representatives of the external view). We quickly drafted a proposal and sent it to the client partner.[65] But, we did not hear much after that. When we followed up again with the client partner, he mentioned to us that the client's priorities had changed.

Around April 2002, our senior colleague in Chennai came to us with an interesting lead. One of his contacts, the CEO of a small biotech firm in Chennai, during a casual conversation had mentioned to him about a biotech innovation which he felt could eliminate vitamin A deficiency related diseases, reduce healthcare costs and transform the dairy industry. He had filed a patent in Australia and was keen to understand whether a large industrial house would help in commercializing this innovation. When our colleague mentioned this to us, we were very excited. We could

---

65 He was supposed to be the formal channel or Single Point of Contact we had to follow; we were not supposed to write to the CIO.

see that this could be very close to what we wanted to do as part of the innovation lab by creating an entirely new revenue stream for DCTS. We asked our colleague to invite the CEO of the biotech firm for a meeting in Pune. When we discussed with the CEO, we understood that the client had an autonomous innovation.[66] This in itself was not going to be a profitable venture. However, if the innovation was supported by a virtual business model it could allow the firm to control the whole value chain of milk products and generate more value. We suggested to the CEO that we could help him with developing the business model and then put a case to our management and group to see if they would want to exploit this opportunity. He agreed to our proposal. I then visited Chennai and neighbouring towns (along with the CEO) to get a first-hand view of the supply-side challenges in the dairy industry, spoke to a few consumers and shopkeepers about the demand-side issues, and also went through the patent documents and the pilot experiments that were being done in Chennai. We also gave samples for testing in the government department. Once I gathered this data, I also did a study on the state of the dairy industry in India, the economics of the value chain, and the competitive landscape and then put together a network type of business model with a strong IT backbone to orchestrate activities of different stakeholders. Our business case showed that it would be a commercially viable and potentially large-scale venture that could also start off quickly by leveraging existing farmers and their cows (without major capital investment). We then requested a meeting with DCTS CXO to present this opportunity and also guide us to a group company which we felt would be interested

---

66 Guided by the typology of innovation and organizational forms discussed in Teece (2000, pg. 63).

in this venture. Our CXO's initial reaction was "so, do you want DCTS to sell milk?" This was a bit disappointing. My colleague and I clarified to him that DCTS would have an opportunity to plan, develop and support the IT infrastructure and applications for the entire supply chain, and this could be a huge business opportunity for the group and would make a visible impact on society in terms of improved health and productivity. He then agreed to introduce us to the CEO of the other group company that was targeting the India market with products like iodized salt and packaged water. Accompanied by the CEO of the biotech firm we then went and made a pitch to the CEO of the group company and explained to him that the dairy business could complement their existing businesses and could leverage their existing distribution model to increase reach in the Indian market. The CEO of the group company said that it was exciting and then indicated that he would ask his marketing executive to visit the site and speak to the biotech CEO. But, nothing happened. We followed up and later realized that they were not interested. No reasons were given. The CEO of the biotech firm also lost interest and became unreachable. We were not able to recover the consulting cost. However, the exercise gave us a very good validation of the business model innovation framework that we had developed, while highlighting the fundamental limitation in making innovations work, i.e., stakeholder alignment. We also felt bad that we were not able to mobilize a good opportunity for an Indian IT company to make a direct impact on Indian society through a commercially viable model.

As we were ruing the missed opportunity, in December 2002, we got a call from the sales head of the e-business group. We were told that the leisure exchange CIO with whom we had interacted in early 2002 was visiting India again and had specifically asked to meet us. When my colleague and I went for the meeting in Mumbai, the CIO asked us why we were still in India, and when were we planning to come to the US. We were a bit surprised and then we realized that the client partner had some difficulty in involving us. The CIO indicated that he was launching a project and wanted us to be part of that team. But, we were not sure about the nature of the project and whether it was in line with the earlier proposal we had given and so on. It was suggested to us that we could share our proposal with the newly constituted team and work out the scope. We did so and then two of us from the lab prepared to visit the US. There was some confusion while filling up the visa documents on the nature of work we were supposed to do – was it consulting, was it innovation, was it part of the ongoing engagement with the client and so on. As the client partner was also travelling with us, my colleague suggested to me that we should be very careful in how we interact with the client partner since the latter was reporting to the e-business head who happened to be one of his peers. My colleague was concerned that we shouldn't send wrong signals.

In the US office of the client we were introduced to three other members of the project – a senior person of Indian origin was the Project Director (also ex-IBM), a person of Chinese origin (and PhD) was the Project Manager, and another person of Indian origin (an engineer settled in the US) was a team member and an expert in process re-reengineering. The BPR expert had some discussions with us on the approach we had sent and indicated to us that this study was about BPR, and our methodology may need to be tweaked. We were told that the project would be run out of a different location and there would be two more team members joining us (a PhD in Marketing and a PhD with expertise in Revenue Management—both

Indians settled in the US). The following week we moved to the new location in the mid-west. We settled in a hotel and visited the worksite. The project director soon called for a meeting to discuss the scope and objectives of the project and also get all the team members on the same page. Different people introduced themselves as experts relating to the project in scope—BPR, Marketing, Revenue Management and so on. When my turn came I said that I had a background in Systems Engineering. The Project Director did not seem to care and quickly inquired if this was my first visit to the US and I said yes. Then he asked me if I knew something about the leisure industry in the US, and I answered in the negative. He then responded saying, "If you are new to the country and the industry, then what can you do? Do you know powerpoint?" I said yes. After that there was a discussion about the scope and objectives of the project. During the discussion the Project Director and others were convinced that it was a BPR exercise aimed at driving process improvements and efficiency and that the scope involved studying their core business as well as certain recently acquired subsidiary businesses. I indicated to them that when the CIO visited us he had wanted us to study the sources of strategic advantage and alternative business models that could boost the top-line. Others seemed to disagree, albeit not strongly, as they were not privy to the meeting we had had with the CIO. Finally, when it came to work breakdown, the Project Director identified three work-streams. One work-stream was headed by the Project Manager and my colleague was asked to be part of it. The other work-stream was headed by the revenue management expert (assisted by the BPR expert), and the third work-stream was headed by the marketing PhD and I was asked to assist him. We then had to put together a presentation outlining the scope, objective, and detailed work-plan for a discussion with the Sponsor (CIO). Since I was identified as the powerpoint person, I was asked to start working on a draft and others would contribute to it. At the end of this meeting, the revenue management expert walked up to us (my colleague and I) and said, "you guys need coaching … you were put on the spot and did not know how to respond." This was uncalled for, so I politely replied that we had worked on projects before and could take care of ourselves. We were not sure, however, why we were being given this feedback by the revenue management expert who was a local contractor hired by the company for this project. Later we understood that the client partner had apparently promised him some bigger role in the organization and wanted him to keep tabs on us, an example of the surveillance mechanism.

After the short interchange, I set about putting together the presentation. Since in my mind there were two objectives of this study—one relating to process improvement opportunities, and the other relating to strategic advantages and potentially new revenue streams—I put down these as two objectives of the project and then listed the rest of the details, team structure and approach. In the approach I had infused my view of how we would look at the strategic objective. Then I shared it with the rest of the team. They had some suggestions, but no one questioned the strategic objective although they didn't seem to understand or relate to it. We started working on the templates for data collection and so on. It was around this time that I wrote a mail to the CIO (Sponsor) indicating that we have arrived in the US and started working on the project; there were some challenges with the team, but we were hopeful of getting things sorted. I had marked a copy of the mail to my colleague and the client partner. A couple of days later the Project Director said to me, in a loud voice, that he did not like my having written to his boss without his knowledge. I explained the rationale behind my mail to the Project Director and suggested that I would keep him in the loop in future communications. Then he calmed down. In the meanwhile, one of the delivery team members working on a different project said to me that there had been some escalation from the client about my work and the client partner would take care of it. After some time the client partner called me. I then inquired how my mail had reached the Project Director. He said it had gone off from his mailbox by mistake. I knew that he had played something foul here. If one looks closely, it was his attempt to keep things under control. He did not want us to speak to the CIO directly. So, he had deliberately forwarded the mail to the Project Director to ensure that such things would not happen in future. This is a typical example of how insecure sales leaders dealt with consultants who could potentially threaten their client access.

A week later, the CIO called a meeting to discuss the project charter. The entire team travelled from Indianapolis to the corporate office in Parsippany to make a presentation to the CIO. After the Project Director completed the presentation, the CIO had a specific question on the strategic objective and indicated that it would be of greater interest to him, but he left it open in terms of how the team would resolve it. This gave some explicit legitimacy to my role in the project. I could notice some discomfort in the team. The supposedly lowly powerpoint work had made its impact (an interesting example of how some simple activities can have transformational impact). Now I had two pieces of work—one was to contribute to the work-stream given to me, and the second was to look into what others were collecting and get a holistic view to address the strategic objective.

Although this was something I had to do on my own, the project structure or work-plan made no mention of it. I had experienced the same issue in an earlier project, i.e., starting in one stream and ending up as the orchestrator of the overall project findings in the end. It was not easy. I was fighting multiple battles within the overall project. Then we set out for data collection, but when we returned after the initial data collection we were told that the scope of the project had been reduced. It did not include the subsidiary, the area that was assigned to us as part of the third work-stream. We were told to help the other two work-streams. This unexpected development was a blessing in disguise for me (another example of an unplanned event changing the course of the project and stakeholder relationships). While much of the data we collected about the subsidiary was not very useful, it did give some important clues about the potential sources of power in such a business. The subsidiary was involved in the business of creating leisure assets (inherent risk in the model), while the core business was a leisure exchange. While conducting research on the subsidiary I had also read more about the challenges in that part of the business.

When I analysed the underlying business model, it struck me that there may be something wrong with the business model or the way we had understood the customer. The model was built on a positive feedback cycle—the leisure asset developers acquired customers, these customers were then given an option to become a member of the leisure exchange so that they could increase their choice, and the members were directed to different asset developers, and the developers gained from the dollars spent by members for various services at their facilities. In the process the exchange had grown in size and was more profitable than the leisure asset developers themselves. Some of the large asset developers were, therefore, showing signs of moving out and creating their own small exchanges. I could see this in the data. And now the client was trying to implement CRM systems to be able to better understand and target the members. Surely, this followed conventional logic, but did not seem aligned with the nature of power imbalance here. Suppliers had greater stake in the business model. While we started consolidating our data and thoughts, one of the team members (marketing PhD) was silently working on something. After three–four days he shared a white paper that argued why this firm should become customer centric and what it would mean to make this firm customer centric. He emailed it to the team saying that this was a document that could guide the thinking of the team as they worked on the findings. This looked like an attempt to shape the thinking in the group and possibly stake a claim for the "strategic objective" of the project. Others responded saying this was good thinking. Frankly, how could anyone contest a concept like customer centricity? However, since my analysis was suggesting that this firm may have to add more value to suppliers at that phase of its evolution, I questioned the basic assumptions of the paper and put forward my arguments. This created a bit of a flutter. People felt I was mad. My analysis did not stop there. I also noticed that the customer (or member) of the leisure exchange was more than a consumer of services. He/she was supplying inventory to the exchange, and was influencing the leisure experience by actually participating and sharing it with others. And there were different levels to which the member engaged in these activities. I therefore suggested that we should take a holistic view of the member and look at behaviour from all the three aspects, as a supplier, producer and consumer. Taking an inspiration from Alvin Toffler's concept "Prosumer",

I coined a term that embraced the three characteristics of the customer.[67] I then developed a model and used some sample data sets to show that this alternative way of looking at members and their segments might be more revealing. This was a surprise to the client's marketing team who were predominantly using the concept of cohorts to talk about customer segments and their needs. But, I think they saw some value in what I was proposing and agreed to share some additional datasets. That helped me develop a couple of other ideas in relation to the inventory and travel patterns. During the mid-term review with the CIO, I spoke about some of these ideas after the rest of the team shared their findings on process improvements. The CIO found what I said interesting. He wanted to know what this would mean in terms of the top-line. I agreed to work on the details. This was the first time that others in the project team as well as the stakeholders started to take notice of what I was doing. The day after the meeting with the CIO there was a perceptible change in the way the Project Director engaged with me. He offered to introduce me to the Finance Director and other seniors in the company. We walked them through the draft presentation and started getting some positive feedback. One day the Project Director walked up to me and said that this was one of the best consulting reports he had seen in the company in the past four years. The word started spreading that there was something interesting coming out in the study. I think what happened here is that by challenging some concepts like customer-centricity or customer as a consumer, I was pointing to the unique characteristics of the organization. Most people

---

67 I had no clue that the term appeared to rhyme with a TV series called Sopranos, which had some negative connotations according to the locals.

who had been with the organization for a longer time seemed to quickly relate to this.

After about four months we were told that the project had run out of budget and we would have to consolidate our findings and wind up. The client partner had suggested to me that I could stay on and work on another project. I indicated that if it was something to do with this project and its next steps I would consider the offer. A week later we presented the final recommendations to the CIO and his direct reports. I presented the key business ideas and demonstrated that implementing these IT-enabled innovations could generate new revenue streams and add 10 per cent to their top-line. During the presentation the CIO kept challenging me on most of the points. Towards the end he suggested that I meet him in person the next day. When I met him the next day he said that he understood what I was recommending, but was trying to challenge me so that his team also got to understand better. He inquired if his team would be able to absorb and implement this. This was a bit ironical. The CIO came from the group company that had acquired the leisure exchange. What we had demonstrated were aspects that were unique to the leisure exchange which people in the company intuitively understood. However, in the eyes of the CIO he was bringing them some new ideas and wanted me to convince them about these. After the meeting I returned to India. This experience was interesting in several ways. It gave me a first-hand experience of the notion of appreciating the uniqueness of a situation from within that situation (making the familiar look strange), and about the integral nature of power dynamics and conflicts in project teams and client organizations. There was very strong resistance within the team, even though the Project Director, the CIO and other CXOs seemed interested. Consensus on the direction for change emerged through a socialization of ideas with key stakeholders. I understood from one of my friends, who continued working with that account, that a few months later the CIO repackaged the study and presented it to the parent company. However, the mindshare and momentum created by the engagement could not be exploited by DCTS to play a more strategic role with the client, since it was viewed with a lot of suspicion by the client partner and the leadership of the account. There seemed to be a constant fear among them that the engagement could threaten their own relationships with client executives.

After my return in July 2003 I got on with other activities. My colleague who was also on the project tried to leverage this case study and interact with some of his peers. One of them happened to be the Insurance practice head. When he heard about the ideas we had delivered in this engagement, he invited me to one of his meetings where they were discussing issues in an ongoing project. We had a detailed discussion on the production support and maintenance issues that the team was facing. We analysed the data on defects and task assignment to people to come up with some views on how problem resolution was linked with knowledge accumulation in teams, and how knowledge accumulation in turn was linked with the breadth of experience that the team had in terms of different components that they worked on. While this analysis did not have any immediate impact on the project team, it proved very useful in my subsequent work. I also noticed that the insurance practice head's view towards me had changed; perhaps he felt that I had proven my credentials in an international client context.

In Oct 2003 I was asked to handle another engagement, this time a service management framework for a utilities services firm in Europe. It was another new domain and a new problem, and I did not have much background for it. My colleague had just completed an engagement on evaluating the effectiveness of SAP investment with the client. This project was an offshoot of that study. I was entrusted with the task of studying the model and suggesting recommendations. I spent about three weeks at the client site understanding how they were operating and then came up with a framework to show how they could improve service management, turn it into a continuous learning model, and use the framework to drive alignment between IT SLAs and business metrics. This again became an interesting case study. These engagements did help me in understanding how to articulate what the client should expect at each step of the engagement.

Differentiation without core transformation

It was around 2004 that there was some movement within the organization towards forming a consulting practice. The new leadership team (Think Tank) in consultation with external consultants identified consulting as a new strategic opportunity that the firm would need to pursue. It is interesting that this realization came after five years of dissolving the management consulting practice. Around this time my colleague had started discussions with a practice leader who was handling the manufacturing and engineering services practices, and had ambitions to play a greater role. The manufacturing practice had been doing some consulting work and had tied up with a renowned consultant from the Japanese market to adopt some Japanese techniques and methods. They also organized some specific training programmes to institutionalize the methods. My colleague and a few others attended these and found them simple and easy to use, and felt that we should adopt these methods. Around mid-2004 there was an announcement that my colleague and the manufacturing practice leader would help create a business consulting practice. My colleague would be the "programme manager for business consulting, and help build a common/unique DCTS way of problem solving". He appeared to have realized his intent of creating the innovation lab (eventually leading DCTS into a new revenue stream that he could manage as a business). There was a flurry of activity mobilizing people who could be part of the team, regrouping the various related pieces of work to be showcased and accounted for under consulting and so on. It looked like the leadership was now forced to re-develop consulting as a strategic growth area, but a form of consulting that would be run by people who had an IT background.

In early 2005 things changed further signalling that power relationships were still unstable. It was also clear that the idea of business consulting seemed a bit different from what the Think Tank had in mind. The manufacturing practice leader left the company after realizing that his chances of becoming the next CEO of DCTS were very slim. A new Global Practice for Consulting (GPC) was launched in 2005. The unit now reported to one of the emerging leaders in the Think Tank. The new consulting practice jumbled together some groups/numbers[68] and claimed that they were contributing three per cent of the company's revenues. It was a sign that the realignment of power in the organization was fairly complete. The new leadership had managed to protect the core and their positioning from the threat

---

68 Some small groups that have been trying to address consulting opportunities from 1999–2004 were brought under the new consulting group. Senior professionals from the quality group found an opportunity to leverage their CMM implementation and six sigma experience to advise client organizations on software process improvements. The Architecture Team found some opportunities to advise clients on technology architecture. The Performance Engineering team got involved in advising clients on improving the performance of mission critical systems. Some teams were advising clients on the selection of ERP or CRM systems.

of differentiation. A potential for creative destruction resulted in elimination of the difference, not transformation of the core organizational capability.

My colleague was side-lined[69] and decided to leave DCTS in 2006. I also did not join GPC, but advised my team to align with GPC to take care of their careers. I preferred to pursue a different theme that emerged out of my work with the utilities client in Europe, i.e., looking at the challenge of co-evolving innovation & client-access in a services context. It also appeared that my interest continued to be in pursuing the problem of developing dynamic or higher-level capabilities, i.e., changing the core organizational capability in existing relationships as opposed to building a new service practice.

Consulting in the ecosystem

The rebirth of consulting in DCTS also coincided with similar initiatives in other Indian IT firms. In fact such competitive moves may have forced DCTS to revisit consulting as a horizontal service in 2003. It was around this time that other top Indian IT firms were also making forays into consulting. In 2004 Infosys, the leader as far as stock markets were concerned, created a separate US subsidiary called Infosys Consulting (Rahman and Kurien, 2007). It was staffed with consultants drawn from top consulting firms like Deloitte and Accenture. Other top Indian IT vendors had taken the inorganic route and acquired some niche consulting firms in strategy or focused on certain verticals (they called it the string of pearls strategy). The underlying idea was that these

---

69 Apparently the CEO, who sponsored my colleague and the innovation lab, wanted my colleague to join the new consulting practice and work with the emerging leader from the Think Tank. However, my colleague had found a different interest to pursue.

skills are different and difficult to grow and need to be managed differently. Even though DCTS preferred to go with an in-house model, it had to offer skill-based incentives to attract people to GPC in the early days. But, how did these models evolve and are they different in terms of their output or value proposition? Most firms saw consulting as a critical element to improve client access—engage CXOs through consultative marketing and position them as end-to-end service providers who could deliver significant cost reduction through a combination of consulting and implementation and win larger deals. There was nothing different in the approach to problems. Most firms adopted similar styles adopted by other consulting firms—"been there, done that", "practical / actionable advice", "strong domain knowledge", "right people". But, the differences between IT services and consulting posed challenges in integrating these models.

Let us look into the case of Global Computer Services (GCS). Both customers and financial analysts had a role to play in the problematic evolution of consulting in GCS. In the initial stages (i.e., late 1990s) analysts had apparently warned the management that GCS being an IT services company should not get into management consulting or software products since both have lower P/E ratios as compared to IT services. They had even suggested that they wouldn't want GCS to balance the portfolio for them. Analysts had also expressed their strong displeasure at one such move by GCS in the late 1990s—a merger of an Enterprise Solutions JV with GCS. The problems started surfacing after this merger. One was the displeasure of the markets with the swap ratio (1:1).[70] The market apparently viewed this as complicating the business model and also felt

---

70 Articles in leading newspapers point to this issue.

that the CEO might be favouring his family and hence pulled down the market price significantly. Second, there was outrage in the rest of GCS. Many leaders with stock-options were angry not only because their stock value had plummeted,[71] but more because some of the senior consultants who came along with the Enterprise Solutions unit got hefty benefits as a result of this transaction. A third development which happened was that most of these consultants did not really persist with consulting and moved into activities that were closer to IT services. One set of people started offering services around enterprise systems (other than SAP, Oracle and BI); others who had good client-facing skills became heads of some vertical units. Apparently, they started making pitches to international clients and win business although these practices themselves were pretty small in terms of pure consulting revenue or number of consultants. Selling consulting was also problematic from the sales team's point of view. They were used to selling large-volume or long-tenure projects. Such projects were relatively easier to manage and the transaction costs involved were low. However, management consulting projects were smaller in tenure and therefore required more negotiations. And sales teams started realizing that higher value or profitability was not a real attractor; one or two small projects were not likely to alter the profitability of an account. Other issues included low conversion rates, salary discrepancy with the ODC rates, domestic market focus (low rates, although some interesting projects were done). Another issue they had was that management consultants could be easily poached by other groups that required functional expertise—SAP/BI teams. Manufacturing was a sector where they could see some value.

---

71 Information provided by a senior friend who was conversant with the issue.

IT Leaders felt that MC can make sense if it is commercially viable and a niche combined with some technology, and they were measured more by ROI and not margins (which the IT services were measured against and the same was applied to MC). Another issue was in the location. While management consulting had to move closer to the client, the overall IT organization was moving the other way, i.e., more towards offshoring. So someone came up with the clever idea of offshore consulting assuming consulting is purely an analytical task. But, that also did not fly. This is taking new forms today under the name of KPO or analytics.

Around 2005–6 GCS acquired some small consulting firms, one in BI Consulting (APAC), a second in Supply Chain Consulting (Europe), a third in Investment Management (US/UK) and a fourth in Strategy Consulting (US). As mentioned earlier this was called the string of pearls strategy. GCS also, based on lessons learnt from its earlier mistakes in acquisitions, tried to be more cautious and applied more stringent rules for pay-off for these acquisitions. While these seemed problematic, some leaders on the side of the acquired firms seemed to have signed off and then left the firm. Others who were left were very angry since they had been put in a very tough situation where they had to be responsible for getting in a certain amount of revenue to get paid by GCS. So, they started working independently. Subsidiary consulting firms struggled with retaining an independent identity (high value, high price model). In some cases where they were jointly positioned to clients, the clients used their bargaining power to demand free consulting or low cost consulting, which the consulting units resisted. In some cases, the IT firms took such risks by internally funding the consulting unit in the hope that the client would give them some downstream IT work. And when such work did not come their way, it became difficult. One of the subsidiaries had been used for a lot of pre-sales activity and after some time it looked that 80 per cent of their revenue was coming from doing pre-sales for the parent organization. There was also not much exchange of people and capability between these units. They struggled to get access to the clients. An interesting point emerges when one compares this situation with similar attempts by other firms. While the attempts of strategy firms such as McKinsey to enter IT seemed partial (and only BCG did this through a subsidiary), it is the accounting/auditing firms that were more successful in scaling the IT services business. One of the key reasons for this may have been that the accounting firms had access to the CFO/CEO of the client companies. A second reason was that IT is rule-based work like auditing/accounting (Armbuster, 2007). Attempts by IT firms to improve client access leveraging in-house or acquired consulting capabilities have turned out to be problematic because their bargaining power is relatively low. In the next section I will discuss a particular experience where I attempted to co-evolve client access and innovation in a more subtle way.

Financial analysts still see a clear difference between consulting-led firms and pure outsourcing vendors. For instance, in a recent analyst call of one of the IT firms, one analyst inquired if Indian IT is better placed to win business in the emerging digital transformation compared to consulting-led firms. Since consulting is still a small percentage of revenue of the Indian IT firms, analysts may not be very concerned.

Conclusion

In this chapter I have provided an account of the struggles that leading firms went through to develop capabilities such as consulting and domain practice. Whenever the model was perceived to be distinctively different and potentially threatening to the leadership of the core business, it did not get much support. On the other hand attempts to grow a consulting service where people were aligned with the core and had resources at their command did not really lead to an overall capability that was distinctive in the marketplace. It might take some more attempts to get this right.

Scale Takes Over:
Glimpses into the Politics of
Strategic Realignment

In this chapter I discuss how leadership change at DCTS in the mid-1990s unleashed chaos in the ranks that persisted for about four years. Out of this chaos emerged a new leadership team that was aligned with the new CXO's line of thinking. The new team capitalized on the inherent global demand for IT services and channelled energies to push DCTS into the league of top global IT firms. One could interpret this as a case where the new leaders demonstrated strong business acumen and an understanding of market realities. On the other hand, it could also be seen as a case where leaders made choices that eliminated the paradox emerging from the pursuit of value, in favour of scale. While my participation in the evolution of Integrative Thinking and consulting gave me some understanding of the micro politics of value and scale, I also got a few opportunities to directly observe the real dynamics of strategic realignment that played out in the background between 1996 and 2004.

Leadership change and realignment

DCTS went through a leadership change in April 1996. The visionary Managing Director (MD) who had led the organization for almost 30 years since its inception passed on the baton to the new CXO, one of the key leaders from the IT services division. IT services contributed 90 per cent of the revenue (in 1996) and the newly appointed CXO had been at the forefront of growing the business in one of the major markets, USA, which accounted for more than 50 per cent of the total revenue. The CXO spent the first couple of years in understanding different parts of the business (especially the non-US business) and getting to know people from different parts of the organization, including R&D groups. The CXO also felt that it was important to adopt a more consensus-oriented leadership style compared to his predecessor, partly because the organization was on a growth path (doubling in revenue every two years) and the aspirations of the people were also growing. But he was a staunch believer that only home-grown and hard-core IT operations people who understood the IT services business would be able to manage the future growth.[72]

In February 1998 the CXO invited about 30–35 senior leaders of DCTS for a brainstorming session on the future of the firm. They discussed several issues such as scaling up quickly, addressing internal systems, rebranding themselves and so on. According to him this marked a significant shift from the earlier era—towards a more consensual approach to developing strategy in DCTS. In May 1998 the CXO along with the former MD issued a note

---

72 To reinforce his viewpoint and authority the CXO had apparently made remarks such as "there were only two senior leaders in the company who had never managed an IT project and one of them is the former MD", or "anyone who is not comfortable with technology may leave the room".

to all the associates, as part of the annual performance review, outlining their plan to structure the organization to enable future growth. The view was that it was time to dissolve the distinction between management consulting and IT services and realign the organization around Business Lines (BLs) and Technology Lines (TLs) and deliver Systems Consulting, i.e., a holistic approach to solving complex problems using IT. This was followed by the setting up of a core team of four to six leaders who would interact with key stakeholders and come up with a plan for the transition to the new structure. The core team that was formed around June 1998 comprised the Professor of Computer Science and Head of Software Engineering R&D, a senior leader from IT services (he was managing a joint venture with a client), the head of one of the regional management consulting units and the Professor and former head of SCC (who was now Advisor to DCTS).

Consensus leads to confusion

The core team interacted with key stakeholders across multiple locations to seek their views and also to firm up the structure. While a great degree of focus seemed to be on the appropriate organization structure, the team (as per the suggestion of the Advisor to DCTS) also decided to do some brainstorming on the organizational objectives and the strategic direction.[73] Since I was working with the Professor and Advisor to DCTS during this period, I was also asked to assist in this exercise. We had some discussions and decided that we could do a few workshops to understand and structure the objectives. We decided to do this using a combination of Nominal Group Technique (NGT),

---

73 There was no explicit listing of strategic objectives in the four-page note circulated by the former MD and the CXO.

Stakeholder Needs Analysis (SNAC) and Interpretive Structural Modelling (ISM). We did an NGT session with the core group to collect the initial set of objectives that they had in mind or had noted during their discussions with key stakeholders. I then did a detailed stakeholder analysis and arrived at a set of 60+ objectives that seemed relevant to the firm. Post that we conducted two preliminary workshops to fine-tune these objectives. One was done with the core team (August 1998) and the other with some managers based in Hyderabad (September 1998). These workshops helped in two ways. First, they helped refine the objectives and shortlist about 35. Second, the structure of relationships among objectives that emerged from these workshops indicated that the overall objective was "to become a top global consulting firm" by "adding value to clients" and "becoming a business consultant". Once we had these dry runs and the core team seemed comfortable, the final workshop with the senior managers was planned. It was a one-day workshop involving 30+ senior managers and was organized in the corporate office in October 1998. We first went through the process of requesting participants to help refine the objectives. Later, we split the group into two teams to structure the objectives using the ISM method (using our in-house tool). I conducted one of these sessions and facilitated conversations about the interdependencies among the objectives. The leaders were kind enough to go through the exercise even though some were visibly uncomfortable with the process as it seemed a bit laborious and some questions posed by the tool challenged the prevalent assumptions. After some time the CXO also joined in, albeit with the other team. Unfortunately, midway through the session, the software collapsed and they had to restart the process. Thankfully, the session that I conducted progressed without glitches and we had a structure to discuss. We displayed the structure on the screen and the Advisor to DCTS made some high-level interpretations. Since everyone seemed tired and eager to leave in order to catch their evening flights, we summarized quickly and promised to send them the final analysis.

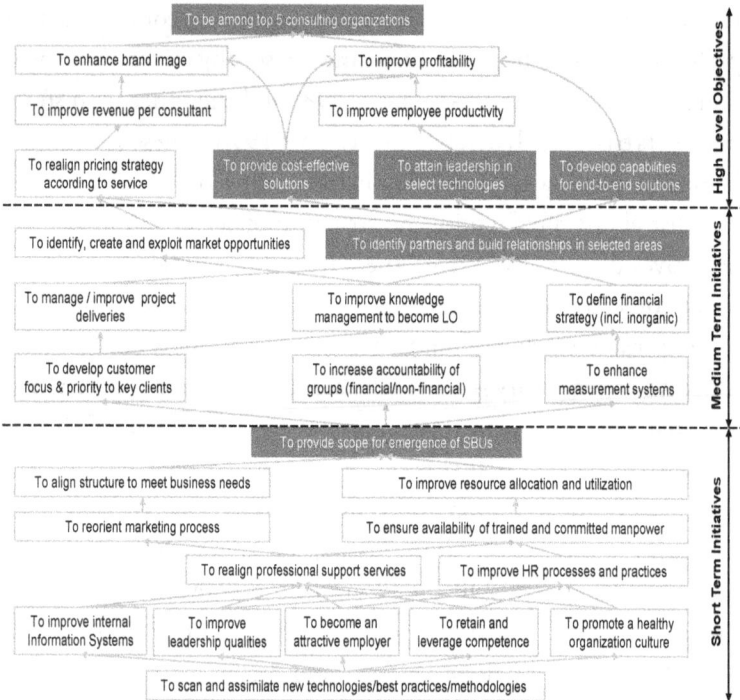

Figure 4: Realignment strategy of DCTS

The final structure (as shown in Figure 4) revealed that the overall objective or vision was to "be among the top 5 consulting firms" by enhancing brand image and profitability (which was already very high). This was in turn dependent on the revenue realization per consultant and the quality of services (cost-effective, end-to-end and leveraging expertise in select technologies). These high level objectives were in line with the earlier model. The model also revealed three paths to realize this vision—marketing, organizational (structure, HR, knowledge) and financial. One element that emerged as a bottleneck was the need for clarity on organizational structure (to organize as SBUs). This appeared to reflect the mental model of leaders at that time. Based on this and other considerations the core committee then proposed a structure to the CXO around November 1998. The report clarified the overall objective of the organization "to be among the top 5 global consulting firms" and also proposed an organizational structure to support a 30,000-strong workforce, the levels of hierarchy, roles and responsibilities and transition into an SBU structure in the future. I was not privy to the subsequent conversations, but there was no corporate-wide communication post this exercise. It looked like the CXO did not get what he was expecting from the exercise or was not confident of discussing it with his board. I felt that the model addressed the two elements of a good strategy, i.e., coherence among the objectives, and pointing to a shift towards higher level capabilities with a partnership ecosystem.[74] However, this view did not seem to resonate with a majority of the IT leaders and the CXO, even though they had participated in creating this model. They had perhaps treated it as an exercise in logical reasoning. The two factors that appeared to dominate their thinking were "becoming a top 5 global consulting firm" and "shifting to a more empowering organization structure". Both these elements seemed to reflect the aspirations of leaders rather than a strategy. Pursuit of scale was clearly emerging as an end goal. The quality of solutions or the problems of scale in the domestic market did not seem to matter. It perhaps reflected the

---

74 For a discussion on good and bad strategy, please see Rumelt (2011).

observation of Agrawal et al. (2006) on leadership challenges in Indian IT—the aspiration gap that emerges when professionals with higher qualifications tend to handle lower skilled work.

As we moved into early 1999, the general feeling among people at different levels was that there was a lot of flux and confusion in the organization and the way the terms BL and TL were being interpreted. The new terms had unleashed a lot of aspirants who felt they could make a mark by picking up a particular BL or TL. At one point there were about 50+ people reporting to the CXO. This was not very uncommon in those days. The CXO seemed uncomfortable with this situation. Heads of delivery centres, however, were not ready to share power with the new aspirants. One senior manager remarked: "there was considerable flux, but unfortunately it was coloured by personal insecurity rather than [being tackled by] positioning DCTS effectively."[75] Ironically, this had no impact on the company. It kept growing at a fast pace, aided by the deluge of work that emerged out of the Y2K bug.

Around October 1999, the CXO hired a boutique Indian management consulting firm to assist with the transition. Not many knew about this company, but they claimed (like most consultants) that they had a unique way to totally align people towards the stated goal. Their framework introduced new terms into the conversations within the organization—voice of customer, voice of employee, and so on. The consultant team went about conducting workshops with people and different BLs to help evolve a new model. At a more subtle level, it was also rumoured that they were evaluating potential leaders for the benefit of the CXO. I got a glimpse of this during one of the interactions I had with their chief consultant during an exercise

---

75 Internal memo of a senior leader.

we were jointly doing for one of the BLs. He pointed that there was a general feeling that the former MD did not give a free hand to the CXO. I was a bit surprised by this observation—what was the consultant trying to do? Was he touching the core issue of power differences? I did not know much about the undercurrents at the top. I kept talking to him about models like the Viable System Model (VSM) and their value in structuring, while he was telling me about the importance of stakeholder alignment. I think he had a point, but the way he was exploring it seemed a bit problematic to me. I tended to view his approach as too political and something undesirable. We finished the BL report and gave it back to the leaders. The report did not lead to any new action, perhaps because it did not help them negotiate structural and boundary issues.

Towards the end of 1999 there was a formal note from the CXO to all the leaders and employees about the new structure of DCTS. In the words of a senior manager[76]:

> To end the confusion that arose from consensus building and having senior people own responsibility for their role in shaping DCTS's business, the CXO mandated a specific structure for DCTS's business: (a) Service Lines, to cover horizontal, across the market services, such as those presented by technology related domains, (b) Domain Practices, to cover vertical markets, (c) Geographies, to cover the location of our customers, (d) Delivery Centres, where our solution production is located, (e) Large Client Relationships, in which mini DCTSs are setup to address specific substantial-client need, (f) Products SBU, which localize on products rather than services and (g) Corporate functions.

---

76 Internal memo of a senior leader.

The idea of Domain Practice or Service Line seemed to be akin to what was being used by some of the global consulting firms. Geography (sales), products, large clients were easily understood. The definition of delivery centres remained ambiguous. The delivery centre was the major source of power, but in the new definition it appeared that it might be reduced to a shell that would hold buildings, delivery processes and so on, but not people.

Emergence of domain practices: The compromise formula

When the CXO of DCTS announced the new matrix structure of Domain Practice/Service Lines (DP/SL) in 1999, he also gave a broad definition of what the practices were supposed to do. The definition of DP as per the DCTS circular was as follows: "DP represents vertical market groups. Its main focus will be business domain consulting and creation and incubation of intellectual assets in the form of components and products". This seemed in line with the notion of practice that existed in some leading global consulting and IT firms. At this time, as part of SCC, I did some internal consultancy work for one of the practices to help them develop a strategy and structure to realize this intent. The view within the team that worked on the banking proposal was that a DP would be an orchestrator of value. It would help the geography in business development, help execute consulting projects and support delivery centres with domain expertise and manage intellectual assets. In other words, it would help integrate and align the services/capabilities offered by different units such as products unit, delivery centres, service practices to the needs of the client and the market. The market/client relationship would be owned by the geography. However, there was no action on the report.

In 2001, when there was still a huge concern about the separation of interests among DP, SL and the delivery centre, the leadership team of DCTS commissioned a core team to brainstorm and share their views on the boundaries of a DP vis-à-vis other units. The core team involved the CIO and heads of four leading practices—banking and financial services, insurance, manufacturing and telecom. And they proposed a certain manner in which to address domain selection and measurement issues, using a three-dimensional framework of vertical markets, functional consulting, IT consulting and others windows of opportunity. This was clearly an attempt to restore the view that which service you offer to the client and what you build as a capability to deliver this service should be central to the discussion. Manufacturing was taken as one of the examples. It was one practice that had made some real headway in terms of combining domain knowledge, consulting and products as an intellectual property-led and consulting-led revenue unit that was addressing core manufacturing and engineering issues of the client. But they still did not have complete alignment with regard to a customer. The non-engineering or manufacturing work of clients was handled by the delivery centres and geographies. This exercise did not lead to any clear consensus about the boundary of a DP. The CIO was probably most disappointed since he had hoped that a consensus on the operating model would help him define a holistic IT strategy for DCTS.

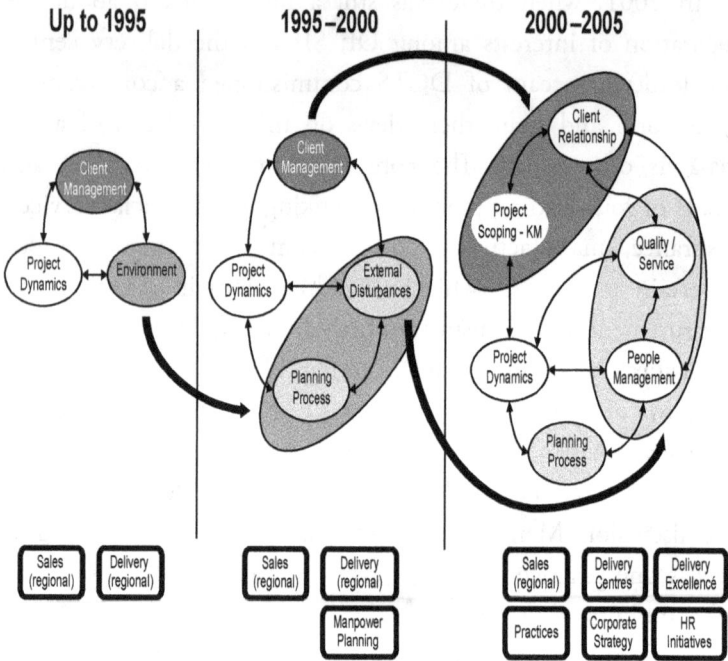

Figure 5: Organizational patterns embedded in a mental model

Around this time in 2001 I felt that in a services model, where there are a number of interdependencies, it may be difficult to draw clear boundaries. I wanted to see if a different way of analysing the clusters of interdependencies might help. I revisited the mental model of DCTS's software development process that was captured in 1995 and tried to analyse the clusters in the model to see if there were any natural groupings based on the relationships among concepts. What I found was interesting—a potential way to explain the organization's evolution over a 10-year period, as shown in Figure 5. When I split the model into three clusters it revealed the early stages of the organization—project dynamics, client management and external disturbances. The first two items relate to points *c, d,* and *e* in the organizational structure proposed by the CXO (referred to on p. 161). When it was split into four, the external disturbances cluster revealed a specific sub-cluster related to the planning process, emphasizing the emergence of corporate functions—point *g* in the structure proposed by the CXO. When the model was split into six clusters, then two new clusters emerged—client management now became Client Relationship Management and Project Scoping-KM (the idea of a practice), and the external disturbances were now split into people management and quality management—the two key sources of complexity arising from people and client requirements. This analysis also revealed that teasing out knowledge-oriented practices from a structure that was based on client management (sales) and projects (delivery) would be a challenge.[77] It also showed the close dependency between sales and practice. Ideally, both should have been onsite, with practice having a central offshore unit as well. Unfortunately, this perspective did not generate any interest. Most firms even today view practice from a cost perspective and fail to see the importance of contextual knowledge.

A peculiar situation that I observed in this particular case at DCTS was that no one seemed happy with the proposed structure. The delivery centres that owned most of the people and client ODCs felt that they would lose control by being responsible for managing delivery practices or physical centres. The DPs/SLs faced the challenge of creating and generating revenue out of assets and consulting—a difficult terrain. The geographies realized

---

77 Most leaders/firms would have had the dialogue about where to anchor a practice. The dominant conclusion is that it should be offshore, and under delivery (since delivery leadership is based at offshore). The model above shows that it has to be onsite and closely aligned with sales. The offshoring companies somehow could not understand that this investment was important. They ignored the view that knowledge and client access are closely related.

that they would now have to share client access with the DP/SL and weaken their own source of power, which was the client (and, to an extent, control over the onsite delivery staff). Generating revenue and delivering value through superior knowledge appeared extremely difficult.[78] A compromise formula that emerged in a fast-changing technology world was that any new technology that was not handled by the delivery centres would be owned by these new groups. Delivery centres would continue to own offshore delivery of ADMS projects. Geographies would own client relationships. Services relating to Enterprise Solutions (ERP, SCM, CRM, and BI & PM), Infrastructure, Engineering would be part of service lines. Further, industry native product competencies and domain solutions were taken over by the domain practices. Another aspect of this compromise was the separation of interests in terms of levels of domain knowledge as shown in Figure 6 (domain maturity was seen as a function of experience, the top-down approach was largely opposed). In essence most continued with a model that they were used to—

---

78 The Domain Practice, by definition, is expected to own and maintain a repository of industry best practices and components. This "knowledge asset" is fuzzy and abstract compared to the more tangible sources of power held by the two other components of an IT firm—sales and delivery (sales owns the client relationship/top line and delivery owns a large number of people / bottom line). And it is very difficult to evaluate the impact of this knowledge asset on the top line or bottom line unless it is translated into some software assets that are actively used in projects. The late entry of Domain Practices into IT services ecosystem has also not helped matters. Over time a compromise formula seems to have emerged where Domain Practices are treated as another Service Line (Horizontal) focusing only on core domain solutions. The sales, delivery and service line managers typically leverage them only when the projects require deeper knowledge of the domain functionality. Where projects are more technology oriented, the Domain Practices may not be involved. So, in quite a few cases there is very little presence of the practice. Where the equations between practice and accounts are good or where the client has demanded strong domain presence, one would see greater presence. Even in such cases, the practice does not have a holistic view of the relationship.

recruiting people and developing competencies in a particular ADMS technology or application like ERP/core banking. The difference between ADMS/Legacy and modern/industry native applications like ERP/core banking was the price at which you got these resources, managing the placement opportunities and the attrition rates. However, in spite of the transition and all this confusion, the company kept aggressively marching towards its short-term goal of $1 billion revenue, largely benefiting from the unexpected Y2K boom and additional work coming from client relationships established during that period.

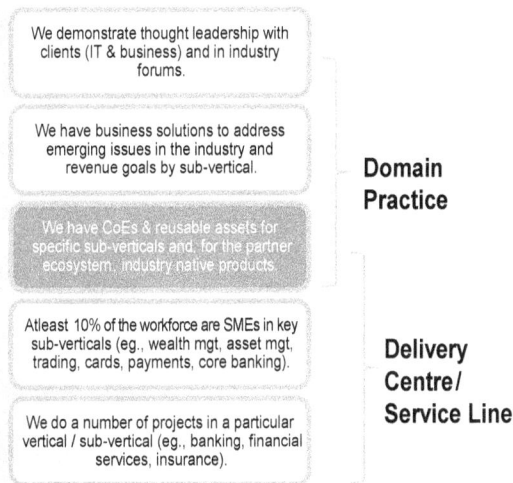

Figure 6: Levels of domain maturity and partitioning of knowledge among groups

This was the first time I started actually experiencing the politics of organization design and change, how the structure is interpreted within the prevalent power relationships among people. If the proposed structure enhanced their position, then they would support it. If the proposed structure put some people in an awkward position then they would resist it. What mattered to people most was what they owned and wanted to own, and the implications for their relationships. Not many would be willing to give up what they owned, and start creating something new that was unknown and uncertain, which could also mean a loss of identity. It seemed difficult to get people to agree purely based on logic or by shifting the power to an external entity like the customer, market and competition, especially when the organization was growing due to a broader trend of technology proliferation and globalization of services. I also started thinking that if people and their relationships were important, then why shouldn't the discussion start with them? The question was, how do we do that? In open forums people wouldn't engage or subvert the discussion since it could turn into a very open conflict. Should one resort to a more informal process? Was the external consultant trying to do this under the concept of "total alignment"?

Emergence of a new leadership team and the rhetoric of scale

Between 2000 and 2001 the CXO also made some key shifts in personnel; he moved some key people from delivery to head corporate functions such as HR and Finance. A vital point guiding these changes was that the company's key functions should be handled by hard-core and home-grown IT operations people who understand the IT services business. And through the process of interacting with several people over three to four years since his taking over as CXO, he also identified a new core team that he would work with and nurture for the future. The total (political) alignment process started by the consultant could have also played a role in this. The new leadership team primarily involved people from the IT services business who had either been part of delivering or growing the business. It was called the Think Tank and comprised the CXO, the newly appointed Finance Head (a trusted aide of the CXO who had taken over the US business after him), the newly appointed HR head (who was one of the members of the initial core team formed in 1998), a trusted lieutenant of the CXO who had been his executive assistant for some time and was currently managing the growing enterprise technologies business, the newly appointed Innovation Head, and the head of one of the largest delivery centres. Interestingly, they all came from a similar socio-cultural background, and through regular interactions and the co-location of some of them in the same building there seemed to develop a close rapport among them to the extent that each could sense what was going on in the other's mind—in other words, there was a sense of collective leadership.[79] They also inducted a well-known Harvard Business School professor to facilitate strategic conversations within the Think Tank with an outside-in view and, more importantly, to enhance legitimacy for strategic initiatives and improve visibility with global clients.

During this period, between 2000 and 2002, another conversational thread was gaining momentum. Some of the top investment bankers had been approaching the board of the subsidiary to explore options to unlock the value from DCTS, and kept engaging them by showcasing benefits that other Indian IT firms had accrued by going public. A similar proposal had

---

79 Rumours are that some of them tried to wear the same cologne or similar suits as the CXO.

been made to the Board of DCTS by the former MD in the mid-1990s. He had argued that DCTS had the potential to double its revenues every two years in the foreseeable future, largely due to the nature of the IT services business, and it was important to give it necessary freedom to pursue this growth. While the Board concurred with this view, they were not keen to let go of control. DCTS had started off as an in-house cost centre for a group of companies. Later it was made an independent subsidiary (but not a public company). The chairman and key leaders of the group had given their blessings and support to the subsidiary's plan to get into exports and grow the IT services business. Their interest and vision started paying off when DCTS started accelerating on the global arena and grew at a very rapid pace (from about $10 million in the early 1980s to $1 billion by 2003). The profits from DCTS were being used by the Board to invest in other group companies. In the late 1990s, the Board worked out a model where DCTS would keep 50 per cent of the profits for its internal expansion plans and the rest would be taken by the group. However, things started changing in 2002–3. Once the new chairman of the group started initiating the global expansion of the group companies, they felt the need to unlock the value in DCTS. In 2002, they finally gave the nod to take DCTS public.

In parallel, the Think Tank met on several occasions to deliberate on various issues using competitive benchmarking data and, after a while, articulated the new vision. This vision was similar to the one that had been articulated in 1998, but this time there was greater clarity on the scope and time-frame: "to be among the top five global IT firms by the end of the decade". They also identified five strategic areas of growth—consulting, asset-based solutions, engineering services, infrastructure services and BPO, apart from the core IT services and solutions. Each of the five bubbles was expected to contribute to a billion-dollar revenue to realize the vision. It was interesting to see consulting re-appear as a strategic growth area since the CXO had decided to wind up a viable management consulting division in 1998. And they had also adopted some best practices like Balanced Scorecard (BSC) to implement and monitor this strategy, and Economic Value Added (EVA) for measuring the profitability of units. One of the Think Tank leaders also launched a digitization initiative for automating internal processes and management reporting. While software CMM and people CMM were already being implemented and the company was eyeing CMMI implementation, the CXO also launched a people transformation initiative in 2002. The consulting firm that had done some work earlier was now running this programme aimed at people alignment and identifying the next level leaders. They interviewed people countrywide and globally, conducting Briggs-Myers assessments and involving people in a culture-change workshop. They even institutionalized this approach in the organization and constituted the groups that would conduct these sessions. And in 2004, when DCTS public listing became a great success, the CXO and the chairman of the group went on a global roadshow to engage the analyst community on DCTS, its strategy, internal initiatives and future potential. It also seemed to have helped in improving the alignment between the CXO and the chairman of the group. More fundamentally, the decision of the Board to take DCTS public gave a sense of legitimacy to pursue scale as the sole agenda in the absence of any clear vision of the kind of value that DCTS would deliver to its clients. However, it may be noted that such a scale was essentially being driven by forces outside the firm, i.e., globalization of services and proliferation of IT.

Around 2005, the CXO nominated one of the rising leaders in his Think Tank as the Chief Operating Officer (COO) thus signalling his potential successor. The action-oriented COO moved very swiftly to streamline the organization, i.e., he reduced the time wasted on thinking and launched initiatives to accelerate the journey towards the 2010 goal. In 2005, the COO announced the formation of a Global Practice for Consulting (GPC) with some consultants hired from firms such as PWC, AXON in the US and UK markets, a sales force transformation programme aimed at converting sales people into trusted business advisors with the help of an external firm and at a cost of about $10 million, and a knowledge management initiative in 2006. Eventually the firm announced in 2009 that they had joined the league of top IT consulting firms in the world in terms of metrics such as revenues, profitability and number of Fortune 100 clients. In 2011, the CXO wrote a book summarizing his achievements and the strategies he had adopted to lead DCTS into the league of global firms. It seemed like the process of establishing his identity as distinct from the former MD was completed. As of 2015, DCTS had touched $15+ billion with a market share of 1.4 per cent of the global IT services market, and were possibly convinced that their focus on scale and cost-leadership had brought them to this pinnacle.

Reflecting on my participation in strategic initiatives
While I played a support role during the period 1998–2000, between 2002 and 2008 I got to participate more actively in some of the key strategic change initiatives—some before they unfolded and others after they were initiated, in different roles, locations, sponsors and parts of the value chain. This active work started in the middle of 2002. I was part of EIL at that time. Another

senior person and long-timer in DCTS who had just returned to India after a stint in Australia as Regional Manager also decided to join the group. While in Australia, he had been closely interacting with the RM of New Zealand and when he relocated to India he decided to work with EIL after considerable back and forth on the scope, expectations and implications. Right at the outset, he wanted to understand the DCTS's Balanced Scorecard (BSC), which was published around May 2002. He asked me if I could help in analysing it and I agreed. One of the first things I did was to compare the objectives listed in the 2002 BSC and the structure with the ISM model that had been developed in 1998. I noticed a lot of similarity in the nature of objectives. However, the BSC of 2002 was more specific, i.e., there were more quantifiable goals around profitability and growth and a clear timeline for the end goal. One glaring difference was in the concept of brand development. In the 1998 strategy, map brand development was seen as one of the key higher level objectives that would make the firm one among the top five consulting firms. In the 2002 BSC, brand development was seen as an initiative by itself. This also possibly reflected the shift in values at leadership level. The issue around structure and ownership seemed to have resolved itself. They were no longer seen as bottlenecks. However, the strategic paths did not seem clear. They appeared a bit straitjacketed by the explicit hierarchy in BSC (Learning→internal processes→customer→Financial). I suggested to my colleague that he may want to relook at the relationships and see if he can drive more clarity around the strategic paths and critical success factors. I took him through an exercise of interactive planning and asked him to put in his views about the potential relationships among the stated objectives. I then analysed and indicated to him that the higher level goals seemed consistent with the overall BSC, but also pointed to some critical success factors that emerged from his perspective—aspects such as capital investments, managing the pyramid, quality management process, customer value management, global account management, brand management and academic and research alliance.

There were also two clear clusters in the model—one focused around global account management and growth, and the other including a number of initiatives in organizational and support processes like quality, global knowledge management, innovation, and these were tied with quantifiable goals such as profitability, market share and revenue realization per consultant. This seemed like an interesting split between sales and operations.

Apart from this analysis, I also tried to understand how the activities of the EIL would support this strategy. I identified the possible role to be played by EIL in the following goals: innovation, developing new business models, diversifying into new growth markets, increasing market share, global knowledge management, and other shaded portions as shown in Figure 7.

However, at that point I could not have foreseen that I would end up participating in these strategic initiatives during the rest of my work with DCTS. It started in a small way in 1999–2000, while helping Domain Practices organize themselves for improved knowledge intensity. During 2001–4, as part of the EIL (Investment in Innovation), I played a role in reviving the consulting business (one of the new high growth/high margin areas), and, through some innovative client engagements, identified new business models that DCTS could adopt. During 2004–6, I moved into key account management, i.e., building long-term relationships with clients and widening the portfolio mix with profitable clients. In this period I also attempted some exploratory work with academic and research institutions. Finally, in 2007–8, I participated in the global knowledge management initiative. It was during this phase that I transitioned from integrative thinking to innovation, which eventually led me to a paradoxical conclusion. I discuss this in the next section.

Revenue Growth
(Double every two years)

Increase Revenue
Generating Assets

Increase Revenue per
Consultant

Adopt New Business
Models

Inorganic Investments

Mix of Geo, Domain,
Service, Product
Portfolio

Diversify into new
high growth/high
margin areas

Increase Market
Share in Profitable
portfolio

Global Product
Alliance Ecosystem

Brand Development

Management
Practices

Global Academic &
Research Alliances

Investment in
Innovation

Global Knowledge
Management

**Figure 7: Strategic objectives of DCTS supported
by the Enterprise Innovation Lab**

Conclusion

In this chapter I have tried to sketch the politics of realignment that went on in DCTS as leaders grappled with the strategic choices of cost-leadership and scale versus differentiation and value, the difference between what they saw as the market need versus what was seen by the earlier leader, and how the new leadership carved out a distinct identity. This micro-politics tilted the balance in favour of scale—there seemed to be an obsession with growing in size, rather than addressing issues of scale that the country was presenting. In the next section I will show how the pursuit of scale and elimination of paradoxes at the senior management level generated new contradictions at lower levels.

Challenges of Scaling in Global IT Service Networks

"Life is a series of natural and spontaneous changes. Don't resist them—that only creates sorrow. Let reality be reality. Let things flow naturally forward in whatever way they like."

—Lao Tzu

Putting the Heart in the Mouth: Co-evolving Client Access and Innovation in a Multi-Sourcing Context

In this chapter I discuss the challenges that Indian IT service providers encounter in engaging with clients in multi-sourcing environments: the interplay of client expectations for increased value, differentiation and co-opetition;[1] differences in knowledge, culture and power between the client and the service providers; and competition among the providers. I take up one very complex scenario where DCTS benefited from three key changes on the client side: (a) a merger between two of its clients, (b) changes in the client's IT leadership and sourcing strategy, and (c) the sale of some portion of the business triggered by de-regulation. I throw light on how DCTS tried to adapt to this scenario by making sense of my own role and how I grappled with the paradox regarding

---

1   Co-opetition refers to a strategy where players are expected to collaborate and compete simultaneously.

the changing perception of DCTS from a low-cost provider to a strategic partner within the client organization and integrating high value consulting with low-cost IT services. I show how my interactions with client managers and with sales and delivery teams iterated over time and improved the positioning of DCTS with the client.

Taking up a new role in a new account model

In 2003, as part of efforts to expand the revenues of our unit (Enterprise Innovation Lab or EIL), my colleague had reached out to different client accounts to identify opportunities for consulting. One of the client accounts that he was actively exploring was in the European utilities sector. DCTS had a relatively weak presence in this client. It was doing some low-end IT infrastructure support work for the group (a majority of the client's business was in a regulated environment), and SAP application support work for one of their small subsidiaries that had started operations recently (and was expected to compete with other firms in a de-regulated environment). Since the revenue was also pretty low (less than EUR 3 million), and the utilities sector itself contributed to less than 3 per cent of the company's revenue, this account and the vertical were not in the radar of the senior management of DCTS. However, my colleague who was strategic in his thinking and had prior experience in sales, sensed that the account and the vertical had very good potential for growth and, more importantly, there seemed to be a very good possibility of demonstrating a consulting-led turnaround in the account. Another favourable point was that one of his peers, with whom he had a good rapport, was handling the offshore delivery of this particular client. In mid-2003, my colleague reached out to the account owners (sales and delivery heads), and through discussions with the IT manager of the client's subsidiary, he generated a consulting opportunity for evaluating the relevance of the group SAP solution for the new business that had to compete in a de-regulated environment. Understanding the challenges faced by the DCTS team in SAP support also helped in positioning the consulting engagement, as a logical extension to the work we were doing. My colleague, along with two other consultants, went and did this engagement. It created a very good impression with the IT manager of the subsidiary. She was able to get some quality work done at an attractive price point. The recommendations of the study also seemed to enhance her positioning with the subsidiary's CEO. Moreover, the engagement caught the attention of the group CIO. It seemed to reinforce their thinking that DCTS could be leveraged better as part of their new sourcing strategy. This alignment of interests helped improve the IT manager's trust in DCTS and she requested our help with another engagement, this time to study the service management framework and its relevance for the new business. I conducted this study in November 2003. I analysed their prevalent Service Level Agreements (SLAs) and pointed to inconsistencies in SLAs across different technology stacks. I also analysed their IT and operations data and showed ways to clarify the impact of IT service on their business, and presented a holistic framework for dynamic service management that could aid three levels of learning (i.e., improve understanding of the how, what and why of IT). The IT manager liked the output and asked me to assist with a few other issues after my return to offshore. These conversations led to the IT manager pointing us to a potential opportunity to position a business consultant with their business. We came to know that they were grappling with challenges in scaling up the new business and needed help in diagnosing the root cause of increasing backlogs. My colleague proposed the CV of one of our young, energetic and analytically strong business consultants, who had also developed a good understanding of the utilities industry and regulatory trends in the six months since joining the lab.

In January 2004, my colleague informed me that the group CIO of the same client organization was likely to visit us in early March 2004 and we would have an opportunity to showcase our capability and explore additional work with the group. He also gave me the background of the client and the account. The group CIO and his team were working towards a more effective sourcing strategy to support their business, which had emerged from a merger of two different types of utilities. They had identified DCTS as one of the offshoring vendors (there were two other offshoring vendors and four consulting partners) since it had been doing some work for both the firms that had merged, had shown potential to do better, and was one of the top Indian IT vendors (DCTS at that time was handling about EUR 3 million worth of work compared to the largest offshore vendor, which was responsible for about EUR 30 million worth of projects). However, the client's group CIO was not happy with the way DCTS managed the account. We had a situation where the Sales Director handling the account had moved out, and a new Sales Director had taken over. The Relationship Manager (RM) role was not resolved; the two people who had been managing the different businesses of the client in the pre-merger scenario were still continuing in the same manner. The new Sales Director also seemed keen to continue with this ambiguity in order to get a better grip of the account—a fairly common practice in Indian IT services. The CIO was concerned that DCTS was not adapting to the changes on their side. The CIO had apparently communicated to the DCTS sales team that they would seriously consider removing them from their list of preferred vendors if they did not show overall improvement in account management. They also apparently gave indications that they would prefer one of the RMs to handle the overall relationship, thus resolving the ambiguity on the provider side. This situation led to discussions between the sales and delivery heads and my colleague. And they agreed with the group CIO that DCTS should invest in the right people, better account management and bring more value. My colleague indicated that they had been planning to position me in that account and therefore suggested that I chart out the entire visit and also interact with the visiting delegation.

When the client team visited Pune, I made a presentation on our work at the innovation lab and showcased some assets and ideas that might be relevant to them. One of our business consultants explained our understanding of how de-regulation was impacting the utilities sector in Europe and its implications for IT. We also showcased capabilities of other groups such as Engineering Services (Asset Management) that we felt would be relevant to the client. In the afternoon I took some of the clients to a few other facilities and rounded off with a visit to the group archives that showcased the legacy of the group[2] to which DCTS belonged. The overall visit went off as planned. The client's IT leaders seemed to appreciate our willingness to learn, engage and contribute. The next day my colleague asked me to prepare to relocate to Europe to be part of the account team. My colleague told me that he had spoken to the Sales Director, RMs (sales team) handling the account, the Head of Europe business, and the head of offshore delivery, who had all agreed to deploy me as a non-

---

2   The founders of the group are well known for their focus on nation building, science and technology education and philanthropic activities

billable consultant at onsite as part of what he called a three-in-a-box model of account management. The account management responsibility was typically shared between sales and delivery heads. Here, I was being introduced as a third element into the ecosystem (under what was termed as a "Think Team") and I was supposed to work along with sales (responsible for client relationship) and delivery (responsible for project delivery) to grow the account and also generate consulting revenues. This was a relatively new model in DCTS, at a time when even the separation between sales and delivery was not entirely clear. In most cases onsite employees were controlled by the RM, and offshore employees were controlled by the Delivery Manager (DM). The closest parallel to this situation that I could conceive was that of a leisure client in US where we had a senior person working as executive assistant to the CIO, with somewhat similar responsibilities (the senior person used to manage strategic engagements, while the RM managed the regular IT services contracts). However, what I was about to embark on was more complicated. Soon I was on my way to Europe, but with considerable uncertainty and ambiguity about my role. Was I there to sell consulting or to assist the RM in selling IT services? How would I do that when I had never been in a pure sales role and did not know much about the utilities sector or the client's socio-political and cultural context? I decided to retain my rented apartment in Pune, since I was not sure how my role would develop and whether I would last more than three months in an unknown terrain.

Entering an unknown terrain

I landed in Europe around Easter time. I started by speaking to different stakeholders to get a sense of expectations. The first was the sales team that was handling the account. There were two RMs from the two components of the merged entity. I understood that one of them (the junior one) was being positioned as the overall RM for the account, while the other (senior) was being asked to be part of the Think Team. I could sense an undercurrent between the two as the senior felt that he was being sidelined and the overall ownership being given to the junior RM who seemed better at relationship management. The junior RM seemed to have the blessings of the client. Both of them in turn were concerned about my role and potential overlaps, and whether I would hijack their opportunities. The Sales Director also seemed a bit suspicious about me and my role. He spoke to me and indicated that I should look to recover atleast one and a half times the investment in my role—about EUR 50,000—on my own, and help him win IT services bids. He did not seem to care whether or not I made any consulting revenues. My colleague, on the other hand, had told me that I should look at generating consulting revenues, and help deploy some of our 10+ team members in billable assignments so that the viability of our lab could be enhanced. Most of the team members in the lab had now spent about a year and a half largely familiarising themselves with different management techniques and tools and developing frameworks for prevalent business problems, and they were keen to get into client engagements.

As I was pondering about how to align the above stakeholder interests, I also started having discussions with the RMs to understand more about the client's context, the nature of relationships they had, who were the supporters and so on. Through this I understood that the client's IT leadership (the CIO and his six direct reports) had largely come from the acquiring firm and there was a general feeling that they were better at managing IT than the acquired firm. The acquired firm did not have much representation in the leadership team. Most of them were positioned at the next level. A portion of the staff had been rebadged to a global vendor as part of a seven year infrastructure transformation deal. The application-related vendors were organized into two buckets—consulting partners and offshore delivery centres (ODCs). Consulting partners (about four) and would be engaged for strategic issues like choice of technology or programme planning, while ODCs (three service providers) were expected to deliver change-the-business and run-the-business projects within the expected time frame and budget and with flexibility of ramp-up/ramp-down. The client was willing to share their order book for the next year and the roadmap for the next two years. However, they expected the vendors to have relevant capabilities and bid for these projects in a competitive way. All this had happened in the preceding eight to twelve months, and now the leadership was focusing on getting their streamlined 200-member IT organization and eight IT partners to compete and collaborate in a multi-sourcing environment to address the upcoming transformation programmes that the business was likely to undertake. Some of them were related to merger synergies (infrastructure and application consolidation and transformation) and others were related to regulatory changes where there were initiatives to decouple distribution from transmission. This latter initiative was likely to spawn new businesses in future.

I spent a couple of weeks assimilating all the above information. Once I had a sense of the client context, their upcoming plans, our presence, competitors and their presence (by the end of third week), I put together a plan indicating what I would target and how I would work with the sales team. My plan was built around the core idea of improving knowledge intensity in our work and relationship. I used this to clarify my role with the other two RMs and showed them that there wouldn't be much overlap between my work and theirs. This seemed to ease the tensions with the sales team.[3] I then prepared to reach out to the direct reports of the CIO to introduce myself and set the context,[4]

I started by requesting meetings with a couple of people whom I had met in India, explained to them my thought process and sought their feedback. I positioned myself as a Strategy Consultant of the DCTS ODC. I put forward a view that while I did not have much knowledge about their business, and my background was not directly relevant to them, I could use this difference to listen and point to some alternative ways to solve the problems they had been grappling with. We could have a follow-up meeting if they saw some value in my perspectives. I used a framework (as shown in Figure 8) to suggest that the problems of mutual interest could be in the grey area between the consulting partners and the ODCs. In other words, problems that require an appreciation of the technical details and the big picture, problems that require building consensus among stakeholders about a technical option, problems that cut across vendors and so on. And this framework seemed to make sense to them as well.

---

3   This was a better start to the relationship compared to the earlier experience with the leisure exchange account.

4   I was not supposed to meet the CIO—he was mapped to the Sales Director and my colleague. There was a tussle there since the CIO was pretty smart and liked to talk to knowledgeable people rather than indulge in pure sales talk. The existing sales leaders struggled to engage at this level, but wouldn't allow someone outside their line function to step in and engage the client. In other words, they would rather protect their lower-level client access and source of power than allow someone to improve accessibility to higher levels in the client organization. This pattern is prevalent at multiple levels even today—individual interests predominate instead of knowledge and trust, and it is a reflection of the nature of leadership in general.

Scope: *Problems of mutual interest*

Client Perspective:
To accelerate strategy implementation;
To facilitate transformation of architecture,
DCTS Perspective:
To improve ongoing delivery;
To better respond to upcoming RFPs &
demand management;
To sell high-end work (Analysis to Advise).

Problem Complexity

High

DCTS Think

Client's Internal Team

Consulting
Partners / SI

Low

ODCs

Low   High

Client's Willingness to Pay a Premium

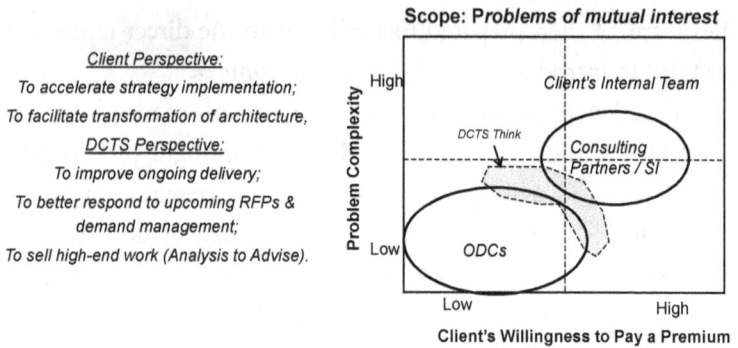

Figure 8: Model used to clarify scope of strategic conversations

About a month and a half into the work, I also started the practice of sending a weekly report to all my stakeholders (sales, delivery and my group) apprising them about the interactions I was having with the clients. In the absence of a culture of maintaining minutes of the meetings, I felt that sending the weekly report would ensure that everyone had the same piece of information. I knew that managers wouldn't give much importance to such a report as the information might be a week old and everyone knows about it. And most managers preferred telephone calls for gathering live intelligence, especially about any new opportunities and deals that they could use to their advantage. While my practice helped reduce the frequency of calls and distractions, I knew that my colleague and the Sales Director were talking to the other two RMs to gather information about what I was doing. However, since the RMs also seemed comfortable with the boundaries I had clarified with them, I do not think they had anything negative to say.

Interaction leads to more interaction
One of the first meetings came up with the client's business in the area where we were working (the new subsidiary that was

finding it difficult to scale up operations). I was told that there was a programme manager requirement, and my colleague proposed that I speak to the client and, if possible, position myself as a programme manager. I did not feel comfortable with this suggestion. I was a bit reluctant to go and make a canned presentation on programme management, and unsure whether I should position myself for that role given that I just landed here for a supposedly different role. I also wondered if my sponsors were really serious about my role. Anyway, I decided to take some time and speak to the client's COO. When I started the conversation with some background on programme management, the COO quickly suggested that they also had exposure to such frameworks and had recently hired a programme manager (I was slightly surprised since our RM had told me that the opportunity was still alive and they were still scouting for a programme manager internally based on a lead given by the IT head of this business), but his problem was different. He said that they were having challenges in scaling up the services business. It was a lean business model with some activities in the service chain outsourced to third parties. Whenever they took on more jobs, some elements in the chain broke down. This was increasing the backlog and they had to put additional resources to clear the backlog (two of our business consultants were helping clear this backlog). He inquired if there was some way he could understand the level of maturity of critical business processes and identify the processes that needed to be re-engineered. It was apparent that his operational metrics and dashboards were not supporting this endeavour. I was not sure if it was a genuine requirement or he was being polite. I indicated that I did not have a ready answer, but could research a bit more and share my thoughts. He seemed a bit taken aback by this response (he may not have got such a response from a typical consultant). Post the meeting I spent some time with our team working on the project to understand the core issues from their point of view. There seemed to be some issues in terms of what was there in the process, what was in the systems and what people actually understood. Also, some of the people hired by the contact centre had never seen the device and were unable to support the field workers. The field workers themselves were exposed to a twin challenge of using their technical skills and learning to operate the computer to record their work. This was also a sort of intrusion or supervision of their activities. As a consequence, some of them were deliberately jamming the device. The device also had performance issues. All this was adding to the confusion. I came to know that the client had hired a business consulting firm to diagnose the issues and advise them and that study was underway. I wondered how we as an IT services firm and as EIL could participate in this situation. I started looking for literature on how new businesses, especially services, scaled up their operations. I found some literature on learning curves in manufacturing firms but not much on service firms. However, it did point to important parameters such as quality of output, production capacity and learning. The other literature that I looked into was related to the capability maturity model (CMM) adopted by IT services firms. This model did not have any reference to the ideas suggested in the manufacturing literature. I checked with a few people in the team and no one had addressed anything like this before. I then came up with a three-dimensional model to understand the interplay between output, capacity and learning. And using the logic of genetic mutation I outlined the different possible states the system could move into. I took some sample data on the first two parameters and showed how one could visualize changes in these dimensions and the different levels of maturity of the business model as shown in Figure 9 below.

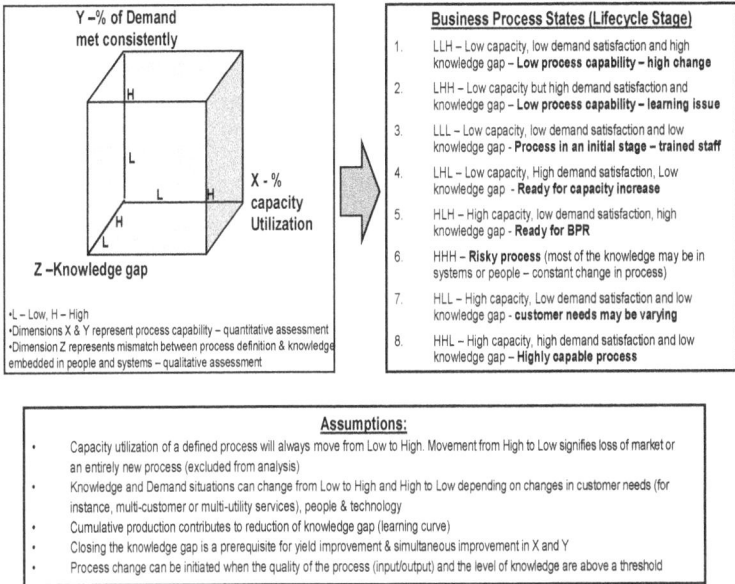

Y – % of Demand met consistently

X – % capacity Utilization

Z – Knowledge gap

•L – Low, H – High
•Dimensions X & Y represent process capability – quantitative assessment
•Dimension Z represents mismatch between process definition & knowledge embedded in people and systems – qualitative assessment

Business Process States (Lifecycle Stage)

1. LLH – Low capacity, low demand satisfaction and high knowledge gap – **Low process capability – high change**
2. LHH – Low capacity but high demand satisfaction and knowledge gap – **Low process capability – learning issue**
3. LLL – Low capacity, low demand satisfaction and low knowledge gap - **Process in an initial stage – trained staff**
4. LHL – Low capacity, High demand satisfaction, Low knowledge gap - **Ready for capacity increase**
5. HLH – High capacity, low demand satisfaction, high knowledge gap - **Ready for BPR**
6. HHH – **Risky process** (most of the knowledge may be in systems or people – constant change in process)
7. HLL – High capacity, Low demand satisfaction and low knowledge gap – **customer needs may be varying**
8. HHL – High capacity, high demand satisfaction and low knowledge gap – **Highly capable process**

Assumptions:
- Capacity utilization of a defined process will always move from Low to High. Movement from High to Low signifies loss of market or an entirely new process (excluded from analysis)
- Knowledge and Demand situations can change from Low to High and High to Low depending on changes in customer needs (for instance, multi-customer or multi-utility services), people & technology
- Cumulative production contributes to reduction of knowledge gap (learning curve)
- Closing the knowledge gap is a prerequisite for yield improvement & simultaneous improvement in X and Y
- Process change can be initiated when the quality of the process (input/output) and the level of knowledge are above a threshold

Figure 9: A model used for discussing process evolution

Two weeks later I got an appointment with the COO. Before meeting the client, I ran the model past two members of my team who were working as business consultants on the project to fix backlogs. They looked at each other and smiled, suggesting that it was too abstract and would not really help. I went ahead and presented the three-dimensional model and possible evolutionary paths to the COO. To my surprise, it seemed to generate interest and we seemed to be on the same page. He inquired if I could present this to his leadership team the next week. When I did that, his team didn't seem so excited, but they didn't reject the view either. Post that the COO asked me if I could help him facilitate a discussion on a change programme they were about to launch and for which they had hired a senior programme manager from the industry (the same role about which I had first gone to inquire). I facilitated a session where we listed out all the programme initiatives and systematically probed the dependencies using the Interpretive Structural Modelling (ISM) method. This was the first time I had used ISM with this client. The workshop took more time than anticipated. It did not seem to converge towards a coherent plan, a reflection of the state of affairs in the client's business team. However, the ISM method and tool did throw up several areas where additional clarity was required, and as a bi-product the tool seemed to generate interest among the participants. The facilitation process also possibly improved the trust the COO had in me. As time passed, our conversations started moving from one topic to another, as I had envisaged in the models (Figures 8 & 9). I had inducted a couple of more people from our team to help the client improve one of the critical business processes. In fact while discussing the solution with the client, I had given them the option to choose their resources. When they said they wouldn't mind if I suggested some people, I gave them a couple of CVs from our team. In a way I had used some of the systems methods to facilitate discussion on issues that were relevant to them and this also paved the way for a deeper understanding of their business, improving mindshare with the client and some business for DCTS. We ended up supporting different aspects of the business change programme in a relatively new domain and for a new services firm (the work done over one year is shown in Figure 10).

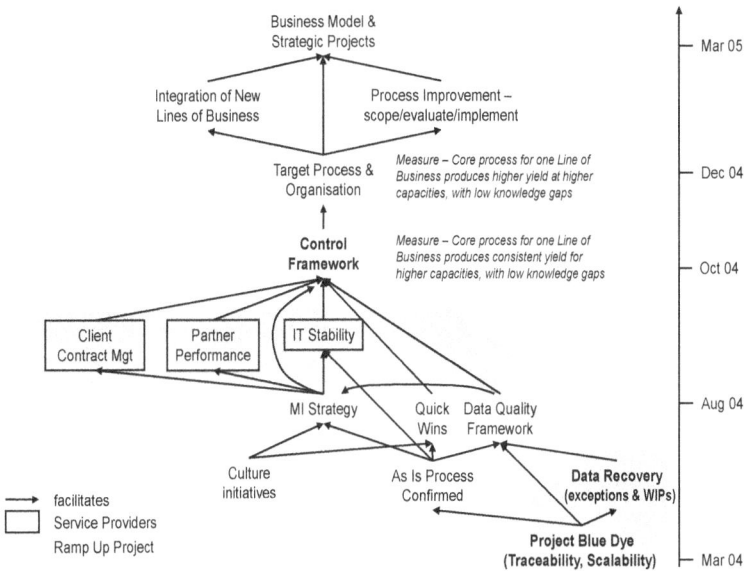

**Figure 10: Participation in a change programme in stabilizing
a new services business**

While this dialogue started developing in one part of the business, the group CIO also invited all the company's strategic partners to present plans for rationalizing the 1000+ peripheral applications they had in their portfolio. Some of the applications were incurring license costs, but were not being used. Others had run out of vendor support, and so on—typical of application portfolios in large firms and especially in merger scenarios. Our sales team had roped in a leader from the e-business practice based in India to help with this plan, apparently because they saw him as a specialist in application rationalization. And they had been discussing and finalizing the approach for some time. As the day for the presentation neared, the Sales Director who was overseeing the account introduced me to this discussion and asked me for my thoughts on the matter. After taking a look at what they were trying to present, I noticed that there was a lot of discussion on six-sigma methodology[5] and some case studies, but very little understanding of the client context. This is typical of most presentations and proposals even today—the offshore consultants do not do enough background research and ask appropriate questions to tease out relevant information, and the sales teams do not have client access that can give them a better insight into the issue. I, therefore, started asking them how the methodology was tuned to the specific problem of the client. The Sales Director and practice head seemed agitated. In fact the Sales Director inquired why I was opposing the views being presented. I explained that whatever we present should be in relation to the specific context of the client. He agreed, but did not like someone challenging their views. I then had a look at the scope of applications being considered, did some analysis and came up with a segmentation strategy indicating how we might tackle those. Having done that, I suggested a way to dovetail it with the six-sigma approach being suggested. I proposed that I could do the context setting/problem understanding using a few slides and then the practice head could present the approach and case studies. When we assembled at the meeting location, we had an opportunity to meet the CIO and his leadership team before the meeting. It was the first time I was introduced to the CIO in my new formal role as ODC strategy consultant. The CIO responded with a quick comment: "You must have done something wrong to be here". Initially, I interpreted this as a sign of power difference. But later I realized that it was a brilliant

---

5   Six-sigma is one of the popular process improvement methodologies. IT firms like DCTS borrowed it from their clients like General Electric who claim to have benefited significantly from its usage

way in which he had communicated the paradox of DCTS. As a CIO he believed that DCTS had the potential to be a strategic supplier, but it did not seem to understand this and was not paying enough attention to this account. When our turn for the presentation came, I started by sharing my high-level analysis and thoughts on how we could segment the applications based on the client's key priorities and the unique characteristics of their business and then passed it on to my colleague to present the rest. There were some questions on the approach and experience. We got a feeling that we had done a decent job, but were not real contenders since most of those applications were being supported by other vendors. Post the presentation our Sales Director got feedback that we had done a good job of understanding the key issues with whatever limited information we had access to and had put up a commendable show compared to other vendors who had more detailed information. I think this started to change the Sales Director's perception of me.

About three months into the role, my colleague also started urging me to engage the group's IT strategy team on the idea of adaptive architectures. We did not do much work in this area, but my colleague had apparently spoken to them about the idea during his interactions and felt that we should explore that conversation thread. I spent some time trying to understand what this meant and using my background in systems/complexity to model the problem in terms of standardizing nodes and relationships. What I derived was a purely theoretical perspective. However, I felt that it might help me start a conversation on a topic where there are ideally no solutions. I requested some time with the IT strategy team. When I introduced myself and started sharing my views on strategy and architecture, the head of IT strategy stopped me and asked what I meant by "strategy". I could feel the power difference. Without getting upset, I shared my view and supported it with examples. The meeting ended with no clear way forward. It became clear to me that the IT strategy team carried a certain view of Indian IT vendors. Subsequent interactions with others also suggested that there was a disconnect between the IT strategy team and the delivery teams. The IT strategy team itself had challenges selling their view to other stakeholders. I was hopeful that I might engage in further dialogue concerning this in the future, but did not see an immediate need for it.

At about the same time, an opportunity cropped up in Human Resources (HR) shared services unit of the client. The manager who was handling the shared services-related work pertaining to HR came to us inquiring if we could look into an issue they were facing in HR. Apparently, the HR business had raised questions about whether their requirements were being given priority and that many requirements were being pushed to the backburner due to a large business separation programme that was underway. They were looking at a short-term solution to combine timesheet datasets from two different ERP systems of the merged entity. A meeting was then arranged and the sales head and I went over to meet the client. We agreed to present an updated proposal, but nothing much happened. Sometime later, I received feedback from the Sales Director that the client was not impressed with me, and since I did not come across as confident, the client was not confident that we could handle the problem. He suggested that we ask my colleague to come and handle the situation. To me this seemed an issue of lack of trust. We were trying to work with the HR unit for the first time. The client was testing waters and did not feel comfortable to immediately start engaging with an ODC partner. After about three months, we got a call from the sourcing head indicating that they needed to fix an urgent problem in HR systems and since we had done some initial interactions they wanted us to participate in the discussion and suggest possible ways to tackle it. For whatever reason, my colleague could not make it, so the Sales Director, sales head and I went into the meeting with the sourcing head, HR business manager and the shared services IT manager. The client seemed interested in having a self-service intranet for their employees. Our team showcased our corporate intranet and indicated that we could build a similar solution. That meeting somehow eased tensions and the HR business manager seemed keen on further discussion. The same person, who had apparently given me feedback, was now inviting me for a meeting to explain his problem. It was not about an intranet or merger of timesheets. He wanted us to build a performance management system that combined datasets of the two merged entities, and made the process of issuing annual compensation letters smooth and efficient. Our sales team suggested that we could use a partner BPM tool. When I analysed the problem, I felt that a simple solution could tackle this requirement without having to introduce any new BPM technology into the mix. We suggested using inbuilt features in Outlook and Word and combining those with a simple web-based workflow for capturing employee validations and so on. We then estimated the cost and submitted a proposal. Once we got the approval, we implemented it. I got one of our team members at offshore to join as a business analyst on this project. We delivered the project in six weeks. The system had visibility right to the CEO level (they had to use it to validate their direct reports), the letters were issued on time, and with reduced effort. This created a substantial positive impact for DCTS (although it was less than EUR 100K in terms of revenue).

Initial success enhances internal trust

The big change in terms of acceptance within the account took place when I was about four to six months into this work. There was a large regulatory change coming up on the gas network. And the client had put out a Request for Proposal (RFP) for the same. The incumbent was another Indian IT firm with a well-established relationship with the client and was making 10 times more revenue than DCTS. They had people who knew the systems in and out and their proposal-making was entirely handled from offshore. We had no presence in that area, except for a few people who knew a bit about the process. Four of us present at onsite (the sales head, two SMEs working in related areas, and I) sat down and discussed how we might approach this. Then we analysed the RFP document and looked into additional information on their intranet, the regulatory website and so on. Finally, we felt we could construct a proposal on the following lines: (a) demonstrating a good understanding of the requirement from both the business and regulatory perspectives—we detailed out the process diagrams and indicated the context of this requirement, where it fit into the context and why it was important for the regulator; (b) looking at the scope uncertainties with regulatory projects and proposing a commercial model that could cap the investment or share savings, with flexibility to start and stop the engagement at different stages. I drafted the core ideas, and the rest of the team worked on the methodology/estimates and then submitted the proposal. We were then invited for the defence. Three of us went and presented our case. We admitted that we did not have prior experience in the area, but had a good understanding of the nature of issues that could come up in the project and could tackle them jointly with the client. This approach and our eagerness seemed to make a strong case for us. The evaluation team was split: should they go with an incumbent or should they allow an eager newcomer? The final decision was left to the CIO. Since the client was also looking at reducing risk/dependence on one vendor and here was a case where there seemed to be a competitive alternative, they decided to award the project to us. It was worth about EUR 2 million with the potential for downstream development and maintenance work. This sent shockwaves through both the competitor organization as well as our own. Our Sales Director's view towards me changed. He could see that I had contributed to winning a sizeable downstream IT project (in the context of the account). The competitor's team attributed this change in decision to my presence at onsite and they started gathering intelligence about my interactions with client managers. The Europe Head came to know about this development and he wanted to meet me.

The Europe Head asked me to join a business planning session they were planning to hold in December 2004. He wanted me to come and share my experience with the utilities account with sales leaders of other accounts. When I bumped into him before the start of the session, he said: "I understand you are doing some good work, what is your billing?" When I responded with a figure, his next question was: "how could we replicate you?" After that we assembled in a small conference room for a discussion on what I was doing in the utilities account. Two interesting things happened during that discussion. First, I was amused to find the newly appointed Global Head of Sales and Operations of DCTS popping in just in time for the presentation and leaving immediately after it. The next day I received a message from the Europe Head's office asking me to send the presentation file. I sent them the slides. It seemed like the Global Head of Sales and

Operations wanted to check what was going on. The climate was one where such developments were closely monitored especially if they were perceived to be part of a different camp. I was sure that the prevalent discourse within the firm would not allow them see the core idea, i.e., viewing interactions as opportunities for joint action, and not just "information exchange, agenda checking or reinforcing positioning". Second, at the end of the presentation the Europe Head inquired if somebody would champion the spreading of this practice to other accounts. I did not respond because I felt that this experience needed to go further before it stabilised. The Europe Head may have been surprised by this response. He had probably been expecting me to jump up and take the lead to improve my visibility. Some of the people in the audience seemed to view this as something that the client enabled, i.e., the client was encouraging this activity and the company had invested in a resource, but they did not have such luxury. Seeing no one volunteer, one of the young RMs stepped forward and said he would take ownership to coordinate and spread this idea. The Europe Head did not seem convinced and asked him if he understood the challenge. The young RM was keen to impress so he took the responsibility. I knew it wouldn't go far. He organized a couple of tele-conferences (in late December 2004 and mid-January 2005); very few people joined the call, and it ended there. What I did not realise was that the Europe Head had been trying to inquire how he could participate in what was going on and possibly contribute to it. We still had a challenge in the account in the sense that we were not really in a good position to engage the CIO. The Europe Head being based locally should have used this as a way to build the relationship. Perhaps he was concerned that the CIO was a sharp cookie and he did not have sufficient background in the utilities sector to engage the latter. It was also the time that my colleague got interested in developing a business consulting practice in DCTS, and wanted to use some of these ideas/experiences to demonstrate how business consulting can pave the way for winning larger programmes from the client. There was no direct correlation here, but the process of interacting with clients on strategic issues of interest had given us an insight into the client's way of thinking/priorities. It had created some mindshare/common ground and these seemed to help fine-tune our responses. The client was also seeing us as a vendor being responsive to their needs, which aligned with their sourcing strategy. Our quality of thinking seemed to improve through interactions and iterations. In a way this enhanced our client access and ability to innovate jointly, or rather these two aims seemed to co-evolve.

Enhancing trust with client and facilitating change

When we won the large regulatory project, it also brought us into close interactions with a powerful programme manager in the client organization. During one of the meetings I suggested that perhaps they should consider showcasing their best practices and I could facilitate extracting these. I then organized an exercise where I requested the five key project managers to list out the most important practices they had adopted in the project and took them through a structuring exercise using the ISM tool. I interpreted the model (shown in Figure 11) and showed that for them, "management style", "rigorous questioning of the scope", and "engaging vendors early in the game" seemed to be the critical success factors. The client team was very happy with what they saw as the output and decided to extend it to other areas.

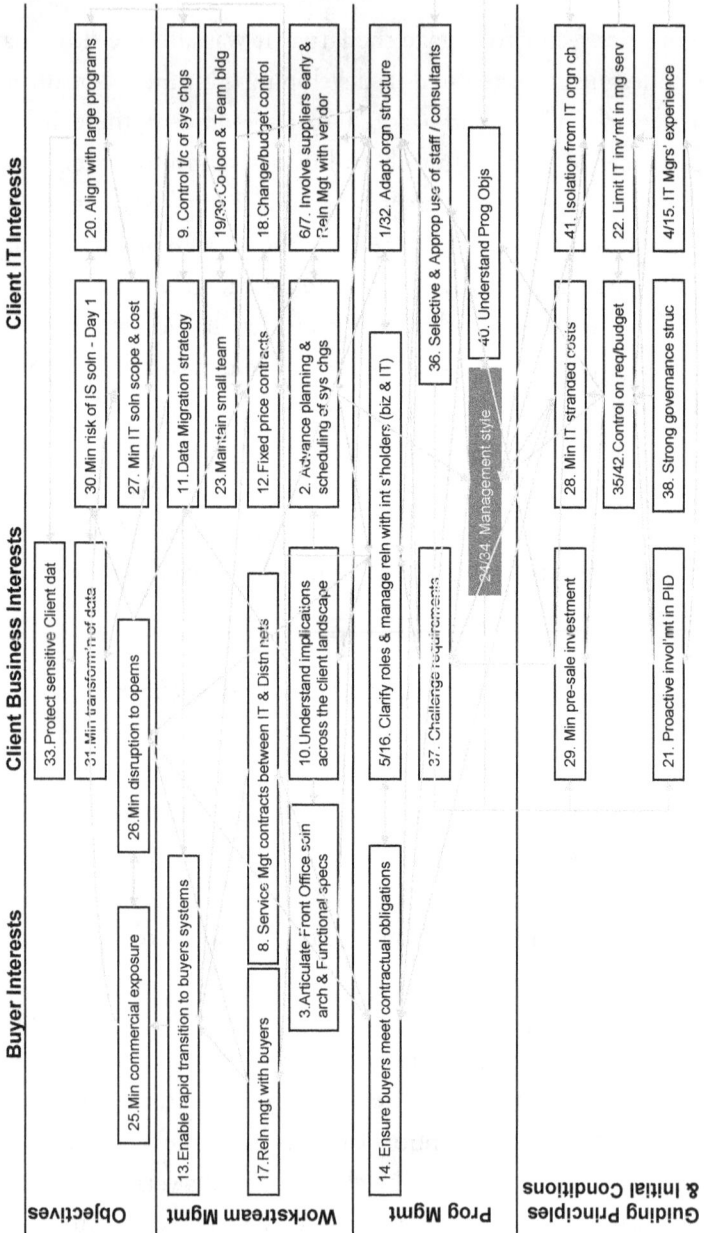

Client IT Interests

- 20. Align with large programs
- 9. Control t/c of sys chgs
- 19/39.Co-locn & Team bldg
- 18. Change/budget control
- 6/7. Involve suppliers early & Reln Mgt with ver dor
- 1/32. Adapt orgn structure
- 36. Selective & Approp use of staff / consultants
- 40. Understand Prog Objs
- 41. Isolation from IT orgn ch
- 22. Limit IT inv'mt in mg serv
- 4/15. IT Mgrs' experience
- 30. Min risk of IS soln – Day 1
- 27. Min IT soln scope & cost
- 11. Data Migration strategy
- 23. Maintain small team
- 12. Fixed price contracts
- 2. Advance planning & scheduling of sys chgs
- 24/34. Management style
- 28. Min IT stranded costs
- 35/42. Control on req/budget
- 38. Strong governance struc
- 29. Min pre-sale investment
- 21. Proactive invol'mt in PID

Client Business Interests

- 33. Protect sensitive Client dat
- 31. Min transform'n of data
- 26. Min disruption to opems
- 10. Understand implications across the client landscape
- 5/16. Clarify roles & manage reln with int s'holders (biz & IT)
- 37. Challenge requirements

Buyer Interests

- 25. Min commercial exposure
- 13. Enable rapid transition to buyers systems
- 8. Service Mgt contracts between IT & Distn nets
- 3. Articulate Front Office coin arch & Functional specs
- 17. Reln mgt with buyers
- 14. Ensure buyers meet contractual obligations

Objectives | Workstream Mgmt | Prog Mgmt | Guiding Principles & Initial Conditions

Figure 11: Best practices in a large transformation programme

Later, I was invited to do a session with the business solutions team of one of the utilities businesses to elicit best practices in feasibility and analysis. This led to another exercise with one of the key ongoing projects in that business unit, which involved making a Go/No Go decision for a call centre rationalization programme. I had facilitated a workshop for 20-odd representatives from other vendors. We had no presence in this programme but participated purely as a facilitator and helped them converge towards critical bottlenecks. Subsequently, when an opportunity emerged for positioning the programme manager for the call centre certification activity, we suggested that they look for a resource from another Indian vendor (as we did not have such a resource). I was requested to facilitate a discussion on another large programme—the infrastructure outsourcing and modernization programme that had been going on for two years and had reached a phase where there was too much finger-pointing going on. The model that emerged out of that discussion seemed to mirror the maturity model for infrastructure management. We revealed critical bottlenecks/conflicts around the licensing model that were impacting the whole programme. I did another couple of exercises for two of their subsidiaries, helping them improve the alignment of their IT strategy with their business strategy, this time using the Analytical Hierarchy Process. I also did a session with the IT sourcing team when they got absorbed under group procurement and had to align their sourcing with the group's procurement policies. In other words, I was slowly becoming one of the go-to persons for some of the complex issues that involved multiple vendors or the internal client team, and the concept of an ISM workshop was gaining traction. Ideally, the client managers should have engaged their consulting partners for these issues, but they probably saw some value in the way I was doing it. This was a case where I was able to position an element of the Multi-Laws approach directly with the client and enable change, largely relying on the nature of interactions and following the interactions and building trust at different levels. I was now in touch with about 60+ out of the 200+ client staff. But, the paradox was not resolved for all clients. During one of the discussions with a senior manager on the future direction of their mobile workforce management solution (the firm had inherited two solutions as a result of the merger and was considering the option of standardizing one), I had presented a framework to facilitate discussion among the owners of the two solutions and explore a way forward. Post that meeting, during a casual chat with the client manager, he remarked that his first impression when he saw my proposal was that either I was a genius or totally mad. This was one way clients made sense of the paradox of high value and low cost.

After about a year's work, I got an opportunity to contribute to a very confidential exercise. It emerged during a chat with one of the senior leaders. I had suggested that they could look at competence management around their projects using a network perspective. He asked me to speak to a team that was currently looking into the issue of competency and leadership development within the IT organization. The team had done a detailed exercise of defining a leadership model and evaluating the 200+ IT professionals against it, followed by a gap analysis and recommendations to close the gaps. I suggested that I could help the discussion by exploring how these strategies aligned with each other and what other insights were possible given the data that they had collected. They agreed to let me assist with this, as a short paid engagement. Delineating patterns of similarity or dissimilarity of profiles, I demonstrated potential ways to construct communities around people with similar profiles and visualizing the architecture of competencies (as shown in Figure 12). We synthesized the recommendations into a coherent set of themes. The team seemed happy and I noted after about six months that they had put together a case study in a reputed journal with a reference to my contribution. This was an instance of perhaps the highest level of trust that a service provider could build with a client organization.

Personally, it was satisfying to see the way my activities were unfolding and the nature of changes that were taking place in the perceptions of stakeholders and the way they related to me and others. I could see a definite change in the "dialogue" between service provider and the client. It resulted in interesting viewpoints as part of "strategic conversations", delivering high-value consulting services as an integral component of traditional IT services (within the constraints of the contractual arrangements) and improving mindshare and trust with client managers at multiple levels. I had also built a rich repository of ISM to facilitate conversations on difficult issues within that context.

Outside work, I also read about evolutionary economics, the roots of industrialization and how Darwin had gathered evidence for his *Origin of Species*. When I read that Darwin used to travel along with the teams that went in search of new territories to collect samples, it rang a bell. I wondered if I could see my work in a similar light—as a researcher engaging with clients on their issues and co-evolving new ways to look at the problems. Combining this with the equation I had established with the account team (sales and delivery), I felt that our joint work was like putting the heart in the mouth of a services firm—an idea promoted by Stafford Beer in *Heart of the Enterprise* on how effective organizations emerge out of the synthesis of intelligence (system 4) and monitoring and control of core operational functions (system 3). This interpretation seemed exciting. I felt like we had discovered a new model of account management that was relevant to the Indian IT services firm and a global service network.

Gap ≤ 0.5 (Do not lose it) Gap ≥ 1.5 (seek external help)

Part One: Core Capabilities

- 7. Rt decision making (1.84) PM
- 1. Result driven (2.00) SM
- 2. Team working with purpose (1.85) BA SA
- 3. Satisfy customers / suppliers (1.82) SM PO
- 4. Influence customer / supplier thinking (1.42)
- 6. Business focus (1.69) SM BA
- 5. Always impro'g (1.79) PM Mgr PO

Part Two: Leadership Capabilities

- 8. Inspire all
- 9. Lead clearly
- 10. Enable others
- 11. Implement well

Manager

- 25.b Setting & measuring targets (2.03)
- 25.a. Managing financial performance (1.78)
- 26. Mng 3rd Party / suppliers (2.31)
- 28. Making significant commercial decisions (2.17)
- 27. Managing people (2.33)
- 22. Programme mgt & delivery (PM - 1.39/PO-0.5/Mgr-2.2)
- 30. Managing change (2.27)
- 29 b. formulate strategy (MR-1.80)
- 29 a Understand Strategy (SM-1.56)
- 23.a. Mng customer relationships, (2.19)

Business Analyst

- 33. Customer Value chain concepts (1.96)
- 34.a BA techs (1.69)
- 34. c. info capture (2.11)
- 34.d.Info model'g (1.76)
- 34. e.Biz characts (1.69)
- 35. Corporate & industry Professional standards (1.83)
- 31. Business proposals (SA-1.8 / BA-1.63)
- 32.a Project plng & cntrl (BA-1.8/SA-2.2)
- 34.b Biz Improvm't (1.67)

Solution Architect

- 13. Analysis / design techs (2.40)
- 12. Appln devp method, techs (2.20)
- 15. Consultancy (2.60)
- 14.c. Std (1.8)
- 14.a Architecture & design experience (2.80) / 14 b knowledge (2.5)
- 37. Research (2.00)

Project Manager/Office

- 19. Resource allocation (1.96)
- 32.? ...ct plng & cntrl (SA.../PM-2.2/PO-1.8)
- 17. Quality mgt / testing (PM / SA) (2.22)
- 18. Structured reviews (PM-2.0/SA-2.6)
- 31. Business proposals (SA-1.8 PM-1.96)
- 32.c Project Mgt Tools (2.19)
- 20. Chg & Config mgt (PO)

Service Manager

- 23 b. Account Mgt (2.06)
- 24. Service delivery (2.06)
- 21. Contract mgt (SM – 1.7)
- 32.? ...& cntrl (SM-1.8)
- 32.? Business proposals (... 4)
- 25.c. Budget (PM-1.96/SM-1.4)
- 18. Structured reviews (PM-2.0/SM-1.6)
- 32. b. Reporting (SM-1.6/PM-2.4/PO-2.3)
- 32.d. Risks (PM-2.3/PO/SM-1.6)

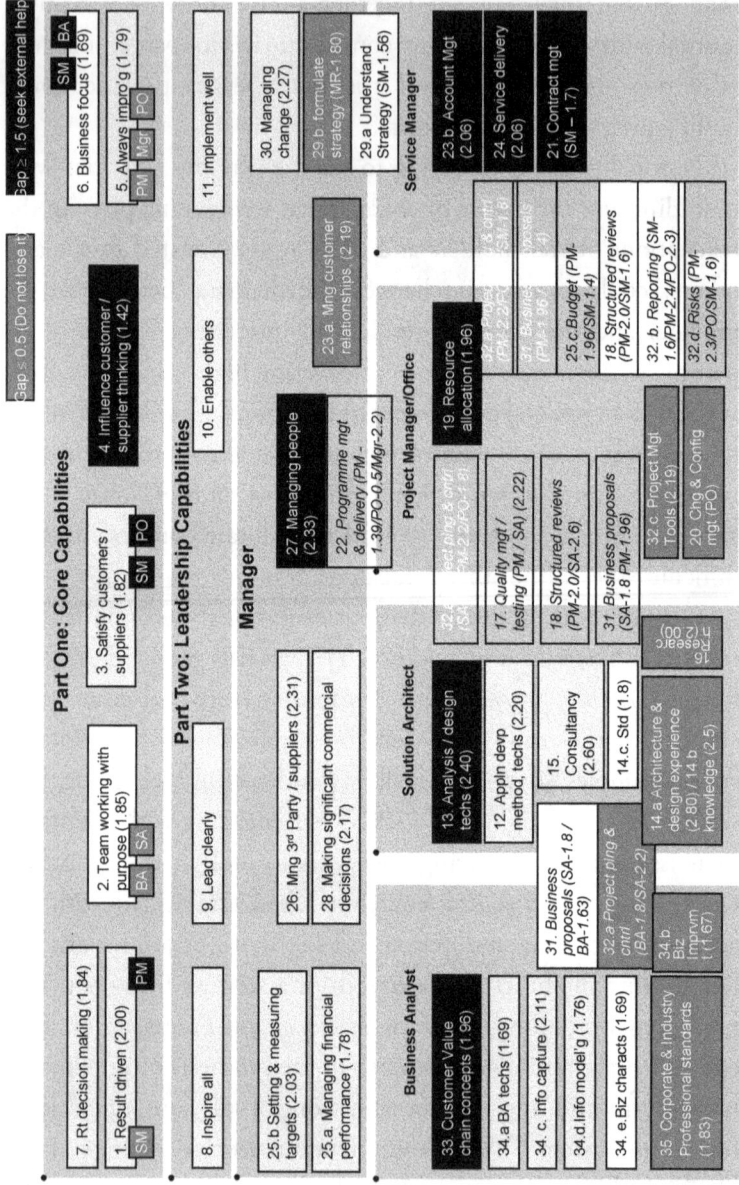

Figure 12: Sample architecture of competencies

Reflecting on the work

After about one and a half years with the account, things seemed to be flowing smoothly. I had started a dialogue with two other business units where we did not have much presence. And I could have continued, but certain changes were made in my group. My colleague who had jumped into the business consulting practice creation in 2004 was side-lined in 2005, with the creation of a new Global Practice for Consulting (GPC). And my own thinking was moving beyond consulting and into the change process, changing supplier-buyer relationships in a multi-sourcing context. Around August 2005 I felt that I should start thinking about life beyond the utilities account (by that time I had put in place some structures, processes and mentored some of them to further the dialogue with the client, although I was not sure how it would work out since the results were so dependent on the nature of interaction between people). I was also keen to put the utilities account experience in the right perspective because I thought people around me were making different interpretations and claims on the model without really understanding the root of the transformation. Some felt it was a structural change and mentoring of junior staff which made the difference, while others thought it was additional non-billable resource that made it possible. The Europe Head seemed to view it as a case of assigning good-quality consultants to accounts, adopting best practices in key account management, and frameworks like Customer Value Management. In 2006 as part of a new initiative to transform the sales process, they went about identifying key accounts that need to achieve 50 per cent growth and started assigning consultants from GPC to these accounts. The expectation was that this move would not only provide client access to the consultants of the newly formed GPC and potential consulting revenues, but would also help them work closely to develop the account. This model may not have succeeded going by what the Head of GPC told me a year later: "Yours seems to have been the only successful case. Can you tell us about the key elements of your model?" I sent him an email indicating the KRAs that I had taken up, but did not hear from them after that.

I felt that these abstractions or generalizations missed a core aspect—the account as a unit of analysis and also the role of strategic conversations. In September 2005, I attempted to summarize my experience in a paper and presented it at a complexity conference. The paper reflected my thinking at that point in time. I presented the pattern of organization (P) as a critical lever for affecting changes in the three dimensions: vision (V), intellectual assets (I), and stakeholder interactions (S). Going by the earlier analysis I had done on the software development process and the experience here I was thinking that client access and innovation (which were emerging as two key areas of improvement for Indian IT services, NASSCOM-McKinsey Report, 2002) are more intertwined and co-evolutionary. One feeds into the other. I also felt that while literature on services and organization science has established that the interface between client and service provider is a key locus of innovation, there has not been much discussion on how client access and innovation can co-evolve in a knowledge-intensive services context. Based on the experience in the utilities account I felt that account would be a good unit of analysis in IT services (unlike projects) since it exhibited characteristics of complex adaptive systems and was also more stable than projects.

However, after the conference and some more reflection and research, I started realizing the difficulty of generalizing what I had experienced. How could one generalize or replicate a process of interaction? As a manager you could create the preconditions, but could one control the process of interaction with some rules?

Many books on sales effectiveness and tools like NLP try to reduce interactions into an if-then-else type of rule book. Even other books that apply psychology to everyday problems, like how to talk to children, are aids but no conversation actually turns out as stated in the book, especially when people with different histories enter an interaction guided by so many other events that they have been party to. I also looked at some of the literature on generative dialogue (like Donnellon, 1996; Isaacs, 1999; Kahane, 2004. Borwon and Isaacs, 2005). They seemed to provide a few clues, but in some cases the recommendations seemed a bit idealistic and appealing to individuals to rise above the ordinary. I was sure from my previous experience with systems thinking that such recommendations would be extremely difficult to implement. After much reflection on my own situation I noticed that I did not benefit from any strong preconditions. Instead, I had to find my way through the situation by interacting with people and following those interactions. When I introduced myself for the first time or presented some ideas they were seen as something different (a potential challenge), and then through further interaction I searched for those transformational moments where some novelty or trust might emerge. There was considerable anxiety, uncertainty and conflict in the process, and I felt that by bringing that into the interaction it could pose a challenge for me as well as the client. I found that it was important to maintain the right degree of difference depending on how much people can really take. It also helped to be open to the possibility of being changed by what the other person might say. I felt that Ralph Stacey's (2000) views made more sense:

> Knowledge is the act of conversing and new knowledge is created when ways of talking, and therefore patterns of relationship, change. The knowledge assets of an organization

> then lie in the pattern of relationships between its members and are destroyed when those relational patterns are destroyed. Knowledge is, therefore, the thematic patterns organizing the experience of being together. Organizational change, learning, and knowledge creation are the same as change in communicative interaction, whether people are conscious of it or not.

In other words, Ralph pointed to the importance of the conversational life of people in an organization in the creation of knowledge. It was then I started realizing that the centrality of stakeholder interactions in the VIPS model. It was "interactions among stakeholders" that played a central role and paved the way for change in the other three factors. My interactions were providing a listening space to the client's senior managers to facilitate their self-interaction and probably helping them reframe their context. Later I also came across a book called *Changing Conversations in Organizations*. I immediately requested a meeting with the author and Professor Ralph Stacey to discuss what I had done and understand more about their perspective. They in turn introduced me to a new body of knowledge— microsociology, interaction rituals (IRs), symbolic interactionism, and creating realities through language. I could see the relevance of the key argument in microsociology, a shift in focus from the individual as a unit of analysis to dynamics of situations or IRs, where individual thinking is determined by the emotional energy and cognitive symbols generated by IRs (for example, see Collins, 2004, p. 4 and p. 147). Collins discusses how the initiating ingredients (physical density and barriers to outside involvement) feed into mutual focus and emotional entrainment, which in turn reciprocally build up to the situational engrossment of collective effervescence. Long-term feedbacks occur when the outcome of one IR feeds back into the conditions that make it possible to carry out a subsequent IR. In other words, interaction could lead to further interaction. This perspective marked the start of a significant shift in my understanding of organization change, i.e., towards finding ways to intervene in an organization's ongoing processes of interaction instead of treating change as an intellectual exercise or seeking idealized interactions, as in most organizational development literature.

The above shift in thinking generated an interest in me to persist with the idea of understanding the "patterns of interaction" that shaped perceptions about DCTS in that geography. I still believed that there might be some common patterns that one could extract, like in the conversation analysis literature. At a conceptual level, I was interested in gaining a deeper understanding of "changing different types of relationships through interactions and conversations" and wanted to explore if the idea of "interaction" made sense in other contexts as well, for instance, business-IT, supplier-buyer, strategy-operations, onsite-offshore, with clients in different industries. This was pushing the researcher in me to formulate a piece of work that could (a) help me look at strategic issues in global services, and (b) gain autonomy to approach it from an interactionist perspective. Around this time I received an offer from my former manager to join the re-constituted Business Systems Centre (BSC). But I was already facing an increasing difficulty with the "recursive-representational" thinking behind systems and cybernetics concepts, the "realist" ontology behind the engineering approach (even though we had talked about multiple models and laws of complexity to understand unique aspects of reality), the difficulty in moving people into action, and limitations of traditional forms of R&D in knowledge-intensive services. Instead of going back to the BSC perspective,

I approached the Europe Head with a new proposition, which I discuss in the next chapter.

In November 2005 when I officially moved out of the account I spoke to the clients and sought their feedback on how they saw my intervention and the general changes over a period of one and half years. The head of sourcing said that what I had been doing seemed a little different from how their consulting partners interacted with them. Other offshore vendors had never tried anything similar either. He was curious to know if it had helped DCTS. I informed him that it had helped us improve our presence in the account and our senior management also seemed happy about the turnaround. During 2005–6 the account became a reference customer for the utilities practice, and we had won a new client and a large transformation deal in the utilities sector purely based on the work being done here, an offshoot of the large industry separation programme that took place with this client. In 2006 I also came to know that the team that worked on internal competency development had published a paper in a journal of the Regional Computer Society about their experience, and they made a reference to my contribution. Several years later, (in 2013,) another manager in the client's supplier relationship team wrote to me indicating that he had started a new consulting firm, advising clients on how to work with offshore vendors, and stated that he had found some luck using one of the frameworks that I had used to explain my role. The interactions seemed to have left some traces.

Conclusion

In this chapter I have outlined the social and cultural challenges that I encountered in my time at DCTS, to improve client access and deliver higher-value consulting services. I have discussed in detail how I grappled with such a situation in one of the client relationships that was initially not on the radar of the senior management, but, over a period of one and a half years, emerged as a strategic account for the utilities vertical. Senior managers, instead of participating and enhancing the process, tried to interpret this development in terms of structures, resources and best practices that could be replicated. One of the questions that was repeatedly posed to me was "how can we replicate you?" My own reflection about the development helped me to understand the primacy of interactions among stakeholders, but I was still too deeply entrenched in dominant modes of thinking. I was looking for deeper patterns in relating that could lead to change. It was through my subsequent work with other accounts in 2006 that I started to move away from entrenched thought processes.

Chapter 7

Making the Familiar Strange: Triggering Strategic Conversations in Key Accounts

In this chapter I talk about the challenges that the senior management of DCTS faced while implementing key strategic initiatives to improve market positioning and shift to a more ambitious growth path, post going public in 2004. I reveal how the leadership in the Europe geography tried to drive this change in marketing, sales and delivery, and how sales and onsite delivery leaders in accounts perceived and responded to these initiatives in the light of their asymmetric power relations with clients. I also throw light on the paradox of control, where both leaders at the top and employees at the bottom felt they had less control on the situation but kept searching for the elusive control. I do this by reflecting on what I observed during my interactions with leaders of different accounts as part of a new role.

Negotiating a new role in the geography
My work with the utilities account from March 2004 onwards

had caught the attention of the Regional Head of Europe. In December 2004 I had an opportunity to meet him for the first time. A little later, in February 2005, the Europe Head asked me to participate in an initiative called Customer Value Management (CVM) that he was launching at the geography level. He had heard about the successful use of the initiative[6] in a group company (an Original Equipment Manufacturer) to change the relationship with their suppliers. I surmise he felt that what I had been doing in the utilities account was something similar, and the CVM framework might have seemed like a good way to institutionalize the practice across all key client accounts in the geography. The Europe Head nominated a couple of RMs as Single Points of Contact (SPOCs) (it is common to find Multiple SPOCs in Indian IT services). They in turn collated templates for operationalizing the framework. They seemed to treat it as a problem of quantifying intangible IT services. I participated in the initial discussions and shared my thoughts with the SPOCs. I suggested to them that communicating the value of a service was just one small solution, and possibly a difficult way of changing perceptions and relationships, especially when a supplier is in an asymmetric power relationship with client.[7] Perceptions of clients are built on day-to-day interactions with service professionals. I

---

6 One of the top five management consulting firms had helped implement this initiative in the group company. Similar ideas have been used by Japanese automakers for supply chain management. The core idea behind the CVM framework was that the client and supplier could collaboratively define metrics, measure and improve the value of the services being delivered.

7 This is different from a scenario where an OEM vendor wants his supplier to improve their capability. Here a vendor is keen to develop a relationship with the client by proposing different ways of improving the client's landscape. This gets further complicated in a multi-sourcing context. If all vendors tried to do the same, then the client would have to exhibit capabilities to synthesize the diverse best practices.

also sent the SPOCs and the Europe Head an internal working paper titled "Pushing customers to the edge" that I had written a couple of years ago, in which I argued about the limitations of such marketing concepts. While the Europe Head responded saying it was interesting, he also reiterated the importance of CVM. Clearly he seemed to value practices that had supposedly been tested and backed with results. In my opinion they were not questioning the underlying assumptions. Later in June I got a call from the Europe Head inquiring why I was not "fully involved" in CVM. I indicated to him that I had had a few discussions with the team and shared my thoughts, but hadn't received any further inputs from them; I had also been on vacation. He asked me to try and reconnect with them. I said I would and sent an email to the coordinator inquiring about the progress, who immediately sent me a set of presentations and some templates, but nothing much happened beyond that.

In mid-September 2005, I requested a meeting with the Europe Head to explain my experience in the utilities account and to find ways to participate more effectively in the challenges faced by other accounts in the geography. I also marked the email to the utilities account management team, the Sales Director and my colleague. While they did not seem to explicitly encourage this, I did not notice any open deterrence either, probably because I was responding to an earlier message from the Europe Head. The Europe Head responded immediately and suggested that we meet at the earliest. I could sense the urgency in his words and arranged for a suitable date (late September 2005) to present my understanding of the utilities account experience. I also invited the account manager and Sales Director. While the latter did not respond to my request, the former reluctantly agreed to participate over a teleconference. I felt that they were not comfortable with what I was doing and may even have seen it as a potential threat. Immediately after setting up the meeting, I received a call from one of the CVM champions inquiring if he could combine his CVM review with my meeting. I was a little surprised. I thought that perhaps the Europe Head was checking if I had something really different to say. I knew that the Europe Head tried to interpret the utilities account experience in the light of the CVM concept, but I did not view it that way. I suggested to the CVM champion that he was welcome, but I would need an entire hour to explain my perspective. He agreed to have the CVM meeting before my meeting. During my meeting with the Europe Head, I tried to present the idea of "putting heart in the mouth of DCTS" —how to enhance the brand in the European market—and tried to explain the criticality of "dialogue", focus at an account level, seeing the account as a special organizational unit, and the ways to enhance strategic alignment using business planning, account structures and focusing on identities of people. He listened to me and asked me to come back with some specifics.

At our second meeting (10 October), he invited the newly appointed Business Excellence (BE) Head to join the meeting. I was amused, and not sure what the Europe Head was trying to do. I took it in a positive light—maybe he wanted the BE Head to understand a best practice in the Europe business or use it to challenge the him to think about improving business planning. This time I presented a more detailed model of the patterns of interaction among three stakeholders—clients, accounts and corporate groups—and how to translate them into win-win-win relationships with an illustration of how we "orchestrated value in the utilities account". I also suggested the three ways in which I could contribute to the emerging themes in the geography. Each of these was aimed at energizing the linkages among clients, accounts and corporate functions at the geography level. The Europe Head indicated that some of these were already being looked into by his marketing and HR leaders, and there were other initiatives being launched at the corporate level, for instance, the sales force transformation programme. He suggested that I define a role that did not conflict with these initiatives.

In the meanwhile, I initiated a discussion with the Head of the newly constituted Global Practice for Consulting (GPC) to transfer my responsibilities and align key consulting resources in the utilities account to GPC. This was done keeping in mind the interests of the utilities account, associates and also to have a clear exit strategy for myself. While GPC at that point was eager to grab any useful resource, they may also have been suspicious about why I was handing over on a platter something that had been painfully constructed. During the conversation I also understood that the Europe Head was planning to assign consultants from GPC to various accounts. I quickly realized that they were being guided by a limited view of the utilities experience—"a structural change"— and knew that they were underestimating the complexity. It was also a sign of the tendency to simplify things in the interest of time, without really getting into a detailed understanding.

I met the Europe Head again on 8 November, for a third time. I expressed that I would like to focus on the "effective integration of initiatives at an account level," both from an "action" and "research" perspective. I proposed to target about 15 key accounts, and also to explore linkages with some academic research centres. I thought this kind of positioning would give me the independence as well as scope to observe and influence how different accounts (by size, age, service, industry) were trying to develop win-win-win relationships and how they were making sense of the strategic initiatives. Further, I clarified my intent of playing a facilitative role through the example of transferring consulting activities and resources to GPC. At the end of that meeting the Europe Head asked me to draft a note communicating my new role to his management team. I suggested the title "Relationship Advisor" to represent the core activities of the role (although I was not comfortable with the word "Advisor" as it might appear elitist, but could not think of a suitable alternative. I was not sure if people would understand a role called "Interactionist". Or maybe I should have used something like what I had seen in London Underground—"Community Support Officer who builds relationships to change neighbourhoods". I was not too concerned, however, because I was not planning to rely too much on the role definition). During the course of these three meetings, I noticed that the Europe Head as a leader and sponsor did not volunteer to summarize the role for me, and I was not clear if he had really understood what I was proposing. I knew that maintaining such ambiguity, a double bind, was a common strategy used by leaders in the face of uncertainty. This way the leader could transfer the entire responsibility of justifying the sponsorship on to me, and he could turn the tables later if the desired outcome was not achieved.

Subsequently during the week, the Europe Head sent out an email announcement to all the Sales Directors who reported to him and were managing client accounts in different industry verticals. It stated:

> In order to achieve aggressive growth targets amidst increasing competition, it is fast becoming an imperative to shift the relationship with clients from "cost" to "value". A number of initiatives have been launched at the corporate and geography levels to facilitate this shift. For instance, (a) Introduction of new services such as business and IT consulting, (b)

Integrated marketing initiatives such as DCTS-Economist thought leadership programme, (c) Sales force initiatives such as Value Advisors, Customer Value Management, Customer Relationship Management and Proactive Account Management, and (d) Organizational initiatives such as Business Excellence, People/Culture and Account Excellence Programme. However, it is becoming clear that the effectiveness of these initiatives in transforming the quality of relationships depends on an appreciation of the unique challenges and constraints faced by each account and effective differentiation and integration at the point of action. In order to catalyse and accelerate this integration, we are creating a consultative role called "Relationship Advisor". The role will focus on developing organizational spaces and offering facilitation services to accounts to help improve the quality of relationships among key stakeholders, i.e., Clients, DCTS EUROPE groups and Associates. Dr Sudhir Varadarajan will take up the role. He will report to me.

As can be seen from the above, the purpose of the new role was to facilitate the implementation of strategic initiatives (connect strategy to operations in that particular geography) so that they could lead to win-win relationships with key clients. More specifically, I was looking at initiatives used to achieve three key objectives in the geography's Balanced Scorecard (BSC): (a) "Win-win relationship with clients", (b) "Nurture a we culture", and (c) "Revenues/profitability". The first objective was addressed through initiatives such as sales force transformation, CVM and client marketing (CSAT Survey, Workshops & Events). The second was addressed through HR initiatives such as value leaders, rewards and recognition, associate engagement (face to face), and learning and competency management. There were others aimed at improving profitability and delivery excellence. Some of the initiatives involved process and technology changes as well.

What was the prevailing context?

Let me start with a brief outline of the nature of the accounts. This is important to understand the challenges in making strategic interventions in accounts. The account is a specific form of organization at the interface between two firms—the service provider and the client. It has a dynamic of its own. This dynamic emerges from the nature of services, differences in priorities and situations of clients, their global sourcing strategies where work is divided across service providers and geographies, the competition among service providers, and the aspirations of knowledge producers (associates in accounts). Associates tend to choose projects, clients and geographies which suit their interests. As a result there is constant flux. That is why we should see it as a Global Service Network (GSN), as explained in chapter 2. Added to this is the fact that accounts have only a very skeletal organization—typically the RMs and, in some cases, the DMs. The rest of the associates usually work on billable projects and are expected to work full-time on client projects. This means that the time available for activities other than sales and delivery is actually limited. People constantly complain about the lack of bandwidth even for their sales and delivery activities. This happens due to various reasons, such as high pressure sales tactics, poor estimation of effort, clients changing their requirements, and a flurry of corporate initiatives (some well-intended and many half-cooked). An overriding perception among most account managers is that they could do wonders if only they had the right number and quality of resources. They believe that this will happen through an alignment with people who have the power to allocate these resources.[8]

What did strategic initiatives mean in such a context? My work with the utilities account had helped me get a first-hand look. Typically, initiatives, in the form of new processes and tools, were introduced by corporate groups as part of the overall strategy. In some cases work practices that were seen to be successful in certain accounts were transported to other accounts as "best practices" (often in partially cooked state). Accounts were then asked to nominate associates who could champion these initiatives. This request was usually viewed as a "nuisance" by the onsite sales and delivery staff because it could potentially eat into their bandwidth (time), and attention and there was not sufficient evidence about how the practice might help them improve relationships with their clients and generate business. It was largely seen as a way for corporate teams seeking more control over accounts. They normally ignored such mails or responded to them from a compliance perspective depending on where the mail originated from and the relative dependency of the account on that source of power. They usually nominated associates who were either eager to participate in such initiatives or were unallocated, i.e., slack resources that were hidden under some billable projects (the double binds created by RMs with specific associates come into play in these scenarios). Corporate initiatives typically required the (time and attention) bandwidth of these associates. The associates would be invited for a workshop on the corporate

---

8   It is probably to change this perception that a new slogan was introduced into the discourse by a formal authority—the Global Head for Sales and Operations—"limited resources, unlimited growth". This statement suggested an end of the power struggle that went on in the background during 2002-05. The Global Head for Sales and Operations was for all purposes identified as the successor to the CXO.

initiative, and then assigned the responsibility of championing the initiative in their accounts, where it would be sustained for some time before being transferred elsewhere. After some time the initiative tended to lose steam. The associates would get some visibility with the senior managers and would be engaged further on other initiatives if they demonstrated "leadership", otherwise they would be discarded. But very few accounts derived any meaningful business value out of such initiatives. My own experience told me that this problem was due to factors such as a lack of shared vision—internally and with clients; a limited organizational structure which did not give sufficient visibility to all those who were taking additional responsibilities; inadequate competencies; and fundamentally, poor dialogue processes at the account level. I also felt that bandwidth was not really an issue. The more pertinent issue was that bandwidth was not available in the timeline of the corporate group running the initiative. All this suggested to me that managers would need to pay more attention to the unique challenges at the account level instead of restricting themselves to macro-level monitoring and planning new initiatives.

How did my role take shape? What happened in the initial stages?

Given the above situation, I started thinking about the different ways in which I could improve the situation and address the goals that I had agreed upon with the Europe Head. My thoughts travelled in different directions:

- Would a managerial approach of setting macro policies and initiatives such as sales training, account organization, and process and technology help? This usually comes under a manager's purview; it This usually comes under a manager's purview; it would not make sense to introduce another manager to manage all the interfaces. In addition, the Business Excellence Head was possibly helping align the interfaces through integrated business planning and BSC metrics.

- Would a programme management approach to change help? As I have mentioned earlier, most of these initiatives required associate involvement, and different accounts had different priorities and a perennial shortage of resources. How would a change programme align these diverse priorities? A considerable amount of time would have to be spent on coordination.

- Would a consulting approach help? Where would I get the high-quality resources for doing such a complex internal study? Will the stakeholders be able to act on the findings?

- Would mentoring or coaching the sales team have the desired effect? Would sales teams see any value in discussing their issues with me when they were already reporting to at least two stakeholders, especially given that I did not have the power to address their resource issues? Would focusing on one person help in improving his/her relational capacity (relational capacity probably depends on group life)? How about changing the relationship between sales and delivery or between knowledge producer (associate) and clients? Did the sales team have sufficient power over accounts, especially in large accounts and those where a significant proportion of the team was offshore? In any case, the Europe Head had hired a sales force transformation consultant to coach his sales team.

- Would a workshop on the dependencies among different initiatives help the account team to understand and implement the ideas? Would such meta-ideas appeal to people at an operational level?
- Should I be spending time with each account, like the way I did with the utilities account? How would accounts justify such a role? If it was a billable activity, then I could be drawn into other activities of the client. Would that be a scalable approach? Could I achieve my target of observing and influencing 15 accounts?

While these questions were bubbling in my head, I gained some clarity about the role—it was not about information exchange (opportunities/threats/gossip); it was not about training or competency development; it was not about assessment; it was not about knowledge management or best practice sharing; nor was it going to be a one-time interaction. But how was I to arrive at an approach that was low-cost, point intervention with potential to generate non-linear connections, anchored in micro-level realities, and in tune with their notion of time?

I thought a good starting point might be to facilitate discussions on the unique aspects of accounts (vision, organization, capabilities and their critical issues) and help prioritize various initiatives. I felt that I could do this without being a full-time member of an account, by participating in their critical conversations at different levels to help them see and make the necessary connections and move their narratives along. I thought this might help address the managerial concern about scalability, i.e., influencing a large number of accounts. But what about the scientific basis of such an approach and the generality and replicability of any knowledge generated? It was clear that I would not be researching the problem of strategy implementation as an external observer. I would actually be intervening in the ongoing narrative of accounts, unlike a pure ethnographic study. Also, I needed to overcome the concerns and insecurities that people might have with respect to me. I had to downplay the role and any perceived power in it, while at the same time using their assumptions about power difference positively. At a more fundamental level, I thought this approach had the best chance of addressing the curiosity of the researcher in me. After spending a decade in consulting, I was feeling the need to look for a different explanation for typical situations we find ourselves in, an explanation that had the potential to help existing people get out of sticky situations and move along.[9] I was keen to explore an alternative approach to human relationships as a function of interactions rather than the parts alone, i.e., see the parts and patterns emerging out of these interactions between people (not abstract variables). Mathematically, I could put it as a recursive equation: Interaction = F (Initial conditions, Interaction), something similar to the Interaction Ritual model of Collins (2004). I wanted to break out of the systems perspective of interactions and order/change, where we are trained to think in terms of self-regulation (setting goals and allocating resources to close the gaps) and self-organization, emerging out of deviation amplifying loops and far from equilibrium situations, and talk in terms of variables that are abstracted from individual experience. But I did not have a clear methodology in place to proceed and was, therefore, feeling very uncertain.

Instead of waiting for a methodology, I decided to evolve one

---

9   Instead of accepting a view that ultimately we need the right people to implement our ideas and therefore resorting to the logic of training, resourcing, recruitment, role definition or incentives; or end up with a conclusion that the problem is with culture or organization or strategy or any other meta idea.

as I went along. I started requesting meetings with the people to whom my sponsor had announced my role. I managed to get meetings with three of them (utilities, telecom and a large global account), a partial call with one (transportation/media), a discussion with a client partner who managed a set of insurance and manufacturing accounts, and with the BE Head. I started the meeting by asking them if they had read my sponsor's email. Most of them said that they had had a look at it, but it had not made sense to them. I wondered why a few lines of carefully drafted and validated statements (in English) would be insensible. When I probed further, many said, "We normally don't give importance to such announcements, because it is probably one among the many initiatives that come and go." I thought they were exhibiting a perfectly rational approach (experience-learning-action). I wondered if that was not inhibiting them from exploring the present possibilities. At the same time I was hopeful because despite the above perception, many of them had agreed to speak to me and then directed me to their next level managers. I wondered if they were responding because they "could not say NO", or they wanted to check my agenda ("not much information in emails"), or if they were really interested in my services. Instead of spending time anticipating their behaviours and planning my responses, however, I decided to focus on the actual interaction with the next level managers (RMs and Delivery Managers).

During the meeting with the RMs and Delivery Managers, I would usually start off with a brief explanation of my role, and how it was concerned with win-win relationships and initiatives in accounts. But, their responses suggested that I was not making any sense. I felt that most people seemed to respond from their own worldviews or assumptions about me, and not to my utterances. For instance, some managers inquired if I would be assessing their account, and quickly suggested that they had been rated well in recent assessments. I was amused by this response. How did they arrive at this conclusion when I had not uttered a single word about "assessment"? I wondered if it was because of assessments such as CMM, BE, and CSAT. Some managers asked if I was trying to socialize practices that may have worked with the utilities client, and quickly suggested that they could also do wonders if they had additional "non-billable" resources of the right quality. I wondered why they gave importance to my previous assignment. Couldn't my thinking have changed? Moreover, how were they sure that it was non-billable, and why indeed would such resources change relationships when "non-billable is usually considered non-value adding"? Some managers queried if I would be mentoring or coaching them and informed me that mentoring had not worked in the past. I wondered why they had reached this conclusion when I had not uttered the word "mentoring" or "coaching". I also wondered if mentoring and coaching one person in an account could change their constrained patterns of relating with clients. To summarize, these initial interactions with managers in accounts and groups, although very challenging and frustrating, did improve my understanding of the prevalent patterns of interaction:

- First, the responses showed that we did not pay much attention to the utterances that emerged during interactions. They were "rationally invisible" to us, thus weakening the input.

- Second, the interpretive scheme in our minds forced us to categorize the already weakened input (for example, what the other person was referring to was "mentoring"). Our social experiences then symbolized it ("mentoring was difficult to measure, so non-value adding") and guided our response ("do not waste time"). As a result interactions were closed, and voices silenced socially and logically.

- However, I noticed that if every interaction was viewed as a "unique moment" and even if one party paid more attention to the utterances/feelings that emerged during the interaction then we could find ways to avoid closure and allow the interaction to iterate and create possibilities in future.

The process of arranging meetings was a really frustrating experience. I noticed that very few people responded immediately to email requests. Some of them got back after some delay and some didn't respond at all. When I tried to call them I found myself talking to their voice mail or they would promise to get back and wouldn't. I had to persist, sometimes wondering why I was playing such roles and not simply becoming part of the establishment and moving with the stream. This would lead me back to the reason why I took up the role—understand how existing relationships could change through the process of interaction. Over time, I arrived at the view that change need not come from directly managing people. One could facilitate change through sustained interactions that create deep listening spaces and allow people to see and make connections in their contexts and timelines, i.e., improve their narratives as they see it (unlike the "sea gull boss" who flies into a situation, makes a lot of noise, dirties everything and then leaves[10]).

My work with the accounts also led me into discussions with representatives of corporate groups in the geography, for example, PMO, HR, Learning & Development, Marketing on the topic of Key Account Management (KAM). These discussions helped me gain access to different data that these teams were collecting to

---

10 I saw this caption in a local newspaper while travelling in a London Underground train.

understand the business and the pulse of the organization. Analysis of this data led me to define the criteria for understanding key accounts (as shown in Figure 13). This exercise seemed to have created an impression on the Europe Head as he referred to it specifically in the half-yearly appraisal. He also sought my advice on a change in the organization structure that he was contemplating. He felt that the creation of a new role—"Delivery Director for the geography"—could help enhance sales in the geography. I advised him against such a role and, more importantly, against the bifurcation of sales and delivery at a higher level; my advice seemed to have been heeded.

While developing interactions with different stakeholders, I refrained from attending official gatherings of managers and associates. There was one occasion when the newcomers to the regional head office were introduced by the Europe Head to the rest of the teams. When the turn came to introduce me, he said that I was pursuing some research interests on my own. It was clear that he didn't want to show that he was explicitly sponsoring my work and wanted that to remain ambiguous; perhaps he was not sure what would emerge out of this exercise and wondered whether it might upset his relations with other senior leaders. I also refrained from participating in the formal forums—for instance, a global tele-conference with senior management that I was invited to and an invitation from the HR to speak at the sales conference. These could have increased awareness of my work, but I was concerned that such exposure may complicate matters if people perceived my work as a potential threat. I also started sending weekly reports to the Europe Head and briefed him every month. All this may have contributed to a basic level of trust with the Europe Head. I think he understood that I was attempting something difficult and in a subtle manner, and did not interfere too much in my work.

Types of Customers

HHH - Very good client for DCTS

HLH - They give business & help penetrate the industry or market, but are difficult to work with

HHL - They consume and produce, but do not actively help penetration in the industry or market

LHH - They don't consume much, but are easy to work with & can help penetration in the industry or market

HLL - They consume, but are not easy to work with or helpful in expanding business

LHL - They are easy to work with, but do not consume or help grow business

LLH - They are willing to help you grow, but do not consume much, nor very easy to work with (highly unlikely except in cases where senior mgt link is strong)

LLL - Inactive customers (or very new)

X –
Consumption behavior of client

Y -
Production behavior of client

Z – Supply behavior of client

H – Represents good behavior
L – Represents poor behavior

HHL

HHH

HLL

HLH

LHL

LLL

LHH

LLH

Measures from BSC, Marketing, HR, Delivery

Example:
Consumption, (revenue, deal size, pipeline, profitability)

Production (product / service fit, process synergy)

Supply (referrals, event participation, mkt leader, % of wallet share)

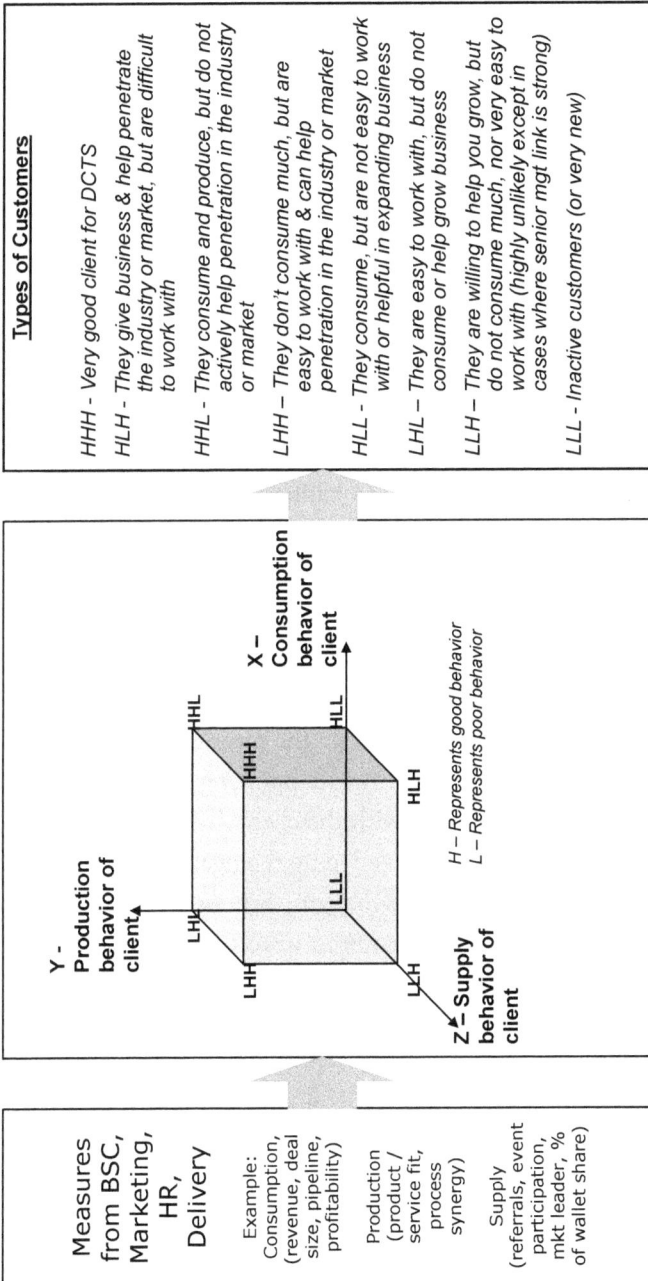

Figure 13: A model for identifying key accounts in IT services

How did the interactions unfold over time?
What was the outcome?

In the Appendix I have provided the details of how the interactions with three different accounts emerged over a period of one year. I started with accounts where I knew some people. For instance, the CVM initiative had put me in touch with the RM of a Global Investment Management client. He was one of the SPOCs identified for this initiative. When I started talking to him about his experience with the CVM initiative, I was surprised to note that they had already tried and given up as it turned out to be too cumbersome. Instead, he suggested that there was a different issue that he wanted to speak about. I went with the flow. The interaction gradually led me into addressing the deeper question of how they viewed the account and the relationships they had with clients and among themselves. The second client account that I had extended interactions for was part of the airlines industry. Here I found a fairly enthusiastic RM who had recently taken over the account and wanted to make a difference. It was there that I was able to demonstrate the meaning of "making the familiar strange" to a team that was supporting some applications but had limited interactions with the client. Through the process of working with the team, we ended up re-engaging the client and also getting additional projects that greatly boosted the confidence of the team. The third case pertains to an account that seemed a bit defensive initially, but its leaders subsequently reached out to me when they faced some challenges. In each of these cases, I noticed that the way in which the teams responded to me provided clues about their patterns of relating with clients. In the airlines account such engagement seemed more relaxed, while with the investment management client it seemed more constrained. In the next few paragraphs, I will summarize the responses that emerged while participating in these conversations with 12–15 accounts. I do this under four broad categories.

First, I experienced that persistent interactions ("rhetoric-responsive" approach) could trigger the "social" nature of human beings, reduce the inside-outside divide between suppliers-customers, strategy-operations, sales-delivery, business-technology, and core-periphery, increase the bandwidth (by enhancing trust in the relationship) and move people into joint actions (Mead, 1932; Blumer, 1969; Shotter, 1993/2005; Stacey, 2003). This happened through "arresting moments" that were spontaneously generated among the people who were interested in interacting (Shaw, 2002) and made use of different devices of social construction (Jocelyn, 2006). Social interaction (mindful or mindless) over extended periods of time created situations where utterances (in the right language—usually in a positive tone, and focused on objects of interest, except in some cases where they were confrontational and directed at the subject) triggered the self-interaction process within the individuals and transformed the relationship (enhanced trust to foster future interactions). Everything could now be seen in a new light. That is what transformation is all about. It is also important to note that such moments arose only in the process of joint sense-making.[11]

Second, continued interaction with 12 accounts suggested that the "Interactionist" role had the potential to help create such "arresting moments" across the global service networks and generate the necessary "butterfly effect" to transform the macro

---

11 We see this in all the family interactions—parents being worried about their children, while children don't want their advice. Everyone needs to figure out the right interaction pattern with the other so that they can also touch each other's self-interaction patterns.

conditions, especially the deep emotions and perspectives that emerged out of cognitive fallacies and conditioned by power (Dalal, 2002). Objects could be introduced at the right moments to sustain dialogue.[12] In other words, interactions among stakeholders could drive changes in the shared vision, pattern of organization and the assets. Conversations and narratives seemed to trigger the social and self-interaction processes of meaning-creation and moving people into joint action. But, for that to happen, I had to interact with people in different organizational spaces, searching for the right situations to say the right things, sometimes directed at the object, and at other times directed at the subject (confrontational). I began to understand the core argument of John Shotter that creating such "arresting moments" by probing workspace identities and experiences should be the central focus of managers/service professionals. It was my Eureka moment. I thought (to rephrase Archimedes) that if given access to ongoing conversations, an interactionist can facilitate change by helping people make sense of their own objects/contexts through improved self and social interaction and interpretation, and facilitate joint action, moving them along, releasing them from impasse-like situations, enhancing vocabulary/languaging, inclusivity of voices, translating emotions into words and vice-versa, clarifying challenging social/power biases, and in a non-intrusive way, helping them to recognize/shape/relate to the objects as they emerge. An interactionist could potentially handle four conversations per day (960 conversations per year) and reach out to about 40 accounts, assuming 24 per account per year.

---

12 Please see Haldane and Bond (2004) for their work on Knowledge and Learning Infrastructure, KALIF.

Third, objects make sense only in the process of interaction. While a general view is that they could help transform interactions, an alternative view is that they can make sense only if there are some interactions already in place. In fact, a certain level of interaction was required before an object could be introduced; after that, the object could indeed help change the interaction. Most strategic initiatives were seen as "objects of control" and not as "objects to facilitate interactions". They were seen as symbols of separation and not integration. Interactions around objects have reached a state where a very crude aspect of the object has become the reason/focus of interaction. For instance, in the case of BSC, accounts relate to them as a scorecard against which to report (no relationship to the underlying strategy). Another example is Sales Force Transformation. This programme was an attempt to transform the predominantly delivery-centric sales force into being more client-focused. This was done in different ways—by introducing MBAs into the sales team, grooming potential "sales staff" from among existing junior members of the staff, and finally, a mega training/coaching programme for senior sales staff costing about $10 million. Did this change the sales force? It certainly instilled some discipline such as focusing on the value to the client, understanding the relationship map, defining value propositions, using standard templates and a common language. But have they become client advisors, especially in existing relationships? Could they "transform perceptions" into "perceptions of value"? My interaction with RMs suggested that it would be a difficult leap. It is not because they were not trying or dumb or were too reluctant to grow. It was a relational issue.

The Sales Force Transformation programme was also accompanied by a greater focus on marketing and consulting, for instance, hiring event management firms or local professional writers or local consultants and organizing fabulous client events, albeit very expensive. This probably helped engage some clients. But did it help the home-grown operational/sales professionals to connect with the clients? Did their worldview of inside-outside change? Was this language really a differentiator in the marketplace? Were they learning a language that could become a strategic disability? What stopped competitors from replicating this training or coaching?[13] I believe (and my belief is reinforced by some RMs) that relationships are a prerequisite for applying many of the techniques taught as part of the training. The techniques will make sense only in the context of interactions. Seeing it as a cognitive exercise where I learn how to present my story, and the sales process as an information/communication process, i.e., right proposition to the right audience at the right time, may have its limitations, especially in existing relationships which contribute to 95 per cent of the revenue. Moreover, in a services context there is a strong dependency between sales and delivery. Therefore, engaging the delivery staff is also critical, and most of these interactions are problematic. If strategic initiatives are viewed as objects of this interaction between geographies and accounts, then it can pave the way for better sense-making and implementation. These objects should not be seen as an end in themselves, but as a means. Instead of standardizing or monitoring them to align with one firm's perspective, initiatives are opportunities for macro teams to listen and connect to accounts, not the other way round. Initiatives could be seen as introducing new words into the vocabulary of accounts so that their dialogue with clients can change, not as instruments of control or standardization. These symbols may be sources of

---

13 After a few years the coach hired by DCTS was hired by a competing firm.

transformation at some points, for instance, the BSC can be seen as an instrument to challenge corporate strategy. I tried to do this using the data being collected by various groups to see if the strategy was working. For instance, there were two objectives in the BSC that related strongly to my work: (a) a high-level outcome stating that "clients enjoy a win-win relationship with DCTS", and (b) a bottom-level driver stating "Nurture a WE culture". However, an analysis of account-level metrics did not indicate any significant correlation between the two, except that "Consultant ESI was correlated with win-loss by value". But, consultants rarely participated in the culture-change sessions and there was a mismatch between their thinking and the thinking of junior staff on most aspects. Discussions with accounts at a micro level also did not point to a strong understanding of how these two could be operationalized and connected. Why? Was it due to inconsistencies in the metrics or the quality of data or was the strategy not working? To enable this, the macro groups needed to change (as much as accounts). At that point they struggled to make use of the data and engage accounts. This was a culture shift for them, because their primary form of interaction had been as compliance managers and messengers of senior management/information brokers. They were not taken seriously by the accounts or by senior managers. It was difficult for them to position themselves in an alternative way (although deep down they may have been concerned about this positioning—their identities were more suppressed than the line staff). They did have a critical role to play in using strategic initiatives as opportunities to engage with accounts and align the corporate and account interests.

Finally, I think the exercise allowed some practical insights on "interactions" and their role in improving alignment or transforming relationships among internal groups and with clients in global services networks. One of the key points was that the interface between clients and service providers (accounts) represents a special form of organization—a global service network. It provides scope for rich interactions among different stakeholders and results in a constantly changing network— like the concept of figuration proposed by Norbert Elias. This interactionist perspective has strategic implications for clients, service providers and professionals because it can pave the way for new forms of learning, innovating and working ethically, and lead to the emergence of new forms of networks. It can help an organization rethink outsourcing from a fresh perspective by focusing on socio-psychological aspects of globalization, services and innovation which are largely ignored in the present techno-economic discourse. For instance, is outsourcing actually reducing the inside-outside divide of the client firm? How do existing people in the client firm find new ways of interacting with newcomers from the new firm and vice-versa? Or is the SLA culture or "offshoring" actually reinforcing the inside-outside divide and limiting inter-firm interaction? Does the new firm (at least the onsite component) acquire new characteristics by being present onsite? What are the implications for open innovation? What are the implications for sales professionals—are they better off as "interactionists" establishing joint listening spaces at the interface between two firms? Other firms are looking into these in different ways (but probably searching for solutions in the dominant paradigm—for example, McKinsey's work on interactions, which supports tacit knowledge workers and IBM/HP's initiatives on "Services Science" where they seek to use scientific methods to model and control services.

How was this different from general advice on strategy implementation?

DCTS leaders largely adopted the mainstream managerial practice. Such an approach entails the following:

(a) Define a high-level strategy—a carefully thought-out plan developed by the senior management after a series of discussions; taking inputs from listening posts like client events/meetings; gathering account-level data through business planning sessions on micro trends by seeking competitive information; and advice from popular faculty at Harvard Business School in the US, where most of its clients are based.

(b) Implement the strategy by setting and negotiating targets for immediate levels—defining key priorities, change initiatives and training programmes at the geography level, organizing open-house communication for associates, collecting metrics, and conducting planned review meetings/governance mechanisms at regular intervals.

(c) Participate in key client meetings and external events (presenting a positive image of the firm and self), review key deals/negotiate with internal groups, organize thought-provoking events, assign actions, push people to comply, coach and motivate staff/recognize key performers/performances, weed out undesirable characters through appropriate policy interventions, and lead the way.

The end result: leaders generally had a picture of where the firm was heading, but were concerned that the growth was not taking place as per the strategy; issues of collaboration within the geography and with others (example of marketing, ODC); last minute compliance (timesheets, billing, goal setting); concerns about quality of content in critical discussions/presentations; initiatives going nowhere; and a general feeling that of inadequate strategic alignment with many groups (line or staff functions), i.e., "both parties knowing what they should be talking when they meet".

In contrast, I started with two questions: (a) how do people in an account (at a micro level) make sense of their environment and how do they contribute to "win-win-win" relationships, and (b) how do macro groups interact with accounts and assist the accounts in their sense-making? I did not do this as a one-off diagnostic study; rather I treated it as an ongoing process where I could move things along as part of the regular discussions. What did I learn about their interactions?

- The people on the ground (below RMs and Delivery Managers) generally did not understand what was going on beyond their work. They may be aware of some account-level activities and some HR-related initiatives such as L&D or Culture Change or Rewards and Recognition. Most of them could think only in extremes—either/or perspectives, for instance, everything was either sales or delivery (exploitative, no element of exploration). Also, they were either totally loyal to their group (practice or delivery centre) or entirely disconnected from other groups and localized in the account (clear inside-outside). They thought it would be difficult to say "no" to client or any source of power (since questioning is seen as a challenge to authority). Generally, most of them were not well connected with clients in terms of intellectual, social or cultural capital. Most were not happy with the appraisal process primarily because there was no dialogue involved. It was perceived by them as arriving at a number which had been predetermined by the supervisor in many cases. They saw RMs as all-powerful since the latter represent the "voice of client and organization" and control their onsite stay, sometimes even in the face of corporate policies of rotation.

- RMs/DMs were smart people who understood most corporate initiatives at a high level, and knew how to present their account as already complying with the corporate requirement or suggest that they did not have enough bandwidth to comply with the requirement. They were afraid to say they didn't understand something or to express concerns about difficulties facing in implementing the initiative in their account. This was because their concerns were often trivialized by comparison with others (for example, when an RM said he could not improve offshore leverage in his account, the Europe Head responded by saying that another larger account had achieved significant offshoring, oblivious to the fact that the client of the larger account had forced it). As a result RMs saw corporate interactions as a source of nuisance (low value); they view interactions only as a means of exchanging information—eliminate threats/show compliance/accept targets—and in some cases, a way to enhance internal visibility.

- The rapid influx of local staff in the regional head office also introduced a new challenge for the "traditional homebred RMs". The interaction of the local recruits with accounts was problematic. This may be because the staff in accounts had built up a decent rapport with clients over a period of time and did not see the local staff making a key difference to that relationship. Local recruits were welcomed if could they help break into a new area of the client but not within the existing relationships. As a result local recruits tended to view account staff with distrust—they didn't trust their information, wanted to construct fresh data and linkages with clients by sending them brochures or invites directly and so on.

- The support groups, on the other hand, viewed the accounts staff as agents who may misuse autonomy and therefore need to be kept on a leash. This was done by exercising control over human and financial resource flows—approvals/technology, raising compliance issues, sensing associates who are well-aligned to management. This was the time when support groups felt a sense of power. Otherwise, they were usually ignored by the management and the line staff.

How did I participate in such situations? From a macro context, I looked for ways in which corporate teams could really listen to the voice of the accounts. I tried to do this in different ways:

- Suggesting changes to the business planning/client events/ sales conference, i.e., make them smaller, more frequent and with participation from local recruits, homebred, clients, prospects, academics, support staff;
- Customizing targets, using data and insights to have conversations with accounts;
- Helping macro groups extract practices that explain certain performances, helping move the practices around, and carrying out the abstractions of specific experiences and relaying them to "senior managers".

At account level, I was helping people appreciate the unique aspects of their contexts; having conversations on problems of interest—internally and with clients/partners; re-connecting them to their everyday work, making the value-construction process work across the service lifecycle; finding ways to use initiatives to suit their priorities or work as tools of conversation with corporate groups and making the supply-demand more continuous; leveraging local objects or other partners, and, in general, enhancing identities. The idea was to fundamentally change their interaction pattern to create space/trust/bandwidth in relationships and help both parties relate to each other in new ways. I talked to them regularly so that they could find ways to construct and enrich their realities (as opposed to giving them specific models or tools to religiously implement) and allowed their self-interaction processes to operate rather than closing them by introducing new objects that may not be aligned with their organic self-interaction processes, which are bound to be very diverse given the variety of people and their contexts. I used the objects as an indirect way to interact with people, but made sure that neither the object nor the subject was the direct focus. I left the objects to their own imagination—to construct, develop and use in the manner they saw fit. Instead of telling a subject what his/her problem was, I was triggering social interactions within the team, letting their self-interaction patterns evolve, and showing them some signs of joint action.

To reiterate, periodic interactions with actor(s) about their vision, organization, capabilities was more useful than engaging them with macro strategies or metrics. In any case, there was no coherent pattern in terms of correlations among key metrics. What I was doing was helping people identify and recognize "objects" in their context, creating spaces for self-interaction/social interaction, and facilitating interpretation that could lead to some joint actions across their value chain.

Don't leaders know how to interact? Isn't it common sense?
Well, it is certainly common sense, but as they say, that is not very common. Interactions are central to any human organization. My interactions with different people from different accounts and corporate groups have, however, not given me the impression that these were common. We didn't seem to approach interactions as an opportunity to "connect" and "make sense". They were only seen as a chance to enhance or sustain one's position of power and were influenced by the prevalent information and communication paradigms. The strategic interventions appeared like different props added to make a problematic paradigm work. I myself have realized that I don't really understand why and how I should pay attention to the "living present" until I have been through this exercise. Let me explain how the prevalent thought patterns and power differences create a number of impediments to even begin these interactions.

I noticed that the reason interactions don't seem to take place is that people appear to be stuck with a number of assumptions. People at the top feel that they have thought their strategy through, but are frustrated that people down the line don't show any "leadership" to implement the strategy, or that they only ask stupid questions when given a chance. They resort to interventions such as "reviews", "incentives", "threats", "resourcing" or other initiatives to improve the situation. Similarly, people at the lowest level feel that their opinions hardly matter; everything is decided and controlled at the top. So, they feel the best way to grow is to align themselves with the right sources of power. Very little attention is paid to the dialogue process itself. The typical pattern of conversations across sales and delivery may be as follows: "We will talk only if there is a real big opportunity that gives visibility"; "We can't talk to the client if we don't have innovative offerings for their problems"; "We cannot develop innovative offerings when we don't have a real understanding of their problems (information)"; "If only the knowledge came from DCTS practices, then the client would respond"; "We cannot get this information or understanding if we don't have a good relationship"; "How can we continue interactions that may have been initiated by experts from practices?"; "We don't have the luxury to say 'No' and still develop the relationship"; "I don't think anybody can beat us on price".

Perhaps there was too much talk on big-bang strategies, maximizing effect with minimum effort ("studying just before the exams"), being aligned with the most powerful for quickly enhancing access to resources (a deep-rooted issue, as suggested by Varma, 2005. Could this be rectified by a sales force transformation programme? I am not sure since we are still stuck in the dominant paradigm, where we are taught to think that situations have to be understood from a customer's perspective (the needs to be met or value to be delivered). We are asked to spend time on thinking about the industry trends, implications for client's, possibilities and solutions. We then see meetings with clients as opportunities to communicate our ideas to match their requirements, or choke the bandwidth of the client to eliminate competitive threats. When this doesn't work, we see that we need to collaborate with the client or partners who are outside our firm. We then redraw the boundary and request the client to include us in their boundary or, with difficulty, include the suppliers/partners within our boundary. We try to engage these groups and complain that if only we had the right people for the event, then we could have had a great conversation. We try to get access to the right people, and inform them in advance about the scope of the conversation and what each is going to speak about. The subsequent story is no different. Once we get the opportunity, we try to break it down into a set of activities, roles, and competencies (knowledge, skills, attributes). Finally, we struggle with the question of how to identify or allocate the right resources, how to develop competencies through accelerated learning strategies, how to get people to work together, i.e., collaborate within and compete with outsiders, how to get people to innovate and so on. In all this, it is clear that most of the effort is seen to be done in isolation (inside the individual or firm) and interactions are opportunities to communicate and convince the other about the need for joint action. The process of interaction itself is fully programmed to the last level of detail, leaving nothing to the imagination.

Interactions are also influenced by power differences. They struggle to take off because most people seem to operate from a power-positioning perspective—people have agendas as if they are hard-wired and static, or have an inside that is different from outside, or use interactions only to seek information that may help them advance or protect their interests and emphasize the power difference between themselves and others. Interactions might be avoided in this context based on the following notions:

- Exploitative in nature: "What would I get by interacting with this guy? I don't see much value—no new ideas or differentiated strategies that I can quickly implement and appropriate credit for myself. I don't see that he would do some work for me, produce assets/best practices, or help me access critical resources. I don't see how he could enhance my visibility internally, or externally, or my strategic alignment."
- Defensive in nature: Typical concerns of RMs include "would he expose my limitations to the senior level? Would he create more work for me? Would he walk

away with the credit for the outcomes? Leave me alone, I already have the right connections and ideas and resources to implement it." As a result, they used different logics to stop an interaction—"let us get on with action". They attempted to prove that the idea was not new by categorizing it and relating it to another initiative that has failed in the past (strong similarity with Farhad Dalal's analysis of the process of racialization, Dalal, 2002), or suggested that they were already doing it.

But how did such situations emerge, given that people who are fresh out of college are typically less used to role-playing and tend to act outwardly in a way that is truer to what they are thinking. The civilizing process within the IT services firm may provide some pointers and this was in the nature of everyday interactions. Interactions influenced associates' construction of their "generalised other" through their experiences (self-interaction) or social interaction with managers. For instance, associates typically got to know about the way customers think from their immediate supervisors/RMs/Sales Directors. One manager used to say that he possessed "customer insight" about "how senior managers think" and "what they expect from a presentation—the next actionable step". Was it straight forward? How would an associate reconcile his own perspective with that of his superior who had access to better information from senior managers of the client or the organization? The conversation was easily one-sided. I wondered how one could generalize about the way customers thought and made decisions. Was it the rational decision-making model speaking? Weren't customers also like us, groping in the dark about their problems? Another instance—in one of the accounts an associate said that managers seem to behave differently with clients and with associates—"you learn to bow to power, or face the consequence—loss of access to resources". Through this kind of behaviour they were civilizing the youngsters in "ways to respond to power". In essence there were many situations of getting stuck and these were emerging out of limited interactions in the available organizational spaces. This was pervasive in almost all the different organizational spaces (I have provided a high-level summary the Appendix). It provided ample evidence that there was an urgent need to focus on interactions.

My attempts to sustain interactions with accounts provided clues that prevalent thought patterns and power relating could indeed be changed. For instance, 12 out of 18 accounts continued to interact. The experience reinforced the perspective that paying attention to local interactions could change rigid patterns of relating and increase "bandwidth" (trust). So, why were leaders and associates ignoring this potential in local interactions and only using/blaming managerial interventions? It appeared that the rational and engineering perspectives of "either/or", "0/1", "measurement-improvement", "walk the talk", "leverage", "replicable-scalable", were not allowing people to listen to the utterances and feelings that emerge in our interactions.

I also had to improvise my strategies to continue with the interactions. For instance, I approached RMs in the following manner: (a) "I am performing-such-and such role, would you be interested?" (b) "We planned to discuss this last time, would you like to discuss further?" (c) "I hope things are coming up well", or "how are you coping with your situation, would you like to talk about it?" (d) "Would you like to pull together some people to have a discussion on issues of interest?" (e) "Can we take a specific problem and see how it goes? (f) I have done a review of metrics, would like for have your feedback/comments—does it make sense to you?" (g) "Can you give me feedback on the interactions we have had so far? What did they do to you? How did you interpret them?" (h) "Can we catch up on what has happened since our last meeting?" (i) "I am coming to your location, can we catch up?" (j) "I could help connect you to another person, would you be interested?" (k) "I know a resource who is looking for an alternative project, would you be interested?" (One tends to meet with a very prompt reply in such cases.) (l) Initiating a conversation with the team member—or whoever is responding.

During the actual conversations, I avoided a review/assessment perspective. But I would still ask: "how do you make sense of these initiatives or attempting to implement them?" I noticed that a direct question like this did not elicit a real response, but an abstracted (copy book)/defensive response. Similarly, if I asked "what do you think is wrong with the current situation and what can be improved", I would get a lot of normative responses that may not have been really grounded. Instead, if I asked "can you describe your best experience in the account or at DCTS" or "tell me about your experience so far in developing the account", there would be a greater chance to observe what objects, interactions, interpretations were picked to talk about—in other words, their sense-making strategies: why and how did they act in those situations? This may be because once they got into the narrative mode and sketched out the story, many things came to life. A small conversation thus became a way of refining and reinterpreting the story, helping them connect dots, and perhaps make a leap of faith through new words. Also, sometimes confrontational points like 'why did you choose to interact with me, but did not continue the interaction?' led to surfacing underlying contradictions. Another thing that I did was to avoid attempting a diagnosis, and, instead, moving on to how they were responding to the situation, what could be done to improve or improvise on the path they were taking. Constructing this dialogue was extremely difficult because we were stuck in patterns that had been established over the years, not just within this firm, but in our business discourse.

How did the stakeholders view this exercise?
Interactions with the sponsor

I should thank the sponsor for investing in such a role. It was very bold of him, but he also took care of it by maintaining a certain level of ambiguity. I sent a weekly report about my interactions to my sponsor, and had a face-to-face meeting roughly once every month. I noticed that my email reports (which I sent every Friday) used to get some replies in the early stages and especially when there was a presentation on a key topic attached to it. He used to respond on Sunday evenings. The face-to-face meetings were slightly different. I was using these to summarize what I had done during that month, discuss the key patterns, and seek his feedback on the next steps (whether he would like me to continue further and, if so, whether the direction I was taking was all right). During our meetings, I noticed that he always sat down with a notepad (indicating that he was interested in recording some thoughts). But most of the time I felt he was listening from an information and communication perspective, to pick up key ideas or contacts that he could leverage, and not to connect or explore the utterances that were emerging in our interactions. I may have also contributed to this because I found it difficult to move out of the reporting/review pattern while talking to him. During the early stages, I used to go prepared with a summary of the work done in the last month, and present it to him via a laptop presentation. But later, I tried other strategies such as using a paper presentation, only using a notebook, and sometimes, as in the case of my appraisal, using a sheet of paper.

Let me throw some light on the appraisal meeting. My appraisal for the first half of the year was supposed to be done at the end of September. But due to time constraints, my sponsor could only get to it in the second week of November. I went into the meeting with a one-page note summarizing my achievements on the three goals we had agreed on. I showed him the note. He patiently read through it. Then he picked on my point that "managers still seem to look at structural solutions". He said "all these interactions could happen only if there was a context. So, wasn't structure important?" I quickly used the back of the paper to show him the four management concepts—planning, organizing, staffing and directing—to demonstrate why interactions represented the fourth one and why it was critical to make sense of the other three or even to shape the other three. He then inquired if it was a question of confidence. "Would interactions be a problem for confident people?" I mentioned that interactions were critical for everybody, more so for confident people because they are the ones who can easily gloss over day-to-day obvious things under the assumption that they have thought about everything, including the other person's move. But human interactions have an element of unpredictability, and therein lies the source of transformation. He then said that he understood what I was saying and pointed out that I had still not addressed one of the points that he had brought up during the monthly reviews—"can you tell us the few leverage points or rules through which we can transform the whole? Now that you have seen the whole organization, what are your recommendations? Do we need ten Sudhirs?" I reiterated the point that if one considers interaction as central, then every interaction holds potential for transformation. Senior managers, by listening closely to their interactions or participating in interactions in different organizational spaces, can trigger large changes. But, I don't think his rational mind was seeing this. He went back and got the latest issue of the *Harvard Business Review* and flipped through an article and read out to me, "a company took about 20 years to solve a problem because they had not spoken to the right people". I could see that he still interpreted interactions as a source of information, only that instead of interacting within your own structure, you interact with different people. I was also intrigued by his response. I wondered what he was trying to communicate by referring to *HBR*. Was he trying to say that what I had said went against the paradigm of management (*HBR*, being a bible for top managers)? Around this time he received two telephone calls. He answered one of them (it was from his superior), but told the other person (his subordinate) that he was in a meeting. This suggested that he was interested in the discussion, although not enough to put off a call from his superior. Then the topic moved to developing innovation. In my note I had suggested that new forms of networking needed to be found at an account level and not at the corporate level. He said they had appointed a Head of Innovation to develop an innovation ecosystem with clients. He seemed to suggest that they were finding it difficult to bring clients into this ecosystem. This was again a little difficult for me. I suggested that such connections happen at the interface between clients and service professionals. So maybe the Innovation Head has to find a way to connect with these. I offered another example to clarify my point—how I went about connecting and did not look for the whole and so on. He immediately responded saying, "I don't want to know how you have done it, but is there a way I can replicate this?" I left the meeting thinking it had taken me about

10 years of action research to realize what I was saying, and that expecting to make the same impact in a one-hour meeting may be difficult.

Response of key leaders and associates

I tried a different strategy to gather feedback from various people whom I had interacted with during the course of my work. I wrote a note reflecting on my experience and sent it to some colleagues to elicit their feedback. A summary of the responses is given below:

- An HR professional: "I think people do understand this but feel it is too simple and it will not get them brownie points, so they tend to give big names to things they do. I am happy you thought of writing this."
- A Senior Consultant: "I read your paper with interest and your courage in sharing these experiences in writing is applaudable though one senses the frustration that you might have gone through while executing your current role, and probably how you overcame that through your process of analysis and synthesis, which in itself is valuable learning. Your observations capture a state that one will find hard to argue against, including the primacy of local interactions. It is in the perspective of why those patterns recur that one may have a different point of view."
- A Practice Head: "It highlights the criticality of local interactions. It very much relates to my own experience, and I believe yours is a very important message. I believe the paper style is predominantly narrative, and hence would be easy for most DCTS people to understand.... Upon permission from you, I would like to use this paper in a current situation."

- A researcher: "I wonder you did not realize that for the last few years an employee's knee jerk reaction in DCTS is 'threat' instead of 'trust'. This is a typical malaise paralysing the system. And it is getting worse. If it is not arrested in time, it could transform into a syndrome. The notion that no man-made system can work without trust is something modern thinkers understand, but do not know how to inculcate. The ancients knew it well, but that goes beyond this discussion."

- A Relationship Manager: "I can connect with every statement you are making… It really captures our reality,"

- An academician: "I think you are talking mainly about enriching the conversation so that people avoid being struck. You are talking about facilitating wider and deeper communication as a major aspect of ordinary everyday interaction while getting work done. You are proposing that we take this seriously—everybody can pay more attention to what they are talking about and how—how they might be opening things up rather than closing them down, how they might be valuing ordinary contact with others, particularly clients… Anyway, I think it is very interesting and look forward to hearing about any response. I think you are doing something quite unusual so don't be surprised if you get a rather muted response. But whatever the response, I think the thing would be to work with it."

- A team member: "Quite ironically, if I re-look at these key barriers they are precisely those tips for effective communication that are taught in management schools and training workshops. As communicators we need to maintain this balance of using such levers towards effective communication as they prove to be double-edged swords. The scenarios you have discussed very aptly demonstrate this."

- An Engagement Manager: "The report has come out very well. I was really excited and thrilled while reading Situation #3. The report captures the real situations in our organization."

- A Vice President: "The entire IT consulting space (including consultants and clients) is by nature defensive— clients being defensive because they feel a sense of guilt of not describing the problem adequately, and consultants feel guilty of the design not meeting even the somewhat-agreed contract... While I agree that abstractions such as score cards cannot drive interactions, how do we create interactions that give meaning to abstractions? A template for day-to-day interactions would sound like an oxymoron." This was an excellent summary and I think he really understood what I was trying to say.

In other words, the feedback that I received on the paper suggested that most of them agreed that our interactions are problematic and need to be improved. But I got the feeling that some of them saw it as merely a "good thing to have" or "being nice" and not as a critical issue. I tried to communicate to them that an "interactionist" perspective can lead to new ways of learning, innovating and working ethically in GSNs—an alternative to the current rhetoric in consulting and services.

Some said that they accepted the primacy of interactions and understood its strategic implications, but wondered what motivates people to interact in the first place. I expressed that this line of thinking is problematic because it suggests that interactions are less natural. Such a perspective would not allow us to come out of a paradigm that has only two strategies: (a) Searching for concepts to shape behaviours from "outside" (for example goals such as "# of interactions", rules, more informal spaces like propel or client events, or meta ideas like vision or culture); and (b) Looking for the right individuals by probing "inside" (values, motives, competencies). Instead, if we see interaction as more natural and central, then it can help us in avoiding the inside-outside dilemma and create fresh possibilities for transforming our patterns of relating and individual behaviours.

Another comment was that the change had to start from the top. They felt that my perspective was bottom-up. I clarified that it was neither top-down nor bottom-up. What I was proposing was that if people strongly felt the need to alter their patterns of relating, then the best thing to do was to pay attention to their next interaction (anywhere, anybody) and the next. A small difference in each interaction could lead to further differences that could transform one's patterns of relating. And, since each manager or consultant participates in many interactions during a day, this can be the leverage that is low cost, practical, and scalable without being replicable!

A final comment made by most was that the paper does not tell them "How/What Next". I was not at all surprised by this comment; in fact it validated my key point. People seemed to be looking at the paper as a source of information for them to act on or to understand my agenda, but were not attempting to interact and share their experience. It is only by interacting that we can try to change our patterns of relating and also appreciate different aspects of interactions. It is easier that way. If you wish to try it, then here are some tips:

- Ask why you should not interact;
- Treat every interaction as a unique moment;

- Sense patterns of talk;
- Listen to connect;
- Avoid silencing voices social-logically; and
- Improvise with local objects.

I even took the risk of sending the note to the CXO. I responded to one of his mass communication email to the employees of DCTS on culture change. I was surprised to get an immediate reply saying, "I will go through it and get back." It seemed a bit like a standard automated reply. I was not sure if he would really be interested in discussing the views presented in the paper. And sure enough, he did not get back. I felt that the leaders were busy with so much in terms of pursuit of large deals, visibility in the market and increased coverage in the media, that they were not really concerned about these micro-level changes. During this period, DCTS in Europe started making huge strides in the world of outsourcing. They won the complete infrastructure outsourcing from a retail client, signed a huge transformation deal (EUR 500 million IT+BPO) for managing closed book accounts, and opened new logos in utilities and other verticals. They believed that their strategic initiatives were yielding results. I wondered how this was happening when people at the account level could hardly relate to these initiatives. Was some broader market trend of cost-restructuring driving these wins despite management-induced distractions?

Conclusion

In this chapter I have discussed how strategic change initiatives were implemented from the top and how accounts and their leaders and employees struggled to participate and make sense of these. Most often they ended up treating change initiatives as fads or the flavour of the month, and did some posturing or filled up templates from a compliance perspective. These were seen as distractions that did not really help them in changing their patterns of relating. I have also shown how I approached this situation, and by merely following up on conversations and issues of interest, account leaders and employees opened up to me. These interactions helped build a level of energy in the teams. It was clear that such change had happened through an ongoing process of interaction and, if sustained over time, can create a sense of vibrancy. I also discussed my learning about complexity and patterning of interactions in unpredictable ways, cases where looking closely at what the teams were actually doing and making the familiar look strange seemed to spawn new conversations and patterns of relating. I have further discussed several aspects pertaining to language and conversations that I observed in my day-to-day interactions.

Chapter 8

Out of Sight, But Not Out of Mind: Enhancing Knowledge Intensity in Offshore Operations

In this chapter I talk about the challenges that offshore workers face in terms of balancing organizational initiatives launched by senior managers (who are largely based at offshore locations) with their client priorities, while coping with the knowledge gaps they have with respect to their onsite counterparts. I specifically look at the Knowledge Management (KM) initiative launched by DCTS in 2006, the structures and rhetoric used by offshore leaders to implement and monitor the initiative, and how offshore teams responded to these. I also show how I got sponsorship for a role to facilitate this process from January 2007 to May 2008 and how I worked with 600+ associates across 100 projects, from 20 key accounts cutting across four industry verticals, to improve knowledge intensity, create some positive experiences in relating to their onsite staff and clients, and produce about 350+ knowledge artefacts.

Background of the KM initiative

KM was one of the strategic initiatives launched by DCTS in 2006. This was part of the overall strategy to push the organization into a new orbit of growth. This particular initiative was aimed at aligning delivery with the transformation in the front-end that I have discussed in the previous chapter. The belief was that there was a lot of experience that the organization had accumulated over time and given that it had grown in size it was important to codify this experience and make it available across the organization for quickly fixing delivery issues or creating new sales opportunities. The need for such an initiative was felt quite some time back (the 1998 strategy revealed such a need). But it got a formal thrust after the emergence of the new leadership in 2003–4. They identified a senior leader from the delivery centre to drive the initiative, indicating the management's seriousness and commitment to it. A team was formed to go through the process of defining the requirement (types of assets to be captured, cataloguing rules to store and retrieve relevant assets, user experience and collaboration features) and then developing and testing the solution. Finally, they were ready to roll out the solution by mid-2006. The solution was branded as KMAX and it was launched with much fanfare and internal branding and communication through mailers and posters in different locations. This was followed by several sessions where leaders briefed offshore employees on the strategic importance of such an initiative and urged them to participate and contribute to making DCTS a knowledge-driven firm. The management also institutionalized a governance structure across all delivery centres to help create assets. They further hired the services of faculty from the Indian Institute of Management (IIM) to conduct train-the-trainer sessions on writing case studies and clarifying the dos/don'ts for other types of assets. Some of the senior leaders took the lead to develop a few case studies and others were supposed to carry this forward and train other people. However, after about three months there was a feeling that the quality of assets being put in the system was not good (it seemed like garbage in, garbage out[14]). In the words of a leader who was overseeing this initiative at the delivery centre as part of the business excellence programme,

> People had interest, but seemed to have no time as they had so many other things to accomplish.

My entry into this context

In the winter of 2006, while I was in the Europe, I was going through a personal challenge and wanted to return to India. Since my work with the onsite staff in Europe was still in progress, I felt that I should persist with it. I discussed with the Europe Head and sought his advice on how I could sustain this activity after moving to India. He told me that some of the accounts that I was

---

14 Incidentally, there are striking parallels between garbage and knowledge in IT firms, at least in Chennai. First, just as increased urbanization and consumption has led to a model where garbage is collected and disposed (after which the garbage out of sight and out of mind), technology change has created an opportunity to move low-end tasks from client organizations into offshore delivery centres that are out of sight for the client managers. Second, just as garbage trucks collect garbage and transport it to the waste disposal sites, buses of IT firms collect their employees from the city and transport them to their respective offices. The IT corridor and Chennai's largest waste disposal facility happen to be in the same location, Old Mahabalipuram Road. Third, while waste-pickers at the collection and disposal sites extract recyclables from the waste, the pre-sales and domain teams extract "nuggets" from the variety of projects done by IT firms at onsite and in the delivery centres. A fourth similarity, pointed out by a colleague, is that college students often compare large Indian IT firms with garbage trucks in the way they source students in large numbers through campus interviews. These similarities will hopefully disappear as the industry matures and leaders and employees realize that the mind is social.

working with had offshore bases in India, and after discussions with his counterparts he suggested that one of the delivery centres may have some options. But, I would have to speak to the General Manager (GM) of the centre and get his buy-in. I drafted a note to the GM. He was one of the key leaders in the corporate Think Tank. He agreed to meet me.

I landed in India on around 27 December 2006 and met the GM. After a brief meeting he directed me to one of his direct reports, who was managing the strategic initiatives in the delivery centre. I met the senior manager and after some posturing he indicated that there were a couple of initiatives where they had some openings. One had to do with improving Go-To-Market (GTM) and the other was related to KM. Both these initiatives had been launched in late 2006, but there seemed to be some challenges in implementation. After some thought I suggested to him that I would like to look at the KM initiative.

Early stages of the process

The process was triggered by an alignment of two interests: (a) my research interest in exploring the transformative potential in the obvious day-to-day interactions in services firms, and (b) the management's interest in improving the quality of knowledge assets. In order to formalize the same I had to put together a Terms of Reference (TOR) and seek sponsorship from the GM's office. After brief discussions with the GM's office and a couple of my contacts on the status of the KM initiative, and revisiting my action research on key accounts and "viable knowledge", I drafted a TOR with the following objective: "To identify, codify and create experiences that can improve knowledge intensity in accounts and help orchestrate the firm's capability as a business advisor."[15] The scope was to help 15–20 key accounts over one year. After a couple of iterations my sponsors agreed and asked me to work closely with the KM initiative leads.

Interactions with KM initiative leaders

I followed this suggestion and requested meetings with the KM initiative leads to understand their implementation strategy. Most of them said that they had processes and tools in place, but were facing challenges in getting associates to understand the strategic importance and contribute quality assets. One of them suggested that I could participate in an upcoming workshop aimed at improving awareness of Knowledge Officers (KOs). I took this opportunity to meet other people involved in this initiative and also better understand the underlying philosophy. The workshop started with a senior management "kick-off" reiterating the strategic importance of KM and the urgent need to improve the quality of assets. The discussions that followed focused on "articulating business value", "need for better processes / templates", "attributes of a KO", "ensuring co-operation from senior delivery managers" and, finally, "culture change". Two points struck me. First, the discussion on KM seemed to be dominated by technical and organizational perspectives with very little focus on the individual-social. Second, the approach to change sounded very familiar (I have discussed its limitations in the previous chapter). I left the

---

15 I realized that the metaphor of garbage probably had a much deeper significance for my work during a casual conversation with one of my friends. I was meeting him after a very long time. We were hostel mates in IIT Madras when I was doing PhD. After exchanging pleasantries, he inquired about my work. I told him that I would be facilitating knowledge creation in some key accounts. He gave a wry smile and inquired if it had any relevance to my earlier PhD work on urban solid waste management. While I smiled at his subtle message, I realized that the reason I might have picked up KM was because it was another public good problem.

workshop feeling that my TOR and the "Interactionist" approach could complement the initiative, make KM more meaningful to the individual and trigger some change in his/her Global Service Network, i.e., the account.

Interactions with key account leaders

Once I got some form of buy-in from the KM initiative leads, I planned to speak to the accounts. However, instead of inviting all the Account Leads to a meeting to discuss content creation, I first sought suggestions from some delivery centre/practice KOs on potential accounts that might be interested in my service. Then, over the next three to four weeks, I met leads from six key accounts. Prior to the meetings I sent them my TOR. During the meetings I did not use any presentation. Instead, I started by asking them how they made sense of the KM initiative, what was their experience in identifying, creating and leveraging assets, and what had they gleaned from my TOR. While most associates said that they understood the importance of KM from an organizational perspective, they did not say much about the value to themselves or the account. Some indicated that they had difficulty in identifying and creating the right assets. Others inquired if I would be training them on developing different types of assets. A few others suggested that it might be better to do this with new projects and inquired if I could help "define a process". In response I briefed them about my role and its focus. For instance,

- That mine was not another initiative. I was trying to complement the existing one.
- That I would not be training them or defining a process, but would interact with them to explore various themes.
- That my focus would be on facilitating asset creation by triggering social and self-interactions in their context.

- I pointed to the possibility of iterating interactions over time so that past, present and future could be connected in new ways, thereby enriching experiences.
- I did not place any constraint on who might attend, but only indicated that about three to five associates (per theme) who were available and interested should be fine.
- I clarified that I did not expect participants to prepare much before the session. I added that they could participate only if they were interested.

In almost all the cases the associates who were present seemed to agree with my proposition. However, I was not sure why most of them had agreed to seek assistance from me. Did my hypothesis make sense to them? Some pointers are available in the participant responses.

One Group Leader (GL) said, "As the account owner, I wanted to increase our contribution to the organization's KM initiative. When, in the first session, you mentioned that the objective of this exercise is not only to come up with assets but to benefit the individuals as well, I decided to participate". While the response shows that targets were forcing managers to seek assistance, it also emphasizes the importance of including the individual. The process of knowledge extraction can also become a process of knowledge creation for the individual (i.e., an opportunity to reinterpret one's experience and reposition oneself in the social context). This is usually ignored in the mainstream thinking on KM.

One KO said:

At the start of the journey I thought this would be another workshop where we will spend some time and there won't be anything that we can take back afterwards. I assumed we would be given generic ideas on creating content and we have to go back and do things on our own... I chose to participate because

> I wanted to check out how the content can be created around themes and how the themes are chosen.

This observation suggests two things: (a) there is an inherent curiosity among associates to know something new, and (b) this curiosity is not nurtured by interventions such as awareness or training sessions or culture workshops. There is a need to go further. The above responses suggest that perhaps my hypothesis touched upon their key interests and hence we could connect with each other.

Interactions with knowledge producers

Even though the account leaders had expressed an interest, I still had to establish a connection with the actual knowledge producers.

How did we make a connection?

The following week I met the project teams to listen to their experiences. Instead of using any presentation, I started by asking them how they made sense of the KM initiative. In most cases I drew a blank. Then I inquired why they valued their present experience—in other words, what did it mean to their careers. Later, I asked if they felt that their experience was strategic for the account or the organization. At the end of the session most of the teams (about 45 out of 50 teams that I had contacted) agreed to participate.

I wondered why they agreed. A technically oriented Team Member (TM) had this to say:

> Initially, I did not have any idea about the session. My Project Leader (PL) said that this is a kind of awareness session about KMAX. I participated in it keeping my PL's request... Actually

> I am not so much interested in this KMAX thing because I felt
> even if we prepare and load something no one is going to look
> at this… Also, I am the kind who is interested in exploring
> technical aspects, R&D—that sort of thing rather than this
> kind of work". One PL said: "I was abruptly pulled into the
> discussion by my superiors. There was no prior briefing about
> these sessions. I chose to participate in the journey as I found it
> to be very useful in terms of understanding the big picture and
> where my project stands in it.

Another PL said: "Frankly speaking, I was sceptical in the
beginning. I wondered what more value could be added to the
existing services that we were providing the customers. The main
reason of my participation was curiosity to learn something new."
The above observations suggest that most knowledge producers
seem to have entered into this interaction with fairly defensive
views.

However, the first interaction seemed to break some patterns
and fan their curiosity. For instance, one TM said:

> In the first session I was totally at a loss of words. The questions
> asked in the session made me think, and it was the first time
> I was being asked questions relating to business and my
> understanding. One question that stuck with me was—how
> do you think that certain things added value to your resume?
> It was then that I felt this journey would be a good learning
> experience and help me discover myself, so I decided to
> participate.

Another TM said: "the first session turned out to be very different
from my expectations. I realized for the first time that there is lot
more than technical detail to be understood and appreciated in a
project. In fact my decision to participate in the journey was to

enhance my knowledge rather than create an asset." It is clear from the above that the first interaction seemed to address some key interests of individuals. In other words, we managed to connect.

In some cases it seems to have triggered further conversations among the participants and drawn others into the network, as pointed out by a TM who could not attend the first session:

> I didn't attend the first session since we had some work to be completed.... But after the session was over, whoever had attended, said the session was very good and thought provoking. They were discussing the session during tea breaks, dinner time, etc. This made me curious to know about it and I decided to attend the next one.

However, it did seem to take another two or three interactions to sharpen interest. For instance, a TM said: "After one or two meetings when it was decided to come out with a white paper I got little interested because I felt it would be a value addition for the team and me." A Project Manager (PM) said, "In the subsequent sessions we had a plan to work towards and were able to visualize the output that we could expect at the end of the exercise".

How did we develop the content?

The initial interactions with knowledge producers helped us identify a few broad areas. Then we continued to meet every week for an hour to discuss the experiences. During these interactions we had to deal with several conceptual and ethical challenges, for instance:

- Identifying distinctive experiences by paying attention to the obvious day-to-day work experiences of participants in a non-judgemental way;
- Exploring different facets of the experience and their interdependencies in an iterative manner with sufficient time for self-reflection (at least subconsciously);

- Linking the experience to the immediate context of the client—IT or business (instead of looking beyond the obvious, like linking software testing to social change);
- Co-evolving human assets with knowledge assets and encouraging them to engage with other assets;
- Involving others who may be part of the project, including onsite staff or practices or possibly clients (by sharing the notes from each session); and
- Separating the service provider's distinctive experience from the overall project experience, and not violating client's IPR.

How did we do this? Did I know everything or plan it all in advance? No! I only paid attention to our interaction, and tried to respond in a manner that would allow us to stay in the interaction and not close it prematurely. Two contrasting examples may help clarify the point. In one instance, a team said they had already produced some assets, including a white paper, and wondered if there would be any value in spending more time on the topic. Instead of withdrawing from the interaction or suggesting that we could look at something else, I said that I would be interested to have a look at the white paper (within the obvious). The team promptly sent me a copy. I went through the paper and noticed that it had an interesting title—"Beyond Testing"—but the content did not seem to match the title. I went back to the team and inquired if they would be interested to close the gap. As we kept exchanging views on potential ways to do this, one thought emerged. I asked if we could view testing from a "technology assimilation" perspective instead of the "defect elimination" perspective. This seemed to generate interest. We ended up developing a white paper on these lines.

In another instance, three TMs came for the session. When I inquired if they knew why they were there, they said that they thought it might be an awareness session on KMAX. Then as we talked further, one of them said that he did not see much value in this legacy project and he was also being released from the project shortly. Another said he had applied for a release. A third said he had just joined the team and did not have much experience. Instead of rejecting the project or being upset with them or their PL, I inquired if they might want to write about their frustrating experience ("within the obvious"). This seemed to trigger some interest. Subsequent iterations led to a significant change in their perceptions and resulted in a white paper and a very good case study. I was surprised to note that the case study reflected a key idea—how interactions can iterate and transform perceptions.

The participants also seemed to understand this. One of them said: "initially the question and answers session was very interesting and we enjoyed being made to think and think hard. The interesting part was how questions were formed from the answer we gave; it was spontaneous, and we were made to find the answers to the questions from our own statements." Another said, "It was the facilitator's patience to answer even the silliest question that we had asked [that made me stay in the interaction]." A third participant said, "In every meeting we saw a perspective that we had never thought of." The ethical questions seemed to help some. One TM said, "a key moment was when this question was asked: 'what did the service provider do to achieve this?' This left an impact on me."

The above observations point to not only the centrality of interactions in asset creation, but also the transformative potential in interactions. Managers or facilitators need to get down to the micro level and look at the participants' reality and improvise from within that context. Imposing some external ideas (as "best practices") through evangelizing, training, and monitoring and controlling using metrics will not move people into action when it comes to initiatives such as KM. Inter-Action is critical.

Why did we continue to interact?

The previous section discussed how the interaction evolved. But, how did we manage to sustain the interaction? The participants' feedback suggests four possible reasons: (a) meaningful re-interpretation of the past, (b) visible improvements and inter-actions in the present, (c) a belief in the future outcome, and (d) deepening of social relationships.

The first reason can be observed in this statement by a PL: "The sessions that we've had so far helped us to organize our thoughts and document them properly." A TM said, "These sessions gave me a holistic picture of our client's business system. I was able to appreciate why a CR was included in a particular release. It was these insights which kept me motivated to attend these sessions."

The second reason was echoed by others. One TM said, "In each session I gained something new that motivated me to join the next session." In a similar vein, another associate said, "the outcomes of these sessions were good and that motivated us to keep going." A PL said, "In each discussion we identified what was needed and who would be assigned the tasks. It was that responsibility that drove the participation." A GL said, "Till date we have had teams who collect information [from us] but [here we got useful inputs]."

The third reason can be found in the following observations. For instance, a Module Leader (ML) said, "my belief that the entire process and output will be different and will reach a wide audience kept my motivation level up." In a similar vein a TM said, "I was motivated to continue participating because I felt that this journey is surely going to help me in understanding the business better." A PM said, "We were also aware that the white paper, once completed, would have a positive response from customers and this was also a motivational factor to continue working on this task."

The social relations seem to have helped some. For instance, one participant said, "My co-workers and supervisor were at each stage motivating me to join the sessions." Another said, "We were working as a team. I think that was a great motivation factor." A third said, "I wanted to be an active participant in creating some useful assets for my project." A GL said, "Everyone felt happy about me participating in the sessions ... one reason why I participated in all the sessions." I also noticed that in some cases the senior associates (PLs) were bold enough to sit along with their TMs to explore their work (not only the positives, but also discuss inconsistencies in their thinking).

These observations seemed to reinforce the idea that social and self-interactions in the present hold the potential to reconnect the past and future in new ways.

How did we find time for this activity?

Here one could see a range of arguments. One argument is visible in this statement by an ML: "spending one hour every week was not difficult for me. As the schedule of the sessions was conveyed well in advance, it was easy for me to plan my tasks." A related thread was highlighted by a PL: "Since the sessions were once a week and most of the work from my side was done in the session, it did not distract me from my other work." An ML said, "I was able to manage time during working hours." A few indicated that they had to put in extra effort: "we sat after 6 for an hour or so to discuss".

The social perspective was highlighted by some: "we had very good support from the team and superiors. Team members were flexible and that helped us devote time for these sessions."… "Generating time was not a big problem, because we divided the work between us and it was easier to spare half an hour a day."

Some felt that they could devote time despite the work pressure. Consider this statement: "It was a bit tough to find time in our already busy schedule to work on this project, but when we are interested in doing something, we definitely find time for it." This point reinforces the core idea in my earlier paper, "Within the Obvious", that interactions have the potential to generate the desired bandwidth and trigger transformation.

What did the participants gain?

One TM said, "I had to think beyond the scope of what I was doing". Another one said:

> At the time we started I hadn't thought about the project in terms of the technology and business. Only after starting the white paper I got a clear picture of difficulties and opportunities in maintaining the application. To a certain extent I can even predict and help address the problems in developing a new application development tool.

One PL said, "this journey brought me out of my technical comfort zone. Earlier, all applications used to look alike to me. But slowly I learned to understand and appreciate why some functionality was present in the application. It helped visualize opportunities for improvement. In fact it motivated me to come back to office to actually learn rather than just performing my job". Another said, "It ignited my thinking process, not only in my work but in every aspect of life ... I got good recognition from my manager and from my GL". This shows that the process contributed to deepening of their work experience.

One TM said, "I got to know about the highlights and contributions of other service lines like development, testing and support. I was able to understand the tight linkage among the service lines and how they together contributed to the business". A PL said, "I learned a lot about project management from my co-participants". A GL said, "the process helped me understand the views of the next layer of people who are currently working in the project. I'm planning to continue this session internally for each key engagement in the future too". This shows that the process has enabled some experience sharing across project teams. This is the route to a knowledge intensive account.

Another TM said "This journey completely changed my way of thinking. ... After two sessions I remember when we were discussing some things two associates made certain suggestions. I began asking them questions and, after a few minutes, I suddenly realized that I was actually copying the manner in which we had interacted in the sessions." This suggests that interactions can be contagious without losing their uniqueness—clues for scaling?

Another TM said, "the sessions have informally provided training about paper writing; they have made us look at our project in a broader and more generic perspective". This suggests that the participants could learn something without being taught anything.

A senior PM; said

> Our team had very few seniors who could understand and get involved in the exercise. Most of the team was very much tied

up during working days. So I couldn't influence them to think on the lines of developing a relevant white paper. But having a mentor from outside the team made my job easier and it gave me great satisfaction that key members of the team not only focused on delivery but also found time to discuss topics other than day-to-day delivery.

The assumption being made here is that an "external mentor" is critical if we have to encourage junior associates to produce assets. There is a problem with this assumption. It leads us to think that defining the "ideal mentor", identifying them and assigning them to accounts will solve the problem. The solution does not lie in the allocation of "appropriate senior resources" to accounts, but instead lies in changing the highly constrained pattern of interaction among participants. Even the PM can change this pattern by paying more attention to the interaction and improvising from within.

In March 2008 there was an announcement that the organization would be restructured into vertical business units to facilitate decentralized decision-making and support growth. During one of the meetings with my sponsor, he asked me how this activity could be scaled up in the new structure. He was now moving into a different role of managing a vertical business unit. I gave him some options of how this could be sustained in the new model. A leader of one of the vertical units (in financial services) inquired if I would work with them. At that point, however, I felt that I was still interested in cross-industry perspectives. I also felt that I had looked at several challenges across the value chain, but there were not many takers for understanding these perspectives. DCTS was on a roll and there was no need felt for any deep listening or rethinking. It was around this time that I reached out to see if other firms were interested in my ideas. One month later

I came to know that one of the firms had shown an interest and in May 2008, I decided to quit DCTS.

Conclusion

In this chapter, I have discussed the experience of several associates who participated with me in a process to explore their work experiences. I have tried to capture the transformative potential in the process and its implications for the way we could Learn, Innovate, and Work Ethically (LIWE) in IT service networks. However, this co-evolution of knowledge assets and knowledge producers is only one part of the story. We still had to find ways to "replay all these assets within the team (onsite and offshore) and to the client", as suggested by a GL and also my sponsor. We tried to build upon this interest and organized interactions among the knowledge producers and other associates, groups and clients. These interactions led to: (a) involving other accounts in this process (20 in all and around 600 people), (b) codifying 100+ project experiences (350+ assets), (c) connecting the project experiences to interpret the bigger picture, i.e., the strategic intent of the client, and (d) in a few cases, sharing it with the clients to seek their involvement in the process, thus contributing to some patterning of their relationships with clients, onsite staff and senior management.

Grappling with the New Normal and the Digital World

"In all chaos there is a cosmos, in all disorder a secret order."

—*Carl Jung*

Chapter 9

Hollow Whole: Strategic Marketing in Indian IT Services

In this chapter I discuss how Indian IT services firms grapple with the challenge of new business development (NBD) in particular and brand building in general. I focus on the perspectives and rhetoric that guide NBD and brand-building activities. These are largely handled by a distributed pre-sales function[1] and centralized corporate marketing unit, respectively. I show how the intent to create a coherent message gets trivialized in the micro-interactions and contributes to an ironical situation where junior staff or the weakest group are held responsible for the interpretation and proliferation of the strategic message. I also discuss how some attempts to bring greater focus on this process of content creation led me to themes and people that had an unexpected value in re-building the confidence of the organization in the aftermath of a major crisis in late 2008.

---

1 Pre-sales activity is an offshore-based support activity that is distributed across sales, delivery, service lines or horizontal competency units, and domain practices.

How did I get into strategic marketing?

Marketing, as is generally understood, has never been of interest to me. I did not play any formal role in marketing or pre-sales functions in DCTS either. However, I got to interact with marketing and pre-sales teams as part of my work with key accounts at onsite and offshore between 2005 and 2008. During this period, I noticed that the corporate marketing function in DCTS was becoming more visible through the nature of high-profile events it was organizing to enable interactions with clients and analysts, and in developing a new brand theme. The new brand theme itself seemed a good attempt to align the internal and external perceptions of what the company stood for— delivering what they promise and promise what can be delivered. I felt that this fresh focus on marketing may be a result of DCTS going public in 2004, hence the commitment to grow further. It was also a reflection of an increase in competition and changes in client-sourcing strategies where questions such as "tell us how you are different" were frequently asked by clients. However, I was not sure about the impact of brand communications on the NBD pipeline or patterns of relating in existing client accounts.

I got an opportunity to work closely with the marketing and pre-sales functions when I left DCTS and joined GCS in 2008. GCS had just scaled to $2 billion in annual revenue. I was offered a role in a newly-formed strategic marketing unit, a small team of four senior people. The aim of the team was to improve the quality of thinking in the market-facing activities of domain practices. Domain practices are called by different names in different organizations, for example, Industry Practices, Service Offering team, and Verticals. It was headed by one of the leaders who had interviewed me and he in turn reported to the President of the US business (who had also interviewed me). After my experience as part of the Think Team in the utilities account in DCTS, I wondered if this was something similar, and was unsure why a separate team was required to think.

During my initial interviews with the leaders, recruitment and induction, I got a feeling that people at GCS were very energetic, vibrant and aggressive as compared to those I had interacted with at DCTS. (In fact the day I joined, I was requested to join a call with the CIO of a large account to share perspectives on measuring the business value of IT.) Through the course of discussions with my manager and other leaders over the next couple of weeks, I understood that the company had a very huge ambition to scale 6X in the next four years. The leaders of the firm believed that smarter thinking could help them grow faster than the industry average (most of the leading Indian IT companies were doubling in revenues every two years). That is why they were keen to invest in a strategic marketing unit and staff it with senior people. I wondered how the existing practice teams would relate to the new unit. My manager also indicated to me that prior to my joining they had had some discussions on where I could be leveraged best—whether I should be part of the solution architecture team, given my background in systems engineering, or part of the strategic marketing team, given my background in research and account-related work. I felt that neither group saw that I was treading a different path, focused on exploring workplace interactions. In the initial meetings with my manager and a few others, I tried to clarify my thought process and suggested that I could be leveraged best as a facilitator or a change agent, but they ignored my suggestion. I got a feeling that they couldn't visualize a role that owned nothing (everyone had to have tangible deliverables). I wondered if managers found it difficult to value the idea of exploring interactions because most interactions they encountered were either superficial (people exchanging courtesies) or zero-sum games (tough bargaining with clients, employees and partners). I felt that I would have to start all over again in a new environment.

4 Ps of marketing in Indian IT services

One of the first things I did was to get some understanding of the nature of marketing activity in Indian IT services. I read through analyst reports that discussed the weaknesses in marketing in Indian IT firms (for example, Iyengar, 2008). I also looked into some research papers that argued that firms of Indian origin have not been successful in identifying and exploiting discontinuities in the market/technologies, unlike some global firms such as IBM (for example, Umamaheswari and Momaya, 2008). I wondered if this was due to an inadequate marketing budget. Would increasing the marketing budget be sufficient? Or were there more fundamental issues that inhibit real market insight? To get a deeper handle on the issue, I started paying more attention to the key activities of a marketing team—market research, analyst relations, thought leadership events, web marketing, press releases, and branding initiatives.

I noticed that between 2005 and 2008, most of the top Indian IT firms launched brand-building exercises aimed at enhancing their visibility in the major markets, especially the US and the UK. The exercises were marked by coining new taglines (often with the help of well-known brand consultants), supporting these with a few client case studies and references, and publishing ads in leading newspapers, magazines and on the company website. This external positioning meant that all instruments of external communication such as brochures, websites, proposal templates, presentations of various internal units had to be repackaged and standardized.

Within a few days of joining, I was asked to participate in one such internal workshop organized by the corporate marketing team. The senior management of the company had decided to position GCS as a "collaborative business transformation partner". The workshop was inaugurated by the Head of Global Marketing. In his talk he emphasized that while branding collateral was an immediate need, marketing teams should actually look at surfacing market needs. To me this *was* the core function of marketing. Why then did he have to emphasize it? The Head also clarified that the corporate brand theme should be given primary importance over verticals or offerings. In other words, the experiences or interpretations at unit level had to be harmonized with the corporate message. What followed through the rest of the day were presentations by the pre-sales and marketing teams of the service lines (horizontal competencies such as ERP, Business Intelligence, ADMS, and Testing). Each group suggested that they were already doing such work (as transformation partners) and showed examples of how they had packaged their collateral in line with the new brand positioning. Most of the comments during presentations focused on refining the statements in the brochures or presentations so that the term "transformation partner" became more visible and integrated with the rest of the text, which, by itself did not seem different from the previous brand positioning. However, there was not much discussion on what they meant by the term "transformation partner" or any details on specific cases where these attributes were really being met. In fact no one seemed interested in exploring such questions at all. The pre-sales teams responsible for developing content also did not seem to bother with the meaning. The mood was "we have given the theme, now we need to get the collateral organized on these lines". I came away from the meeting with several questions. For instance, was it a real capability or an aspiration? Could transformation mean the same thing to different types of firms and in different industries, geographies and market conditions? How would clients perceive this brand positioning in the light of what they actually observe in their day-to-day interactions with sales/delivery staff? Will it lead to better price negotiation or have a counter-intuitive effective, i.e., further weaken the bargaining power? How would this brand positioning generate interest among the NBD prospects, who may be hearing about the firm for the first time?

A few weeks later the marketing team launched a campaign to promote this brand in different forums. One such forum was an international thought leadership event organized by a technology publishing website. The president of our business unit was invited to make a presentation on the concept of "collaborative business transformation". The event was coordinated by the marketing team. The president asked us (the strategic marketing unit) to help with preparation. My manager told me about the requirement and suggested that we put together a presentation by collating relevant case studies. We contacted different verticals to check if they had some case studies that highlighted our capabilities in "business transformation" and got hold of a few. When I started analysing these cases, an inherent pattern emerged: each case study indicated transformation at a different level of business, starting with process, then business unit, enterprise and finally industry; and in each case there seemed to be a set of enablers in the form of tools and the leverage of the partner ecosystem. We then put together a framework explaining what business transformation might mean (based on GCS' experience) and had a call with the president and the marketing team to share our thoughts. The president seemed happy with our interpretation and also added some perspectives to further enhance the presentation. I then consolidated these ideas in the form of key criteria for business transformation. The marketing team arranged a call to review the presentation. After the presentation was reviewed and signed by the president, the marketing team took the responsibility to improve the look and feel of it. They improved the formatting and added some good visuals for each of the slides, although I was not sure if the visuals were appropriate for the themes.[2] After the event was over, the marketing team sent out a message that the presentation had been received very well, with a special thanks to the speaker. One noticeable feature of this entire exercise was the minimal contribution of the marketing team in shaping the content. There were two senior marketing executives throughout these meetings (one at offshore and the other at onsite). They seemed to be keen to manage the process, coordinate the event and get the presentation polished, but not really influence the content. This exercise, along with the previous workshop, left me wondering why marketing was a mere spectator to the process of content creation. Why didn't they play a role in shaping the content? Was it not integral to brand-building? After all, the topic we were discussing did not require any deep understanding of a particular domain. I was reminded of process culture in software development process (where client gives the content).

As time passed, I kept up my discussions with different domain practices and their sales counterparts about their understanding of the market and the emerging trends in the industry, and how they used the research of analyst firms to improve this understanding. Most domain practices complained that they did not have access to relevant analyst publications, even though the firm had subscriptions with two or three analyst firms (some funded by the corporate team,

---

2   Visuals used in presentations sometimes communicate the opposite meaning.

others by the practice teams). When I probed further I noticed that there were two types of issues. One type was where the marketing team periodically sent the domain practices a bunch of analyst papers based on the alerts that are created. Invariably, the domain practices claimed that they were too occupied with their work and did not have the time to sift through these papers and pick relevant information. The second type was where the domain practices asked for research reports on a particular topic or a customer. In such cases the marketing team expected the domain team to give the details of the specific publication so that they could download it for them. This was frustrating for the domain team. They felt that the marketing team was not able to understand and respond to their needs. One may also notice here that the content (market research) was typically outsourced to analyst firms, which have been quick to exploit this market for research and advice, especially with smaller IT firms. However, irrespective of size, the general issue I observed was that there is no firm specific market research and synthesis other than the discrete signals collected by the sales and practice teams from their interactions with clients or by searching the web. Also, since most of the analyst reports typically present views at a macro level and are also available to competitors, there was no major competitive advantage in having this information, other than making their presentation look well-informed.[3]

The above situations seemed to reinforce research findings that marketing in Indian IT services is largely transactional in nature. I also felt that the entire focus was on promotion. Marketing had very little role in shaping the other three 'Ps'—product (offering), price, place (geography, target segment). There was very little value-add in terms of identifying new trends, developing thought

---

3   Analyst firms usually survey clients and technology providers and summarize emerging trends; this can sometimes result in self-fulfilling prophecies.

leadership and creation of new service offerings. The expectation of all the stakeholders was that the 3 Ps were to come from the pre-sales function of domain practice. But, how does domain practice help in these areas, how does it interact with marketing, sales and delivery, and other entities to bring a deeper market understanding into the conversations? To understand this I started engaging with the different domain practices in GCS that focused on banking and financial services, insurance, public services, retail and travel.

Domain pre-sales: Expecting the tail to wag the dog
In this section I discuss the way the pre-sales function is typically organized and perceived in an Indian IT firm. I would do this by presenting day-to-day situations where perceptions about this function are constructed and sustained; for instance, its role in advising on industry trends, creation of collateral and branding, and developing analyst relations. In the case of GCS, the pre-sales function was housed under the domain practice (also called SO or vertical team). The pre-sales function typically involves activities such as responding to Requests for Information / Proposals (RFIs/ RFPs), preparing collaterals, and supporting analyst interactions. They are typically equipped with IT staff who have handled IT projects in a certain domain/industry over a reasonable amount of time, or lateral entrants from respective industries who have knowledge of say, the banking business and operations, or IT professionals with experience in developing/implementing domain solutions such as core banking products. Some practices also have staff with domain consulting experience, for instance in risk management. But this is generally small, and even if present, resides in the consulting units in these organizations. Domain practices are also responsible for solutions (which includes

solution design, developing domain expertise, maintaining a pool of business analysts, and managing alliances and competencies in industry native products). The distinction between pre-sales and the solutioning function is usually fuzzy and a source of conflict. My focus in this chapter is on the pre-sales function. I discuss the domain solution-related challenges in the next chapter.

The pre-sales function and domain practices generally have a poor image within IT firms. One of the reasons for this is rooted in the origin of the pre-sales function. The domain pre-sales functions (as I have discussed in Chapter 5) evolved after the evolution of the delivery and sales functions. Initially, this function was supported by people on the bench, i.e., non-billable resources. Non-billable is usually considered non-value adding. Over time these teams were staffed with people who had done IT work in a particular domain or with domain SMEs/business analysts hired from the industry and organized as a cost-centre at offshore (to keep non-billable costs low). This has further limited their understanding of client contexts and markets that they are expected to support. The poor image of the pre-sales function is also due to a mismatch in expectations. While they are staffed with people not seen as adding value, the expectation from sales and delivery teams is that the pre-sales team should address the complexity that sales and delivery are unable to handle. I noticed this pattern even in DCTS. For instance, around 2006, DCTS launched a major initiative to transform its sales force into a proactive and consultative sales team. The sales force was trained in the concepts of demand creation and given tools to proactively identify opportunities from industry trends. In the business planning session that followed it was obvious that the sales teams were struggling to really understand industry trends and explore the implications for their clients. They started suggesting that this required more research and involvement from the domain practices. As a result a GTM (Go-To-Market) team was created at offshore to facilitate this. However, the domain teams struggled to interpret the trends and translate them into meaningful opportunities that were aligned with the client. In other words, the expectation was that the support team at offshore, which doesn't have any real sense of the context, should know it all. I haven't seen anyone reflect on this irony of expecting the weaker team to handle a more complex challenge. Even when this is acknowledged, it is translated into "we need more budgets to build the right team". What I observed through my work was that a good understanding of the processes and technologies in a particular industry was necessary but not sufficient to generate better insight into the business and industry trends. Such knowledge can only be developed through research, consulting and sustained interactions with clients and industry experts. In the absence of a model that allows people to actively combine practical work and research, this capability is lacking or weak.

The prevalent attitude towards research within practice, sales and delivery teams also does not help matters. Let me cite a couple of instances here. When we established the strategic marketing unit to cater to the needs of a few clusters of verticals such as Banking and Financial Services, Retail and Travel, we started receiving requirements from the sales and practice teams. One of the requests was for some detailed research on a set of prospects. During the conversation with the sales/practice teams I was constantly questioned on whether I would be using some paid research databases such as Hoovers to provide additional insight. When I responded that I would use a particular framework to analyse customers and rely on information from a variety of sources (including Google), a sales person seemed uncomfortable.

He suggested that he also had access to Google and had looked into all searchable material, so what else could I provide? This shows how sales/practice teams viewed market research, i.e., access to paid research. Intelligent and systematic data collection, analysis and synthesis of information did not seem to have any value. I could see that even if the sales or practice teams had access to all the information, thanks to the RSS feeds from different websites, there did not seem to be a way to synthesize and enhance the strategic alignment between external opportunities and internal competencies.[4] Let me illustrate this with another example. As part of the planning process in the banking vertical, the practice teams had indicated that they sensed a strategic opportunity in core banking and had developed alliances and a talent pool around certain core banking solutions that had good potential. They requested the sales team to pursue opportunities in that technology/vendor. However, the sales team came up with an opportunity with a different core banking product where the domain practice did not have sufficient skills. During the discussions the practice head indicated that this was not in agreement with the earlier plan and it would not be easy to develop this competency within the suggested time frame. Immediately the sales team escalated the issue to the business unit head and the business unit head slammed the competency teams for being inflexible and not understanding the market, i.e., choosing right partners/technologies (the sales team's understanding of the market, however opportunistic, is of primary importance). Finally a decision was made to source these competencies from the market. About 10–15 people with the requisite skills were recruited. Later it was found that the

---

4   Today there are tools based on semantic technology that could facilitate the synthesis of different pieces of information.

project was likely to be delayed and the sales team had oversold the immediacy of the requirement. The people had to be deployed elsewhere. A key issue here is the absence of a collaborative and continuous market-sensing approach in the face of significant external variety (clients and their choices of technology). And the distributed model of work adds to the variety. I felt that these gaps were impacting the ability of GCS and other Indian IT firms to sense and proactively shape market needs. As I was grappling with these issues, we had our first major shock.

Global financial crisis creates an opportunity to adapt

In September 2008 we woke up to news of the bankruptcy of one of our leading financial services clients. There were rumours of other clients getting acquired and several others going into some form of crisis management in the wake of the global financial crisis. This set off a flurry of activity within the firm to rethink our positioning in the new situation. The new brand theme of "collaborative business transformation" was the first casualty. No one seemed confident of talking about this theme and it was clear that it was more about what we wanted to be, not what we were actually capable of. As we were going through this exercise there was a banking client visit in November 2008. The banking team had reached out to me to inquire if I could help with some insights on how the industry might emerge from the crisis and innovations that could make sense in such a context. I was a relative novice to banking. I did some research and then put together a framework to explain how the industry might evolve. I had used the model as a way to synthesize the different perspectives that were emerging at that time and trigger relevant conversations. Some of the predictions that I made using this model were about the type of financial firms that might use this situation to drive growth, the priorities of large complex financial institutions, and the functions that might attract new players and potentially evolve in new directions (for example, payments). When I mailed this presentation to the team that was preparing for the client visit, it apparently created a lot of tension. One of the senior programme managers called me and inquired if I could join them over a call and explain my presentation. I did so, but it didn't seem to help. I got another call in the evening asking me to join the preparatory workshop the next morning and participate in the client visit the following day. Since I had joined a few months back in Chennai, and this meeting was happening in Hyderabad, I was meeting several people for the first time. When I went for the workshop, people started inquiring if I was a banker. I told them that I did not know much about banking. I had only analysed the literature and used my systems modelling experience to develop this perspective. They didn't seem convinced. How could I talk about future scenarios without being a banker? Also, they were trying to grapple with the model I had used. Soon after lunch, during the client presentation, I was given a 15-minute slot to present my model. It did not invite much discussion, but there was no major disagreement either. I wondered if this kind of research had any value at all.

Later, I thought that it might be a good idea to develop this perspective on the future of banking industry into a white paper. I did some research into the nature of responses and strategies that were being taken by leading global financial services firms. One thing that caught my attention was the contrasting responses of two leading firms on the future of the universal banking model. While the chairman of the European bank suggested that the universal banking model was not sustainable (and the bank was considering selling off its investment banking division), the US-based bank's CEO did the exact opposite—he reiterated that the the bank he represented would persist with the universal banking model. When I probed this a bit further, I noticed that there were two thought processes at work. One line of thinking argued for a complete overhaul of the financial system, while the other placed the blame on the people who ran the system. However, I noticed that the global financial crisis of 2008 did not leave any type of firm untouched. The US-based firm had also suffered great losses. In that case, should we blame both people and the system? I wondered if this conclusion was helpful. Would such reasoning help evolve a more robust financial services industry? A financial services firm, whether it is a retail bank, an investment bank or an insurance firm, is fundamentally built around the concept of "trust". Added to that is the "service" characteristic of these firms. While regulatory and technological interventions do provide some guarantee and have enhanced the transparency of financial firms, these are clearly not sufficient (as we have seen in the present crisis—firms that were stated to be leaders with good balance sheets suddenly collapsed). Trust essentially evolves from the process of human interaction. Unfortunately, this process of interaction has been greatly disturbed in a global financial services context. The model of global capital markets decouples the players to an extreme level when compared with retail banks. Based on this insight, I developed a white paper wherein I argued that finding ways to enhance the process of human interaction in a global financial services context will be crucial to evolve a sound financial system for the future. This kind of change can come about in all types of financial services, and with all types of customers (retail, private, SMBs and corporate). Financial firms should try to initiate a fresh conversation with their stakeholders—employees, customers and shareholders. Instead of trying to "overhaul the system" or "removing barriers to allow new entrants", I think regulators should try to introduce interventions that encourage financial services firms to relook at the process of human interaction and trust-building in a global financial services context. I then shared the white paper with a few people from the banking practice and sales. Some of them thought it was a good angle to argue with the executives of clients, but did not feel they could engage their immediate client managers who were largely handling IT. Their client managers were interested in whether we could cut costs further or come up with some innovative ideas that could help them protect their IT budgets.

Developing a holistic view of the market

The global financial crisis also pushed me to revisit the frameworks used to understand the market. We tried to develop a framework that could provide further scope for understanding trends within an industry in a holistic way and also explore convergence opportunities across industries. For instance, the convergence in financial services around aspects such as micro-finance, the convergence of banking and logistics in supply chain finance, the convergence of banking and telecom for mobile payments or the convergence of banking and healthcare (health-wealth). However, we also felt that such frameworks alone would not be sufficient. Some organizational spaces also needed to be created for people in vertical silos to pursue these opportunities. My manager discussed this with his counterparts and the president of the unit and canvassed for a new organizational space called "affinity forums", where we could bring leaders from different verticals to explore cross-industry opportunities and service offerings. We used a unique framework to show that while Banking, Financial Services and Insurance (BFSI) had remained one unit in several

IT firms for a long time, there was very little sharing of service offerings and tools across these. Neither was there any holistic view of the market (apart from industry classifications such as the North American Industry Classification System) that could help identify niche sub-verticals that we could focus on. We presented similar possibilities for retail, travel, healthcare and public services. The vertical leaders listened to our presentation and made some remarks, but it appeared that they did not see much meaning in what we were proposing. They seemed too engrossed with protecting their reduced portfolio in the wake of the global financial crisis.

Understanding client-supplier networks

A second framework that I introduced in the ongoing discussion within domain practices and marketing was a network model of the IT services industry. I felt that such a perspective could help unearth key trends and weak signals. For instance, analysing the network of connections across clients, technologies, partners and competitors, could give us insights into areas where there was strong clustering. It could also help in understanding sourcing and acquisition strategies, knowledge flow across firms (transfer of best practices), competitive or collective advantage, role models (competitors and clients), customer ecosystems, entry points and ideas for designing effective service offerings and value propositions. I carried out an analysis of the IT supplier-client contracts database (published by one of the leading analyst firm) in the BFSI sector.

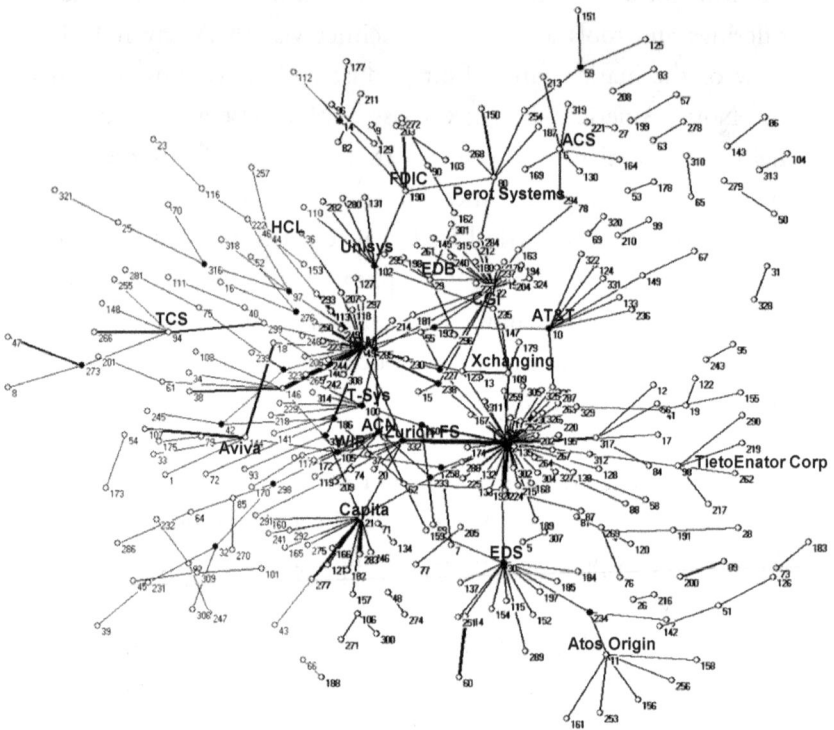

Figure 14: Client-IT provider relationships in the insurance sector (in 2008)

The analysis of the supplier-client network in the global insurance industry (shown in Figure 14) revealed the following: (a) CSC and IBM are industry leaders, followed by Accenture, CGI and Capita; (b) most customers of players such as Atos, EDS, Capita don't seem to have multi-sourcing (exclusivity for vendor); and (c) customers such as Aviva and Zurich Financial Services seem to have strong multi-sourcing strategies (the latter client was presented as an ideal case by Gartner in one of its reports, see Da Rold and Karamouzis, 2009). I used this to trigger dialogue with the insurance and banking sales and practice teams. The response was muted. The NBD sales teams also struggled to make use of this information; they didn't have any contacts with the identified prospect. The existing business development (EBD) sales teams felt that such insights would not help them repair their existing relationships. It was clear that deeper insights by themselves were not of much value under constrained patterns of relating.

Intelligence at sub-vertical levels

A third area that I explored was to develop market intelligence at a sub-vertical level. I felt that branding efforts would have to move from the corporate level to the vertical and service-offering levels. A key aspect of this was to understand competitive differentiation at these levels. This would not only help the firm understand its position better, but also position itself effectively with its clients and analysts. I did some research on these lines. For instance, a comparison of solution accelerators in the BFSI vertical revealed certain aspects where competitors saw opportunity in building accelerators that have the potential to translate into products and so on. Similarly, we analyzed brand visibility of competitors through a comparison of web presence, event participation and media releases to understand the relative strengths and weaknesses, and identify any emerging trends. We consolidated these into a competitive intelligence report which we shared with leaders of the domain practices/vertical teams.

While about four months of efforts in strategic marketing did not seem to change the thinking of sales and practice leaders, it did seem to improve interactions with them. This was clearly evident in the area of market research where I emerged as the go-to person. For instance, there was an increasing number of cases where requests for the same piece of information came from four different groups (domain, pre-sales, sales and delivery). There was also a tendency for the pre-sales teams to view the strategic marketing function as a bridge with the corporate marketing team. This gave me a glimmer of hope that I could navigate the new landscape to further the dialogue and help the firm evolve a creative response to the financial crisis. While I was trying to build on this momentum and develop a dialogue with the practices, we encountered the second major shock and this time, it came from within the firm.

Internal financial crisis changes the network

In early 2009, GCS came to the brink of near failure following a revelation that the promoters of the firm had been manipulating the books of the company for about five to seven years. The firm was saved by the government and was taken over by another Indian IT firm called Think Big (TB). By July 2009, the new management had taken over, retrenched a number of people and restructured the organization to not only bring it in line with the actual revenues but also better understand it. This meant that many non-billable groups like the one I was working for (strategic marketing unit), were dismantled. Some lines of business that seemed small, unprofitable and had a low probability of turning around quickly were liquidated.[5] And out went the branding

---

5   The leadership of the acquiring firm (TB) reviewed the performance of several groups and took a call on the ones where they did not see much strategic value. One such group was the Public Services unit that had lost a key client during the crisis period. And in the absence of financial statements the TB leadership believed that there was very little possibility of getting work from government and public bodies. An interesting thing happened during the evaluation. I was surprised to see the team use the positioning statement that I had presented to them sometime in September 2008 to convince the TB leadership that they had a strong vision for this vertical. However, this seemed to come too late in the game.

exercise as well (nobody would dare hire this company for business transformation). My manager and his manager (the president of our business unit) both left the organization. I was asked to become part of the Financial Services (FS) practice (into an undefined managerial role). I did not know why, but I guessed that it might be because I was relatively new to the firm, had been interacting with the FS practice in the immediate aftermath of the crisis, and a couple of senior people who were finalizing the list of people to be retained had interacted with me (during my interview, and later while helping the FS practice to align its thinking in relation to the changed market scenario).[6] I had survived the crisis, but

---

6   After the crisis came to light in January 2009, there was a lull in activity for two months. After my manager quit (mid-February), I was for a short period reporting to the president of the unit. The president was also under scrutiny due to the investigation, so there was no interaction. In such an environment, two of my colleagues and I continued to keep ourselves busy doing market research and trying to understand how a firm could respond in such a situation. I looked at how most banks started treating employees as high-risk customers and reduced credit card limits and so on. I felt that they did not have a micro-level understanding of a customer and were using a general rule for all the employees. So, I started looking at ways a bank could actually look at understanding risk profiles of individual customers. In April 2009, after a new Head of Sales was announced for financial services in North America, the sub-vertical leaders reached out to me for assistance in formulating the overall financial services strategy. Until then there were three separate domain practices in financial services. Now they were being asked to frame a unified financial services strategy. They were facing difficulties in synthesizing to make this happen. I began helping them with some market and client research and identifying commonalities. During this time one of my colleagues called and said that a list was being prepared of those who are likely to be retained and he said that my name was not on that list. I started thinking that I might get the pink slip in a few days. A few days later one of the senior leaders (who had earlier interviewed me) asked me to meet him. I was not sure if I was going to be asked to leave. I went and met him. He told me that they were planning to take me into the FS practice. The next day, my colleague who had warned me about my name being missing called me and said that his name was now missing from the list. Then I told him about the development on my side and asked him to speak to the senior leader. After a couple of days he came back and said that his name was also now included in the practice. During this period I felt that some of the people in the FS practice who were left out were

faced my second identity crisis. How would I re-establish my relations in a new context, a new domain and a new role?

The new management (from the acquiring firm TB) started speaking to different teams to start thinking about the future. I was pleasantly surprised to see that the leader assigned to improve the financial services business was someone with whom I had worked in the early 1990s. This was totally unexpected. We had shared a good rapport while working together at my first job with one of the earliest software product firms in India. We started exchanging notes and discussing the financial services strategy. The model I had developed on the post-crisis scenarios of the industry and my ability to hold and stitch together a coherent story from the diverse pieces of information seemed to make a big difference in facilitating the dialogue on strategy. I also sensed that the sales and delivery leaders seemed comfortable with what was emerging as a strategy document (primarily because they started seeing the new BFSI leader from TB as a conduit to the company's senior management, and the document seemed to help ward off uncomfortable questions from the senior management). This also appeared to change the dynamics within the domain team and my equations with leaders in delivery and sales in a small way.

Sensing the urgency among the new leaders to get things back into action and the call that we should start looking at building a billion-dollar vertical, I prepared a note on the following lines in September 2009:

The financial crisis of 2008 has triggered forces that could alter

---

questioning my credentials to be part of the FS practice. I did not have any domain expertise, but had a consulting and research background and in an interdisciplinary topic. Did someone see value in this?

the global economic landscape in a significant way. There is already a talk of a "New Normal"[7] that is characterized by an increased role of the government, decline in consumer spending and increase in saving, and increased role of internet and social media. This emerging context poses new challenges for all industries including the Indian IT industry. Over the past few years Indian IT firms have been addressing growth issues by adopting both organic strategies, such as corporate branding, sales force transformation, account mining, verticalization (of sales/delivery or independent business units), and inorganic strategies, such as acquisition of vertical or horizontal competencies. While these may be helpful in sustaining growth, the "New Normal" will fundamentally test the way IT firms sense and respond to market needs. For instance, the financial crisis and recession have impacted different industries in different ways (for example, a recent IMF report indicates that global trade in goods has suffered more, compared to services). Within an industry, different firms have been impacted to different degrees. Within a firm, different business units have performed differently. These differences suggest that it is no longer sufficient to analyse macro-level data or segments to spot trends and opportunities. Instead firms have to develop capabilities to sense and respond to micro trends, weak signals at sub-vertical levels and for specific roles (this is being increasingly recognized by analysts such as Gartner and Forrester). But how do firms do this? Can they do this with their present structures, processes, and patterns of interaction? It is time to rethink if the present model of marketing is relevant for IT services in general and the "New Normal" in particular. There may be a case for making marketing knowledge intensive, or it has to be tightly coupled with the domain practice.

---

7   A term popularized by Mckinsey consulting

I also pointed to the issues that I had observed in the earlier setup and suggested that we avoid a structural solution, but look to trigger interactions on key issues. For instance, both marketing and practice development were stuck with problems in thinking and relating. Leaders have struggled and continue to struggle in their attempt to facilitate changes in these two units. They usually try to create additional "Strategic Support Units" to enhance the thinking process (like the one I had joined). However, such interventions rarely succeeded since they are considered overheads by both the existing units and there is a constant struggle to clarify boundaries. Such "Strategic Support Units" are either rejected for the lack of domain/geography-specific insight, or avoided in case they have some real insight to offer, probably due to the fear that the insight provider may gain visibility. The possibility of co-creation is rarely explored. I suggested that these gaps could be addressed in three ways: (i) developing an integrated model, i.e., embedding a strategic marketing function for a cluster of related practices, (ii) adopting new analytical frameworks that can generate micro-level insights, and (iii) adopting an interactionist approach to develop and sustain a dialogue with core-value creating units (sales and delivery teams of existing clients). The third point, to me, was the most critical aspect. While the analytical frameworks can help generate insights, making sense of these insights and acting on them requires an interactionist approach. In other words, we need to pay attention to the utterances during an interaction, amplify voices that have the potential to generate emergent patterns, and find ways to sustain the interaction. And this can be done in the interaction between marketing-practice and others such as clients/sales/delivery teams. For instance, when marketing-practice teams interact with delivery teams to capture the case studies, it is essential to see this as a two-way process. The process should first help the delivery people in enhancing their knowledge and customer focus. The case studies should be seen as a bi-product. Similarly, one should look for sustained dialogue with sales teams. Sales teams tend to be opportunistic and secretive. They may not acknowledge any proactive information sent to them. And even if they request any information, try may not reveal the context they are likely to use it in. While a mismatch of the information with the immediate need may be one reason, a real concern about sharing the credit with the source of information is another. These interactions could be extremely frustrating in the absence of adequate levels of trust. The engagement should go beyond meeting their need for a proposal to constantly engaging them in other forums including business planning. Constant polling along with an ability to demonstrate knowledge yet revealing ignorance simultaneously and facilitating the emergence of key patterns in an inclusive way will be critical in developing and sustaining the dialogue.

I shared the note with my new manager and a couple of senior leaders from the financial services business. However, I did not receive any response. They probably found it impractical considering at this point the firm was trying to rationalize costs and eliminate duplications. I felt we were missing an opportunity to adapt to the "New Normal". Nevertheless, I went about internalizing some of these ideas in my work and focusing on my interactions. I discuss this further in the next chapter.

Conclusion

In this chapter I have discussed the challenges with strategic marketing in Indian IT services and translating these into NBD opportunities. I have drawn attention to a particular problem that is deeply ingrained in Indian IT firms—the dominant focus on process and inadequate attention to content, a result of the process-orientation in software development and how this impacts the ability to sense and respond to dynamic market changes. The irony is that the weakest link of the organization becomes responsible for a very strategic function.

I have shown that even when GCS tried to improve the marketing function, they sought to address this problem by creating a separate team for strategic marketing. The expectation of the sponsors was that this team that would not only produce new market insights, but also align all the stakeholders in a new direction. I tried to address these two expectations by producing certain insights and embedding this in the interactions among practices, sales and delivery. Within the first three months I could sense that it seemed to improve the centrality of the strategic marketing function. The global financial crisis did create any further opportunity to change the patterns of relating. However, a new disruption in the form of an internal financial fraud led to the firm getting acquired by another one which further led to a simplification of structure and breakdown of relationships. The process that seemed to be gaining some momentum was disrupted, but took a different shape. What was this shape? Did it help us to adapt to the new normal? I discuss this in the next chapter.

Chapter 10

When NOTHING Matters!
Innovation in a Disrupted World

In this chapter I will reflect on the managerial discourse that played out in a very unique scenario—the process of reviving GCS, whose fabric of business relationships was torn apart by two significant events in 2008–9 (discussed in the previous chapter). First, the market situation that emerged out of the global financial crisis; and second, a near-death experience triggered by exposure of an internal financial fraud, and subsequent acquisition and merger. Five years later the firm appeared to gain some sense of stability, but a majority of revenue came from a few clients that had stayed through the crisis. During the course of five years, the firm oscillated between order and anarchy and increased frustration for managers because most managerial interventions such as strategy and execution (structure, people, process, scorecards, governance, values, communication, leadership) didn't seem to follow a neat logic (like Stabilize >> Invest >> Grow) or deliver desired results (35–40 per cent+ annual growth and above industry average) in a three–five year timeframe. Having participated in this journey for over five years in a fairly reflexive manner,[8] I realized that this "new normal" situation was clearly exposing the limitations of dominant management styles, beliefs and ideologies that are prevalent in Global IT Service Networks (GSNs).[9] Instead of diagnosing what is wrong with the strategy or execution, which can be a never-ending game when desired results or successes are not achieved,[10] I am more interested in reflecting on how these interventions/abstractions were produced, accepted/rejected and proliferated/stalled through day-to-day workplace interactions in a highly uncertain environment. For instance, how the interactions developed, took different paths or stalled through the interplay of agendas, ideologies, power differences among different stakeholders when there was nothing spectacular in the financial outcome. I will articulate my views by drawing upon key interactions that I participated in with internal groups and

---

8   When I survived the crisis and ended up in the FS practice, my main motivation was to see how managers and associates might respond to the crisis, and whether it could open possibilities for qualitative change.

9   Indian IT services have now become an integral part of the Global IT services networks. There are strong dependencies between clients and service providers at an operational level. The language of clients invariably seeps into the conversations of managers and associates of service providers. This is more pronounced in the case of servicing financial services clients, especially investment banking jargon and behaviours.

10 Management concepts are largely built on a very strong cause–effect logic [Desired Results=Strategy*Execution]. If the desired results are met, then one can retrospectively say that the company had great strategy and execution capability—the stuff of best practices and case studies. If the desired results are not met, then either strategy or execution or both are flawed. A typical response in such a situation is to push the strategy or execution levers hoping that things might change for the better. What if it does not? The process continues as long as the service network is alive. In such a scenario it is extremely difficult to say what is right or wrong. What the dominant group says becomes right, and No Result becomes a powerful weapon to include or exclude people in the formation of the dominant group. Further when included people drop out of this due to the high level of uncertainty, it creates more flux leading to search for new allies.

external entities, mostly aimed at developing differentiators and rebuilding relationships for the financial services business[11] that contributed to about 20 per cent of GCS's revenue, and suffered the most due to the two discontinuities.

In the next part, I will show how the dominant management discourse (logic, metaphors and jargons) was used either to simplify the situation by focusing on what is tangible/known and diverting the unknowns to a catchall unit (one way of handling complexity) or to push the system towards anarchy by expanding the scope of solution search, but very rarely to foster generative dialogue and change. In the rest of chapter, I will show how some possibilities for generative dialogue and change emerged by exploring the complementarities with the parent company and linking them with the themes emerging from client interactions. Some of these had the potential to push the firm into new strategic paths but were constrained by a situation where innovative thinking was being reduced to "talking points" by senior managers and sales teams to gain access to clients. They did not significantly alter the growth trajectory of the organization. The vertical grew by about 12-15 per cent CAGR during this period.[12] A significant proportion of the growth came from the expansion of work around existing projects/clients and resulted in a long-tail scenario, with no major change in the quality of revenue. However, the market cap of the merged entity grew manifold and increased shareholder value.

Disruption and Uncertainty: All roads lead to domain

---

11 It may be noted that the financial services vertical is not one formal organizational unit with P&L, but a collection of units that cut across different geographies, each with a different P&L. The FS domain practice packages these different pieces to present a unified picture of the vertical.

12 Competing firms that did not suffer similar turmoil reported equivalent growth rate on a much larger base (almost eight–ten times).

In early 2009, when the CEO of GCS admitted to an internal financial fraud, there was a huge upheaval in the Indian IT industry. Everyone started distancing themselves from the company. Clients started leaving or putting their commitments on hold. A number of employees whose identities and assets were strongly tied with the company suddenly felt abandoned; many started leaving. Competitors were distancing themselves from the firm in public, but in private were actively poaching clients and employees. The government had to finally step in, reconstitute a fresh board and facilitate the takeover by another IT firm, TB, which found value in complementing its strength in a telecom vertical with the multi-vertical capabilities of the beleaguered firm. During this period, a number of passionate managers and associates spent a lot of time speaking to clients and associates in an effort to arrest the tide, while others preferred to secure their careers either individually or in groups. The period between January and May 2009 was a state of complete anarchy.

Once the company got acquired and a new management team had been announced, the focus shifted to right-sizing the organization in line with its revenues. In July 2009, about 8,000–10,000 associates cutting across different levels were served notice. This was a painful experience, possibly happening for the first time in the context of Indian IT services firms. The employees of Indian IT firms had been used to the scenario of taking over client-employee roles in outsourcing partnerships, but not many had seen a situation where they may be stopped at the entrance of their own office one day and asked to swipe a card to check if they should be permitted inside or asked to meet HR. Two of my junior colleagues found themselves in that unfortunate situation and I was helpless to do anything about it. Those who survived that situation heaved a sigh of relief only to see another round of pruning in August 2009. By September 2009, the organization was "optimized" in terms of the number of people and a new structure[13] was announced. The entire focus was now on making the business profitable again, i.e., increasing EBITDA from a very low three per cent to the analyst expectations of 20 per cent. The New Business Development (NBD), pre-sales and domain competency teams were reduced to a bare minimum as the likelihood of acquiring new clients seemed bleak. Those who were on billable client projects were the safest and also the most valued.

In parallel, as the impact of the global financial crisis was becoming clear it was forcing clients to cut down on IT expenditure and consolidate their vendors. For most clients where GCS was not a key vendor, it became an ideal candidate for elimination. Some of the reasons cited included—"vendor instability is risky for our business … we will reconsider after your financials are restated". The NBD engine had almost come to a standstill; there were no major RFIs (Requests for Information) or RFPs (Requests for Proposal) except for some sporadic requirements. Neither was there any investment into training the sales force for the changing market scenario; the management focus was on profitability. Management called it the period of stabilizing (2009–11). Existing business teams (sales and delivery) were busy sustaining their projects and retaining people. This turbulent situation seemed to have a counter-intuitive effect. It started improving client satisfaction in certain cases—higher quality metrics were reported in some projects during this period. Two

---

13 There was considerable debate to decide the appropriate structure. One of the senior leaders commented that the simplified structure was designed to help the new management control costs and reduce risks, but not necessarily to help the firm cope with the situation that it found itself in. All approvals were centralized at the CXO level to ensure tight cost control.

client accounts benefited by absorbing experienced people, who would have otherwise been in non-billable pre-sales or practice activities, as SMEs/business analysts. There was more value for money for the clients.

From April 2010, efforts were initiated to rebuild sales teams by inducting people who did not carry the "scars of the past". Some joined with idea that this could be a great turnaround story that they could be part of. However, it was not clear if they brought any new capabilities or relationships that could help in a changed market scenario. Having proven strength in delivery, the reluctance of clients to engage in the absence of restated financials, and a rejig in sales led to an informal consensus on the challenge faced by the company—domain knowledge and innovation was the only way the company could stay relevant in the marketplace, i.e., not only help deal with the questions asked by clients, but also build new relationships. It appeared as though the key sources of power in the organization (sales and delivery) knowingly or unknowingly had found it easier to transfer the uncertainty to the domain practice, which was now becoming a catchall unit. This message was reinforced in different interactions. Typical observations made by new sales leaders included "We have lots of capability ... we need to articulate them in business terms ... all it needs is effective packaging ... we need to develop right set of collaterals to take to prospects ... existing collateral lacks punch ... it is the responsibility of the domain team to create innovative propositions to sell these capabilities". This seemed like the typical rhetoric used by political parties claiming that they could help society in recreating its glorious past. New entrants also introduced new terminology and templates such as "pitch books", "play book", "cheat sheet", "battle cards" and these dominated day-to-day discussions. As a result, there was constant repackaging of collateral and internal awareness sessions for new sales people who came and went on a frequent basis. Some case studies were amended so much that when they were re-played to the delivery people who actually did those projects they struggled to recognize them. The process of repeating the same content to different people and getting feedback that the content "lacked punch" became the daily routine for the domain team. Not many paused to think that the organization may not have accumulated any unique dynamic capability in the first place.

Similarly, "domain solutions" was another topic for which the domain practice became an attractor. Solution itself was a very vague concept—it could refer to anything that could help convince a client to give business. In existing businesses where the "farmers" were finding it difficult to plough the parched land, the feedback from the sales/delivery teams was that "clients are asking us for proactive solutions ... we have teams who understand their technologies, the domain teams should sit with delivery teams to identify strategic opportunities/proposals that we can take back to clients". Whenever the pressure on these proactive pitches increased, a host of people would be invited to a virtual teleconference (sales, delivery, pre-sales, domain competency, horizontal competency) and the call would start off saying, "We have a once in a lifetime opportunity to meet a very senior person in the client organization and we should ensure that we capture the client's imagination with some innovative propositions that no one else has presented and the client cannot refuse". Most people attended these meetings without any preparation hoping that someone would bring in new pieces of information to make it interesting. These calls typically ended with a search for that one person who could look at all angles, synthesize different competencies and then come up with a proposal that would be differentiated, innovative, with quantifiable business outcomes, and that person had to be from the domain practice. The NBD sales teams ("hunters") added to this challenge by saying, "Clients are no longer looking for technology capabilities ... it has become a commodity ... clients are expecting differentiated Domain/Business Solutions."[14] The technology competencies too joined

---

14 I can recollect an experience in prospecting for a global cards brand. The sales person (fresh from the success of closing one of the global cards interchange) wanted to quickly move on to a new logo, even before the ink on the first transaction had dried. I had suggested that it would be better to concentrate on the customer we had acquired, but there didn't seem to be any takers. Around September 2011 the sales leader reached out to us saying that he planned to target this new logo and wanted us to package our ideas and approach. We then had an opportunity to speak to the client manager who was interested in understanding how we could help reduce risks in a new customer acquisition in the mobile-enabled business model. We did some ground work and proposed some relatively new ideas. These were thrown at the client and that led to further discussions with other stakeholders. I then involved one of our team members, who had some background in cards, to support further discussions. Several other people from other competencies like architecture and analytics were then roped in by the sales team in furthering the dialogue. A central issue in these preparations would be the lack of detailed domain understanding. The architect and analytics expert would tell the sales person that if they had a granular view of the client's business, they would be able to add more value and unfortunately they did not see this coming from the domain team. This went on for about six months. I started getting a feeling that things were not making much headway. However, the sales person seemed confident that he was just one step away from closing a deal and all the senior leaders seemed to buy that. In April 2012 the sales leader had organized a call with his manager, the delivery head and my manager, and the unit head to review the support from Domain Practice for this logo acquisition. The sales leader mentioned that there was an impending client visit that could help us clinch the deal and we needed the right team to handle this. We were told that the client was interested in seeing our mobility offers platform, and he was expecting the domain team to get the mobility practice that owned the platform to put together a good show. I had indicated that this did not have anything to do with the domain from a solution-design point of view. It was a coordination problem where the sales and pre-sales teams were not able to get support from the mobility team. How would a domain person solve this problem? The sales team insisted that since it involved integration to a payment system, it was a domain problem. I stuck to my stand knowing well that it had reached a breaking point, and in all probability I would get excluded. It happened. My stand seemed to make the situation extremely uncomfortable for all the stakeholders. I was excluded from further discussion

the chorus: "Our partners are looking for domain solutions ... if only we had the right domain SME, we could readily build a differentiated solution on a popular technology platform." Paradoxically, this is an extinct species in a knowledge-intensive IT services company. There was no discussion on the possibility that client access and delivery capability may be areas where real change was required.

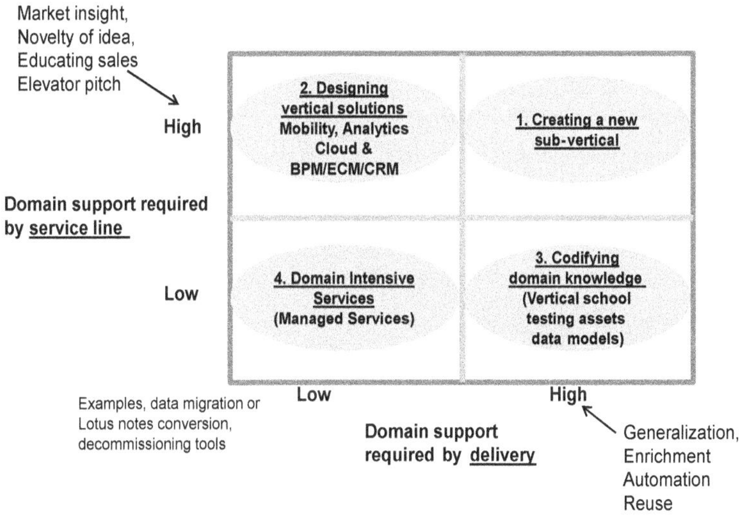

Figure 15: Expectations from the domain practice under uncertainty

and it led to a new alignment of interests between my managers and the North American sales team in the payments area. My manager suggested that he would work along with my team member and the mobility practice to address this requirement. In other words, the power imbalance could not be broken even in such a situation, even when it was clear that there was really no need for the domain team. This hunt for the large logo continued for another six months, and they even declared a victory and celebrated it based on some email sent by the client. Congratulatory messages flowed around and everyone started highlighting their part of the success story. Eventually, after one and a half years of pursuit and realization that there was no possibility of getting into the client, the sales leader was asked to leave. What did this pursuit leave behind? Tired minds and some collateral that is either gathering dust or has been archived.

Inadequacies in other units were translated into a domain problem (Figure 15 summarizes the typical expectations from a domain practice). Not many in sales or delivery or horizontal competency wanted to re-look at the way they had conceptualized problems, or question their approach to scoping problems or estimating efforts or collaborating with groups. Let me share one example here. It was an opportunity to help a leading bank in the ASEAN market to leverage its investment in a document-management software. It was in October 2011, just before Diwali. Our partner had got a lead from the bank. The client wanted to extend the use of the partner's document-management tool for other business processes in the bank. They had hit upon cash management as an area to start with. The client's analyst had put together his view on how the tool could be used for cash management and inquired if a consultant could validate this and suggest alternatives. The sales team had translated this into a domain problem since it was about "cash management". I assigned one of our banking team members to take a look and advise. He came back saying that it was a normal account opening process and there was nothing much to innovate or suggest. On the other hand, the technology competency team had started working on the estimation and came up with an estimate of about six calendar months with six people to implement the process. There was a feeling that this estimate was far higher than what the client had anticipated. The sales teams said that the domain team should validate the estimates. Our team said they did not have expertise in the tool to do so. And the key people went off on Diwali leave. Now the ball was in my court. I only had a high-level understanding of the cash management process. I started analysing the information that was shared by the client. I noticed that the client essentially wanted to use the tool for the cash-management account opening process.

And when I looked at the proposed solution, I found that they were only duplicating information between existing systems, and not really using the new tool to improve efficiency of the process or customer experience. I put down some ways in which the process could be simplified and shared this with the team. After that we revisited the estimation model and were able to bring down the effort to one-sixth of the original estimate. This case highlights the weaknesses in the problem-solving capability in the organization and how this got translated into a "domain problem". There were umpteen such cases where a common-sense approach to problem-solving could have made the proposition sharper and compelling without complicating matters. However, it appeared as though the more powerful groups resorted to transferring the complexity to the domain practice. In other words, everyone was suggesting that the domain team should play the role of a client or an industry know-all, and that it could, sitting in an offshore location with only Google as its saviour, identify the business issues faced by customers and have sufficient level of detail to be able to work as an SME to develop solutions. Those who struggled to engage in this game were quickly excluded.

In cases where the domain practice accidentally developed a new perspective, it was suggested that "PPTware" was not sufficient, and that we need to have a Proof of Concept (PoC) to "Show and Tell". And when some "Show and Tell" PoCs were developed with great difficulty (almost pleading for help from the service practice), the response was that there was no "wow factor" in them. When these discussions resulted in a large number of offerings and were difficult to comprehend, there were repeated calls for creating an inventory of offerings and evaluate them like the BCG matrix—big bets, game changers, premier league solutions (an interesting selection of words that suggest that organizing may be interpreted as a type of game). New tools were designed to facilitate evaluation, categorization and tracking the pipeline of offerings across the organization. This ritual was repeated as and when new sales heads came into the system. While I have not really seen much change in the quality of the solutions, it appears that it certainly bought time for sales teams and reduced the noise for delivery units. In other words, it seemed like an anxiety-reducing ritual. The domain practice had no choice but to go through this ritual (a drudgery) because "they are the support team and have the luxury of being a non-billable resource", a clear reflection of the power imbalance in the system.

This power imbalance actually flowed from the client and was pretty steep.[15] The sales and delivery teams (of the Indian IT firms) usually accepted and fulfilled a variety of requests from clients. This "flexibility", in some cases, was glorified as a key differentiator. The reality was that most managers and professionals struggled to say no to the client (or anyone who had a higher bargaining power against them).[16] However, there was a basic difference in the way clients and staff of the Indian IT service provider viewed power and human interdependence. While some clients used their power difference to demand more quality and strengthen the interdependence,[17] most sales and delivery teams assumed that clients might use power to exclude them from the

---

15 The power flows as follows: Client > Onsite teams (sales and onsite delivery managers) > Offshore delivery teams > Service practices / Horizontal competencies > Support teams (Presales and Domain).

16 When there are no results, the sales teams would argue that we should take any opportunity that comes our way, however distant it may be from the current capability.

17 A similar situation exists between sales, delivery and service practice teams— they appreciate their mutual interdependence, even though there are power differences between onsite and offshore teams.

interaction, either at an individual level or at the firm level.[18] The domain team members who supported sales and delivery made a similar assumption. They thought they were powerless with respect to sales and delivery teams and feared that they could be replaced by another SME. In such a scenario a typical response from the weaker group (domain team w.r.t sales/delivery or sales/delivery w.r.t client) was subservience or withdrawal from the interaction.[19] Associates in the domain team did not understand that they had a great opportunity to change the power relations, provided they could enhance their capability and also leverage the dependency that senior managers had on this unit in providing a holistic picture of the vertical. The two managers under whom I worked during this period understood and leveraged the senior management dependency to establish better equations with sales and delivery. I also understood this, but made a conscious choice to stay away from the executive level due to the following reasons. My initial interactions suggested that the executives seemed too preoccupied with their categories and I did not seem to conform to their notions of a leader. I also felt that I would have to spend considerable time in reducing the anxieties of new leaders and building rapport with them (show that I was more "aligned"). I did not want to do that since the need of the hour was to pay

---

18 Clients do have the power to change vendors and more so when the nature of work was T&M or body shopping, and some have exercised that.
19 It will be interesting to observe the variety of practices used by domain teams in such situations. For instance, there is an interesting case of the nature of interaction between white women and black women at the check-out counter in toy stores (Williams, 2006). White women tend to use the interaction to show the black women in poor light, as incompetent. Some black women apparently address this issue by making it clear that they actually solved a much tougher problem. Similar examples can be seen in the relations between land owners and labourers in cultivation. It is during the harvest season that labourers resort to mass desertion to negotiate a better deal for the next year. Such negotiations are also ritualized in some cultures.

more attention to uncertainties in the process of value creation. I was aware that this approach would result in my getting excluded from the network sooner or later.[20]

In summary, sales, delivery and service practices were expecting domain practice to trigger interactions and help rebuild relationships in the marketplace. When such interactions provided possibilities to sell the existing competencies, they readily exploited them, and attributed it to the strength of sales and delivery. For example, the domain team is used to wow a client with some innovative ideas and then use that perception to seek out some opportunities in CRM or testing. The domain practice is not informed about this since there is no way to correlate these. When their interactions did not translate into potential sales, they blamed the lack of "differentiation" and this was directly attributed to the domain team. Differentiation was understood to be in the ability to "get through the door", not in the underlying capability. In other words, the tough questions posed by the market were transferred to a catchall unit with the hope that when normalcy returns, the core units can get back to what they did best. Nothing else signified this view better than the sigh of relief that most leaders heaved in 2011 when, after the announcement of restated financials, one of the executives said, "We are a normal company". But, unfortunately, many did not seem to realize that we may have entered a "new normal" that demanded change in the core sales and delivery units. Senior managers did not seem to have a view on how this change could be facilitated other than by replacing people or asking for more

---

20 The exclusion process started in mid–2010 and was formalized through a structural change after two years. However, I noticed that the weakening of the network primarily happened in terms of internal managers, not in terms of relations with associates or clients.

processes, metrics and reviews. In the meanwhile, the gap with competitors widened further. How did my focus on interactions shape up in this situation? How did we deal with two key challenges—addressing problems of high complexity and low probability of win (Black Swan opportunities?), and attracting talent when no one wanted to be part of this non-billable unit for fear of getting fired any time?[21]

Making connections in an unconnected world

From September 2009 to 2011, I was supervising the FS domain practice, a random collection of 10 people, some with pre-sales experience and a few SMEs, i.e., people with operational experience in Indian banks or insurance firms. Considering the high gap between expectations from the unit and the capability of the team, the difficulty in attracting quality talent into the team, and the absence of clear financial goals, I decided to focus on enhancing the quality of interactions around the problems that were thrown at the unit and encouraging the team to develop expertise in one of the 12 functional areas of interest. These were identified as a part of the discussion on financial services strategy between April and July 2009.[22] In August 2009, I was formally included as a part of the FS practice. It was also around this

---

21 Only two bold souls joined the team in 2010. In addition, I took a person with expertise in core banking. He also had a personal interest to move back to India.

22 I was not a part of the domain practice when the financial services strategy discussions started in April 2009 under the leadership of a new sales head. After a few iterations among themselves when they did not seem to be making progress, the new sales head asked me to help the team think through the strategy (I had interacted with him earlier in September 2008 in connection with a presentation we were preparing for a board meeting). In order to help the financial services team prepare the strategy I had researched and shared some relevant pieces of information with the team.

time that one of the senior leaders from TB who had joined GCS as part of the transition strategy started taking specific interest in reviving the financial services vertical. She started having discussions with the leaders from sales, delivery and the practice. As I have mentioned in the previous chapter, during our initial discussion over a teleconference I was pleasantly surprised to know that she was the same person with whom I had worked almost 20 years ago in one of the first software product companies in India. This unexpected development helped in establishing a quick rapport between us. Other leaders in delivery and sales also seemed to be comfortable with her. We then collaborated and gave shape to the financial services strategy document. The intent was to look at how the firm could build a "billion dollar vertical" in financial services over five years. We knew that it was an unrealistic expectation, but treated it as a direction to think big (in line with the rhetoric used by the new senior management from TB). Since we were in a state where we did not know how much revenue we were actually making in financial services (barring the revenue from the top 10 clients), we refrained from talking numbers and instead looked at the strategic themes that could make the organization competitive in the marketplace. Here we were going beyond the traditional boundary of a practice and taking a holistic view of the vertical and how we could position different competencies to address the business and IT issues of the financial sector. Such a synthesis was possibly happening for the first time in this firm, and it pointed to three potential themes: (a) showcasing higher level capabilities by integrating diverse technology and process competencies with appropriate conceptual frameworks, (b) creating innovative point solutions using niche technologies, and (c) inorganic acquisition of client assets that could give us access to customers or help launch new offerings. This strategy was then socialized with several stakeholders from sales, delivery, service practices and senior management. The responses of the stakeholders suggested that it did not make much sense to them, a key reason being lack of a financial goal or target; most leaders felt that talking about "strategy" without a financial number attached to it was meaningless. Indeed, very few seemed interested in the qualitative themes, even though we were in a situation where there were no numbers to talk about and the company was on the brink of failure. The document was largely dismissed as an academic exercise. To me, the lack of financials was a blessing in disguise. It allowed us to focus on the qualitative aspects of the strategy and explore synergies among various themes. One of the most important bi-products of the strategy exercise was retention and sustenance of organizational memory. The initiative was triggered by a senior delivery leader. I, along with a couple of team members, spent a lot of time in understanding, analysing and categorizing more than 150 ongoing and past project experiences by functional areas and industry themes. At a personal level knowing this history proved to be extremely beneficial while rebuilding the confidence of internal sales teams and repositioning the vertical with clients/prospects.

Accidental entry into a new sub-vertical
As we were socializing the new strategy document with different teams, an interesting opportunity emerged in November 2009 (which we had not anticipated). We had an opportunity to engage a senior executive of a global investment management firm. He was well known to some of the senior managers of TB and when they reached out to him he gave us an opportunity to talk to him.

Management used this as an opportunity to validate our financial services strategy with him. At first this appeared to be a strange move. Why would a supplier want to validate its strategy with a prospective client? But, this turned out to be a master-stroke. Based on this discussion, the client executive inquired if we had some capability and strategy to get into the wealth and retirement benefits administration business. Since we did not have this capability, I did some research to check what was happening in the industry and to my surprise found that there might be value in looking at this segment (an area that had not emerged in our earlier discussions on strategy). I then put together a presentation articulating why this could be strategic for us and constructed an innovative proposition to address the client's need. The proposal was then jointly developed with the BPO unit. The proposal had elements of integration, innovation and inorganic (a possible JV option for a joint Go-To-Market in future). The client executive liked our proposal and indicated that it was differentiated from competition. This was followed by discussions and negotiations with multiple stakeholders before the client team visited us in March 2010 for a more detailed discussion. On the eve of this visit, my manager who was also leading this deal organized a call with the senior leaders in the firm to brief them about the deal and take their advice, primarily because there was a possibility of a joint venture. In the initial few minutes of the call, one of the leaders asked what was the size of the deal and when he heard that it was about $3–5 million per annum, it became evident that it was not big enough for him to engage further. Nevertheless, my manager and the rest of the deal team went through detailed discussions and after two months in June 2010, we were awarded a five-year $15 million contract for an integrated IT+BPO managed service for their retirement benefits administration business in Australia.

This win was unique in several ways. It was the first integrated deal (IT+BPO), it involved an entry into a new line of business (wealth and retirements), with the possibility of a platform in future, and it was led by the domain practice.

The transaction also generated interest among sales teams across the world, even though it was not a big deal and not in the biggest market (US). Sales teams wanted to know about the deal and how it was won. To many it was a surprise how domain practice could influence such a deal. People were quick to observe that it was the relationship at the executive level that had won us the deal. They were right in saying so. Relationship at the top helped us get into the opportunity and close the opportunity. The in-between journey of justifying why it was strategic for us and how we could make a difference to the client was fulfilled by domain practice with support from the BPO unit. The client also clarified that they found our proposition more aligned to their interest (especially integrating IT and BPO under one umbrella), while other competitors like DCTS had treated these as two separate pieces or had capability in only one piece, for instance BPO. All this suggested that we could replicate this model in other geographies provided the sales teams had such relationships. Unfortunately, this did not happen. As things seemed to gather momentum and there seemed to be a real possibility for altering the power imbalance between domain and other groups (sales, delivery, horizontal competencies), there was a setback. In June 2010, my manager faced some personal constraints and decided to move into a part-time consultant role and restrict herself to building the retirement benefits administration business. I realized that we might have lost a great opportunity to alter the course of the financial services business. In November 2010, we had a new FS Practice Manager. He was my fifth boss in two years.

The success of this superannuation deal spawned several similar pitches to customers—integrated IT+BPO for client reporting, wealth management, market data distribution, customer support for payment gateways, AML fraud detection, trade finance, claims processing and other processes. None of these translated into projects. In the meanwhile, the superannuation team in Australia continued to build their capability and persist with their sales efforts and entered into discussions with several prospects and product vendors. While it did not translate into any new business until 2012, the first engagement matured and won a prestigious award for best IT+BPO model in the ANZ market. My manager and the delivery team had to put in a lot of effort to ensure that the transition was done right, and their stringent SLAs were met. Through the course of the engagement they realized that the client's IT and Operations were not integrated and this was inhibiting the effectiveness of our integrated IT+BPO model especially in terms of implementing process improvements. Nevertheless, they continued working with the parameters and sustained the morale of the team and this helped in targeting new prospects in this area.

Integrated deals gained momentum again in early 2012 when we won a 10-year $100 million integrated production support deal with a financial services firm in India (covering trading applications and infrastructure). This was significant since it was the first case in financial services where the synergy with the parent firm had made a visible impact in terms of a large deal closure. The parent firm's strong capability in Infrastructure Management (IMS) was combined with the Application Managed Services (AMS) capability in financial systems and the pressure exerted by the client to put our skin in the game, i.e., taking a stake in the client's subsidiary,[23] contributed to this win. The above experience along with an earlier pitch on integrated IT+BPO for data services opened up the possibility of bidding for a data platform with a global asset manager. This culminated in the acquisition of a Data Services platform in June 2013. In July 2013, the superannuation business in ANZ also got a big boost through the closure of a multi-million, multi-year deal for managed services (IT+BPO) with a mid-sized firm. It also involved monetization of some small assets of the client. Some of these small battles around inorganic strategies also pushed the firm into a "big-ticket" M&A deal in 2013 that fell through in the final stage. We were now seeing the interplay of two strategic themes—integration and inorganic—in the above transactions. Most of these inorganic strategies had the blessing of the senior management. The rapport established by the practice leader with the senior management was one of the critical factors for the closure of these transactions. However, after two years people started realizing that these transactions had not changed the game

---

23 I was not directly involved in this decision to take a strategic stake. The infrastructure group was exploring an opportunity with a large diversified group in India with interests in financial services and healthcare. Around mid–2011 the deal team had asked for help from an FS SME to help with the proposal. I deployed one of our team members for this and also requested help from the head of the US delivery team to assign a program manager to help with the estimation process. When the deal came to the final stages, a meeting was organized between our executives and the client's executives. There was concern that the value proposition did not seem to be compelling. My manager, who was involved in the final stage, requested for my suggestions. I analysed the group and suggested that there might be a possibility to expand the relationship into a strategic partnership with a joint GTM with the financial products subsidiary. During a subsequent discussion, the client apparently insisted that they would like TB to have a skin-in-the-game, and this translated into a decision to take strategic stake in the firm (the business case was put together by the SME and my manager). At that point no one had an idea that this would lead to a joint product development in the area of compliance.

as anticipated and disillusionment started creeping in around some of the investments. The particular client relationship was no longer of interest to the senior management and the data services platform was becoming a topic of contention.

Joint product development with an unlikely partner
While the global financial crisis may have been the result of too much financial innovation, the crisis also resulted in a shrinking of IT budgets and unleashed a lot of talk on innovation in the IT community. The client IT executives wanted their vendors to come up with innovative solutions (perhaps some of them were transferring their uncertainty to their vendors). Sales, delivery and service practices were urging domain practice to deliver innovative business/domain solutions. Since we had embedded innovation as a key theme in the financial services strategy, we attempted to develop innovative domain-intensive frameworks using technologies like Enterprise Content Management, Business Process Management, Business Intelligence, Cloud and Mobility where we believed there was an opportunity. We were clear that we would focus more on frameworks and not on full-fledged products.

In October 2009, we started off with an attempt to develop a cloud-based document platform and homed in on claims document management as a pilot. We had done similar work for a health insurer, a partner was willing to work with us, we had an SME with detailed knowledge of the claims process, and there was inclination from sales to support this (albeit no formal commitment). We also knew that insurance companies who are extremely risk-averse may not want to consider this from a company that was itself considered risky. The technology competency team did not seem too interested since they felt that this partner solution was not state of the art and they would find it difficult to go to market with it. They were used to riding on the popularity of proven platforms, but agreed to put in some effort since the sales teams were pushing for it. With all these ambiguities, we managed to build a decent prototype in a year's time. However, it ended up in cold storage after about a year since the sales leaders who had sponsored the solution had left by the time the solution was ready for demonstration. One year later it was a reverse scenario. The technology competency team agreed to build a project finance solution along with a leading technology partner. The sales teams pushed the ball into the domain team's court saying they would sell provided the domain team approved this investment. I had communicated that this investment may not yield much benefit since the market was very small for such a solution. Nevertheless, the technology team went ahead with this and even won an award from their partner for the best solution in the financial sector in 2011. However, it did not translate into any sale.

A third attempt was forced in 2012 and this turned out to be more successful. We had an opportunity to target a new regulation that was introduced by a US regulatory body. One of our largest customers in North America initiated plans to comply with this regulation and inquired if TB had a solution. Since one of the technology partners proposed to develop the solution along with a competitor and fearing that this would allow a new vendor into the client landscape, the account team decided to go with the technology of the product firm in which TB had taken a strategic stake in the early 2012. This firm was an unlikely partner. The business case for the strategic stake was primarily built on the potential to leverage the partner's domain products. However, this compliance solution was to be developed on their in-house technology platform that was not necessarily state of the art. It was also not a technology that was attractive to TB's service practice and delivery teams. There was no explicit market for that skill. Nevertheless, with great difficulty the joint work resulted in a product, a seed client and revenue to show. After this breakthrough, the product was socialized with several other prospects and it helped win some new logos in 2013 and 2014. The two bold souls who joined in 2010 and my manager who also joined in 2010 played an important role in this joint product development. Managers seemed happy that their strategic investment had paid off, but employees associated with the product delivery had other views.

SCAM powers a new digital vision

As a part of the innovation agenda, I also started taking a close look at mobility (mobile technologies). I did not know much about mobility until about October 2009 when I was introduced to a company that was involved in inter-operability of mobile networks/devices. We were supposed to talk about "use-cases" relevant to the financial services industry. I did a bit of research, had discussions with the partner's solution team and we created a few use-cases that could be relevant. Nothing much happened with this partner since the parent company who had introduced us lost interest in this partner. However, these discussions led me to research the mobile banking space a bit more since I also felt that mobility had the potential to influence micro-interactions, an area of interest to me. When I probed further to see why many banks were showing great interest in mobile banking and what they were actually implementing, it was clear that mobile banking was ripe for innovation especially in terms of how they influence consumer financial behaviours. I could see that there was an opportunity in creating new use-cases and this could give us a way of engaging customers, given that we had technical competency in mobility in the parent company. We designed a few use-cases and also informally validated some of them with a Senior Manager of one of our clients.

It was around this time (January–February 2010) that we were presented with an opportunity to present a proposition to a global credit card interchange. We got the opportunity due to a very senior connect at the group chairman level. The one-liner sent to me was that "the client was interested in a JV". When I researched this firm, I found that there might be an opportunity to help this firm in cost-reduction in their dominant market (US) and explore innovative models for the emerging markets. We proposed an innovation lab for low-cost experimentation in emerging markets. This led us into discussions with the Head of their Innovation Labs. While he had his own concerns about involving an offshore vendor in the innovation process, he wanted to see how we would develop creative ideas. We proposed a pilot exercise at a nominal cost and he agreed to give us a generic problem statement—"improving payment experience on a mobile without dis-intermediating cards". We carried out this exercise in an earnest manner using a combination of bottom-up and top-down approaches. The process and the concept of a semantic model to tie up different ideas were appreciated by the client. However, he expressed some reservations about the novelty of the ideas and negotiated for another exercise on a different problem. We were aware that if he had not seen some value in what we had done, he wouldn't have agreed to another pilot. We delivered the second pilot. This time he said that he liked the ideas and they would take it up for an internal prototyping workshop.

These two exercises helped us to socialize our services with different business units of the global credit card interchange and also to other prospects. While it did not lead to any new revenue immediately, these exercises pointed to two important possibilities: (a) we could now see a different model to engage with clients in open innovation, especially at the start of a client relationship; and (b) it gave me a deep insight into the implications of mobility. The insight was that mobility could transform traditional outsourcing models. The reason being that the success of mobility depends on the variety of use-cases; these use-cases mostly demand an integrated approach to emerging technologies; and this is in turn would require different kinds of partners and outsourcing arrangements. In January 2011, I articulated this in a white paper, which was used to facilitate a CIO forum in UK. I also coined an acronym called In-MACS (Integrated approach to mobility, analytics, cloud and security to deliver personalized solutions) and defined a logical architecture based on the dependencies among the four technologies, i.e., mobility related use-cases would require real-time analytics and lighter applications, which in turn can come from cloud-infrastructure and this whole set would require unique security technologies. Not many knew that the acronym had a dark side as well, when read in the reverse.[24] The concept soon caught the imagination of several stakeholders and was used in different client conversations in the financial services vertical. By mid–2011, after validating with 10+ clients, I started realizing that through interactions with a diverse set of people in a crisis situation we might have hit upon an idea that could be a game changer for TB. And it had an early mover

---

24 In response to run-of-the-mill questions on differentiation, we used to often joke that GCS' differentiator was in SCAM. When I was preparing a presentation for newly joined sales leaders in the US, it stuck to me that In-MACS was reverse of SCAM.

advantage.[25] It was also coming across as a creative response to clients grappling with the financial crisis and had the potential to disrupt the SCAM-tainted company's image in the marketplace. We used the momentum to align and channel some investments from the mobility competency team into PoCs that supported this idea. We ended up building four PoCs, one each for investment management, wealth management, auto insurance and branch digitization to support discussions in different sub-verticals. However, convincing executives to see this possibility and invest in developing an integrated capability seemed extremely difficult. Typical questions would be, 'Would this give us large deals?' Are we sure no other competitor has this capability?"—questions that reflect their anxiety more than anything else.

In early February 2012, when the parent company TB formally announced a merger plan, they were in need of a strong proposition that they could present to the market about the value of the combined entity. During one of the brainstorming discussions between marketing and senior managers, one of the leaders suggested the idea of In-MACS. The executives and senior marketing managers seemed to like the idea. The marketing head wrote to me soon after inquiring if they could use this idea for some corporate communication while announcing the merger. After I had given my consent, the idea went through further iterations and finally emerged as TMACS to accommodate the "Telecom Network" capability of the parent company. Then there was a plan to communicate this to the analyst community. The CMO and CTO offices took over the initiative to drive enterprise-

---

25 Analyst firms and leading competitors started recognizing the interdependence only after mid–2012. It is now referred to as SMAC (Social, Mobile, Analytics, and Cloud). To me "Social" was irrelevant since I went with Norbert Elias's view that individual and social are one and the same.

wide branding around this theme and forcing other verticals to recast their experiences in this line. It reminded me of the earlier branding exercise, the dominant managerial view prevailed.

In the meantime I continued socializing the concept with senior leaders in client organizations, especially in Europe and the Middle East. The typical response of clients was that while the concept was good, they would want to keep the mobility capability in-house. At the same time they expressed their concerns that they were finding it difficult to keep pace with their competitors. These discussions led me to a very powerful insight—can mobility be a change agent and help bank employees participate in the change process and rebuild trust with their clients? Based on this insight and a specific requirement to engage with the CIO of a global bank headquartered in Europe, I wrote a white paper articulating how these technologies could be transformational for a bank, and the type of role that a company like ours could play. However, the initial draft of the paper seemed to suggest a consultative role which was not intended. When I showed the draft to the executive of the Investment Management firm, who was on a short consulting assignment with TB, he suggested that I should try to emphasize the design aspect and downplay the consultative role. I thought this was a very sharp observation on what the firm should aspire for. I refined the paper and shared it with him. He went on to share the paper with the executive of TB (his sponsor), and the executive in turn shared it with other leaders (a mass email). The response was muted. I could sense the discomfort among some leaders. By late 2012, the momentum that was created in the financial services vertical was losing steam since attention and resources were shifting to proliferation of the concept across other industries rather than to enhancing the integrative design capability within financial services. After a few months of struggle on who should own the initiative and a realization that competitors started talking more aggressively about SMAC, the initiative was transferred to a senior "business leader". He was given the mandate to create a new revenue stream around this concept—a rather difficult endeavour of creating an integrated technology solutions business. The new leader did not appear to understand this complexity. He gave his own colour to the initiative and created a consultative digital solutions pitch in 2013 (exactly opposite to the advice given by a client executive). He started calling for meetings with different vertical, sales and delivery teams to make TMACS an integral part of business planning. Once TMACS became part of the business plans, there was a lot of debate on what constituted an ideal TMACS solution. The compromise driven by sales and delivery leaders was that any solution that had more than three elements of TMACS was a digital solution, i.e., they reduced the unknown to the known and showed that digital solutions were already contributing to X per cent of revenue.

Another attempt at engaging the core

After spending nearly three years trying to co-evolve strategic themes, improving capability within the practice, and facilitating innovation and client access, in September 2012 I started to take a closer look at the issue of delivery capability enhancement. I wanted to see how differentiation can go beyond marketing or competency teams and be institutionalized in the delivery capability of the organization—in essence, invite the delivery team into the change process. I had done some of this in 2010 while re-packaging some of the project experiences into new offerings for corporate banks. However, that process couldn't be sustained because I was pulled into multiple transactions and my colleagues were not able to listen and engage at a deeper level and also easily got distracted by other requirements (we were 10–12 people at that time). This time around I adopted a two-pronged approach to engage delivery teams. The first one invited delivery teams across the organization (including other verticals) to contribute ideas to some themes of interest to financial services. As a part of the second approach, I started looking at ways to enhance commodity services like testing and managed services. While I was not fully sure where it would lead me, I drew comfort from the fact that I had played a very similar role in the earlier company.

I started with a rough idea of the themes I should use for the innovation campaigns. I started with one theme on customer service, which drew about 100+ associates to contribute ideas. I then involved some senior delivery and competency associates to evaluate the ideas. While this was done to comply with the process, I was more interested in using this process to involve associates and sensitize them to the ideas so that they could use them in their discussions with clients. The process resulted in shortlisting the top–10 such ideas. I also tried to tease out patterns underlying the 100+ ideas. We married these two to finalize the top–three ideas. One of them was in the area of self-service, the other around mobile security, and the third around APIs (Application Programming Interfaces) in mortgages. I then used this output to trigger a discussion with the security practice and engaging the associates on the mortgage API which led us to revisit the mortgage space. I also created two other themes for ideation—one focused on APIs in financial services, and the other on service delivery. Suffice to say that while these campaigns themselves did not produce really new ideas, they did point to problem areas that could be of interest to the organization. It also invited more people to participate in the corporate innovation contest (we had about 20 entries in 2013 as against one in 2012).

In parallel, I also tried to enhance and further the discussions that the delivery teams had started on testing and managed services in financial services (following the loss of a large[26] RFP). The testing practice had also started a similar initiative on industrialization (largely driven by the parent company's experience with a large Telco client) and planned to have workshops with the delivery teams. The discussions that I had with the delivery teams helped both sides share their views in the testing workshop (in a way I was helping re-connect the testing competency and the delivery teams which got broken in 2009 as a result of the new organization structure). These activities manifested in a consolidated pitch for testing in financial services; we had delineated the areas that needed attention to enhance industrialization in testing— specialization, standardization and automation. I also realized that the emerging banking industry standard could provide a strong foundation for this industrialization effort. We then did a similar exercise for managed services and brought together capabilities in networks and security into the discussion. When we finished this we realized that we had some strong experiences in Channels (online, mobile, ATM, IVR and branch) and some interesting experiences that could add strength to the managed services story (for instance, use of big data tools in network monitoring). This along with the outcome of the innovation campaigns pushed us to explore the area of channels in greater detail. Given the nature of IT spending and outsourcing

---

26 The parameters of a large deal vary with the situation and size of the firm. For some firms $50 million and above would be a large deal, while for others anything above $5 million could be a large deal

arrangements around these, we felt there may be a case to push banks to rethink outsourcing models around channels. This resulted in a white paper. I requested the Executive Director of the banking industry body to review and give his feedback. He readily obliged and even suggested that they could publish it on their website (even though we were not a member of the Industry body). Indeed, the paper was published on the banking industry body website. This pushed us to look at technologies such as model-based testing and big data to power commodity services like testing and managed services, and subsequently leverage semantic technology to address challenges like client interaction management and operational insight. These initiatives led to a new perspective to approach run-the-bank- and change-the-bank-related IT initiatives and point to a new direction in application development and maintenance for the digital world. They also pointed to a new way of dealing with three types of changes faced by delivery units, i.e., improving offshoring, domain intensity and automation.[27]

---

27 For most of the Indian IT firms, these challenges came in a linear manner. It was around 2004–6 that leading firms such as DCTS faced the pressure of increasing offshoring and shifting to more fixed-bid engagements, some forced by clients and in other cases by competitive and profitability pressures. This was followed by a phase (around 2008) where attempts were made to improve knowledge intensity (including domain) among the workforce. Since 2012 there has been greater focus on automation. However, the situation now in the financial services vertical in TB is where all the three pressures are operating at the same time, and unfortunately, the teams do not seem to understand that it is a fundamental change issue. A recent account-planning session in one of the largest client accounts threw some light on how sales and delivery leaders viewed these challenges. The discussion flowed in the following manner. The onsite leaders (sales and delivery) complained that they had a number of testing opportunities in the client's LATAM operations, but they were unable to fulfil these as they did not have the right resources and were unable to reuse their experience in other parts of the bank. They were suggesting that some of the resources were deployed in building a new capability in automated testing that was not producing the desired results. They went on to suggest that this

However, all this did not seem to meet the expectations of senior managers in terms of market-making signals or financial results. There were constant messages from senior management that the team did not have "salesy people", "business leaders", "market makers", "McKinsey types", and "those who could walk into client organizations, change perceptions and close market-shaking deals". I wondered why they were expecting domain practice to carry out the sales function. Were they searching for the key where the light was?

"Yeh Dil Mange More": The unrelenting rhetoric of senior management

"Yeh Dil Mange More"—this Hindi phrase (meaning "give me more") in a way encapsulated the overall message of the senior management (executive level) of the beleaguered company. Becoming big quickly appeared a key aspiration at the top (much like what I had observed in DCTS). This message echoed in management meetings and open forums even though a corporate group banner in the reception of each office says, "It is not how big we become, but how we become big". Management briefings typically involved statements such as "Smaller IT service companies

---

strategy to develop this capability had a number of problems—the choice of the tool was a problem, getting the client to buy the tool would be another problem, and it was taking far too long to get people trained on the tool apart from the initial project having delivery issues. When the offshore leaders tried to defend the situation, the conversation shifted to the problem of reuse or the need for business analysts to be part of the projects. What people did not realize was that some of the newer tools were trying to eliminate downstream efforts and provide greater power to business analysts. Instead of training business analysts in using this tool and producing a new breed of highly skilled resources, the delivery teams were training low-end manual testers to become highly skilled business analysts. This would be a tough gap to close. This is another example of how patterns of power-relating create ironical situations at a grassroots level. And people fail to see these contradictions or accept them.

don't have a future ... If we don't have scale we cannot take up larger and complex deals that in turn can attract more customers and talent".[28] An unstated concern was that if the company did not grow aggressively, then the stock price would stagnate and the promoters of the parent company would revisit the rationale for acquisition or at least challenge the leaders who had promised synergy from this acquisition. One could see this view unfold in several ways—in goal setting, definitions of leadership, and pursuit of differentiated solutions. For instance, senior managers exhorted employees to be more ambitious and think big through statements such as "We need billion dollar verticals ... we need big, hairy, audacious goals ... we need to focus on large/strategic deals that will capture the imagination of industry analysts/ investors ... we should be in the magic quadrants of analysts ... we need to win awards in industry forums ... we should add scale by buying out captives ... why can't we grow if the competition is growing and the offshoring business model continues to be viable? ... Why can't we scale up in financial services when competitors do as much as 40 per cent of their revenue from this sector?" The BIG agenda in terms of differentiated solutions translated

---

28 Perhaps there is an element of truth here. Most Indian IT service companies have typically grown by adding headcount (body shopping). Increase in headcount increases the diversity of skill base, and has the potential to attract more diverse customers. This in turn attracts partners who wish to leverage this talent pool to grow and support their customers. That further adds to the scale in skills that are in demand in the market. This logic helped large Indian IT players achieve superior growth rates in the last two decades and during this journey they did make some shifts from bodies to delivering projects and programmes. However, a key point that is largely ignored in this particular context is that many of these firms have not had a situation where their engine of growth was disrupted for two–three years and had gone back a few years in terms of size and relationships with customers and partners. Even the leader took close to 10 years to achieve a 10-fold increase in its revenue ($1 billion–$10 billion).

into "we need blockbuster solutions/big bets … we need solutions that no competitor has … we need big global alliances with niche product vendors … we need to co-innovate with customers … we need to create a fund to support innovation – internal or external start-ups". In terms of people, it translated into "we need business leaders, not just thought leaders … we need domain guys are who are more salesy … we need sales people who can talk business and domain … we need to identify and unleash ambitious young leaders … everyone needs to sell".

How did the sales and delivery teams respond to these aspirations? They followed the same strategy they had adopted while dealing with market uncertainty; transferred the unknown variety to the domain team. Two examples illustrate this point. First, let us take the case of account reviews. A client account that increased its revenue from $4 million to $10 million in a year was asked why they are not doing $50 million. There was not much exploration or appreciation of the difficulties in achieving the $10 million, the quality of $10 million revenue, the unique capabilities being developed and whether it presented a case to rethink other strategic investments and so on. The account managers (sales and delivery) in turn translated the difficult questions into a set of action items for the domain team to pursue, until the next review. Second, we seemed to have very quickly democratized the idea of inorganic strategy, so much so that most discussions on proposals/transactions started off with a talk of inorganic options such as asset monetization, some per cent stake, JV and M&A that made me wonder whether we were "leading" or "dealing". One of the North American financial services sales leaders was fired on the grounds that he was into more deal construction than lead generation. This point was also reinforced by an external consultant who was hired by the organization in 2013 to suggest ways to revamp the vertical and sales engines. It was only then that some corrective action was taken (mandating that only executive level should handle M&A related communication). However, there were also cases where some client relationships prospered largely based on the trust that had developed between the client and the onsite sales and delivery leaders. There was also a sense of coherence that started emerging in the North American team between 2011 and 2012 when some new sales people were brought in. However, this was short-lived and got disrupted after the sales head was fired in 2012.

The FS practice also saw some structural changes in 2011. The senior management decided to create a new role called the Vertical Competency Head and indicated that all practices would now report to this new role. It seemed to be a good move indicating the importance given to vertical solutions in the organization. A similar attempt was made in DCTS in 2004, but it fell through since none of the senior practice heads wanted to report to a relatively junior person who was being positioned for the role. However, no such thing happened here. The person brought in was a fairly senior person and was the head of a major service line in the pre-crisis period. He had left the company just after the takeover by TB and now decided to re-join. The practice heads (including FS) now started reporting to the new leader for vertical competencies. Initial discussions with the new leader raised a lot of concerns on both sides. He felt that the teams had no strategy (clarity on financial goals, agreement with sales and so on), structure and naturally believed that absence of these was not allowing them to achieve big results that the senior management expected. Vice-versa, many people in the practice felt that he did not have any experience in financial services or in managing domain practices.

The new management of the vertical team spent close to a year searching for a big goal for the unit and "one throat to choke". It got finalized after a strategy workshop with an external consultant in August 2012. The workshop was designed and facilitated by me and it involved people primarily from the FS practice, Vertical Competency Head, and senior delivery leaders from financial services business. The key difference between this strategy exercise and the previous one in 2009 was that this one had a revenue target articulated, and more importantly was blessed by a consultant (former client) who was trusted by the management. Now the senior management felt that they had a "clear strategy in place and it was down to execution". This was followed by defining a new organization structure,[29] role definitions and recruiting the right set of people. The intent was to create a practice that would be a market maker and a key influencer. Once some senior leaders had been recruited,[30] the management started assigning Key Result Areas (KRAs) and gave them the freedom to manage their teams and lead the change. Key beliefs that shaped KRAs included "Number focus will drive actions ... everyone should have a number ... there should be a single owner for everything ... every initiative should be in the KRA".

The reviews usually started with the statements like "numbers

---

29 The structure appeared to address problems in other parts of the organization (sales and delivery) more than enhancing the core work of the unit. For instance, to improve visibility of global sales pipeline and drive focus we had sales enablement team and similarly to provide delivery oversight to projects delivered by different regional teams we had delivery enablement. But, no one asked why the respective teams were not doing their job? The structure finally resulted in a scenario like the story of the ant (*www.cse.cuhk.edu.hk/~jlee/ antFableEng.pps*).

30 The company became more attractive to employees in 2012 compared to 2010–11, but most leaders still came from smaller firms and usually at higher cost to the company. They were possibly taking a higher career risk, but were they better than the people within the team?

are sacrosanct ... we are behind targets ... we need to do more ... unless we become paranoid about the numbers it is not going to work", and then moved on to "outcome/results are everything... if we don't have results then either the effort is lacking or the thinking is not right or we don't have the right people". It usually ended with "we need new initiatives, 30–60–90 plans and reviews". Motivational talk was replete with utterances such as "We need to be market makers ... we should drive domain led growth ... we should do what it takes to close a deal ... we should coach and enable the sales teams (apart from supporting them) ... and enable delivery and horizontal competency teams (package the delivery capabilities, and verticalize horizontals) ... engage analysts ... drive innovation and thought leadership". Preparing for reviews itself became a laborious task. Every time there was a different template depending on what was important at that time, data quality was poor and unstructured; the task was usually outsourced to lower levels, and there were multiple iterations before the final presentation. The reviews usually focused on the initial slides and rushed through the rest due to lack of time. These reviews usually concluded that "we should do things which we have not done ... we should reach out to new set of teams or partners" or indulged in management posturing such as "Tell us what are your asks and we will enable ... You are the expert and it is your job to think through and come up with a solution". This was a subtle way of saying that they had limitations in influencing the rest. The net result was a flurry of activities and new initiatives, and another 30–60–90 plan to review these. This only expanded the number of cells in the matrix for which people were responsible at a faster rate than the number of people added to the team and resulted in a situation where everybody was responsible for multiple things and without any real authority to influence the outcome (Leadership without Authority). Whether this management approach and posturing resulted in any greater alignment at the top is questionable, but it definitely reduced motivation level within the team. In applying the idea of leverage (changing a small unit to achieve a non-linear impact on the rest of the organization), senior managers seemed to under-appreciate the difficulty in getting a tail to wag a dog.

After three years, it appeared that the vertical solutions, leader could not satisfy the aspirations of the senior management. In 2014, he was replaced by another leader and the story started to repeat itself (new goal, new organization and more leaders[31]). The new leader spent some time in understanding the organization and key stakeholders. A year later he started to make his interventions. He sent across a note saying that he wanted a plan for 2.5X growth in the financial services business, with a scanned attachment that showed a back-of-the-envelope calculation of how 40–60 per cent growth over the current revenue could get us to the goal in three years. I put down an outline, and suggested that it cannot be an excel sheet exercise. I listed some questions that would need attention. His response was that "this is too rudimentary" and he called for a meeting to discuss this further, and invited some of his young leaders (possibly suggesting that they might be able to do a better job). The conversation proceeded on the following lines, "We have a goal (that is given by the executive level). Can we figure out how much we need to grow every year and where will the growth come from? Can we grow in this sub-vertical or that region and by doing what?" I went back with the revised numbers based on assumptions that one sub-vertical may grow

---

31 TB in 2014–15 became more attractive for prospective employees from larger
    Indian IT firms

faster organically and in certain markets. However, I also made an observation that the plan would not be feasible if we did not pay attention to the nature of customers we had and were acquiring. The leader retorted by saying that "diagnosis is not enough. We need a solution that will work." In other words, the target was non-negotiable. We should somehow find an answer that looks convincing. In this conversation there was no acceptance of the difficulty in changing existing client relationships or internal patterns of relating. After two–three iterations I started wondering if the leader was actually looking for a justification for the inorganic strategy that seemed to be in his control. Unrealistic expectations and the difficulty in changing large client relationships and influencing large deals with new clients introduced new behaviours from the next-level leaders. One of them focused on acquiring a large number of smaller clients (using his earlier connects) under the promise that they would deliver future growth. Another leader tried to take the inorganic strategy to an extreme, where people started talking about M&A pipeline as opposed to sales pipeline. Other leaders trivialized the change issue by treating it as a resource allocation problem—we needed more resources to support existing relationships. The net result was that at an operational level, employees were forced into tasks that were neither connected with their interests/values nor translated into tangible outcomes that they can relate to, thus increasing their anxiety and stress levels. And the managerial solution was to treat this as an individual's psychological problem and hire professional counsellors to support the employees. In other words, listening to employees (the fundamental aspect of workplace interaction) got outsourced.[32]

---

32 As I was finishing this book, I saw a newspaper article that said that firms were now adopting a new best practice, "outsource exit interviews". The logic was that employees would give frank feedback to an external entity.

Conclusion

One can see from the discussion in this chapter that several possibilities for generative dialogue and change emerged through everyday interactions during a period of extreme uncertainty. However, the opportunity to translate the emerging themes into strategic capabilities was not fully exploited. In the face of extreme complexity, most managers and groups used the managerial concepts to transfer the uncertainty to a catchall unit with the hope that when things get back to normal, they can get back to their routine. Unfortunately, there are increasing signs that Indian IT services firms may have entered a "new normal". This chapter should provide enough evidence for leaders and managers to understand the limitations of mainstream managerial thinking and find ways to effectively participate in the everyday workplace interactions.

Epilogue

A confluence of key trends led to the rise of the Indian IT services industry. These trends emerged from interactions among various people in governments, academia, global clients and the Indian IT industry over a period of 50–60 years (as documented by Sharma, 2009). Increased IT adoption in the global market and resistance to IT in the domestic market in the 1970s forced the pioneers to take the export route. This was not easy. The leaders had to find innovative and cost-effective ways to convince global clients that Indian professionals could deliver IT services and also do this from offshore. They also had to create an ecosystem to attract and develop IT skills at offshore. Once the huge global demand was unlocked, several firms made inroads, and by the late 1980s the IT services industry was riding the global outsourcing wave. As the firms scaled up, managers adopted quality processes to control the delivery of IT services, and organizational/HR practices to attract, retain and control a highly aspirational workforce. Managers and employees demonstrated tremendous resilience at different phases in this journey to overcome various types of challenges to the offshoring model.

However, one area where they have consistently struggled was in developing higher-level capabilities such as consulting, products, domain solutions, executive relationships and innovation. It was not because leaders did not think ahead or lacked business acumen. Through a reflexive inquiry into my experience I have shown that the problem was in the way managers and employees dealt with paradoxes that emerged from the complexity of human interaction in global service networks.

In Section II, I have shown how a committed and visionary leader of one of the top firms did recognize this challenge in as early as 1980, when the firm had less than 1000 professionals. The leader visualized the need for integrative thinking/design capability for delivering effective IT solutions, and took the necessary steps to incubate and institutionalize this capability through research and training. He also actively encouraged project teams to adopt these practices and urged professionals to rise above the ordinary. However, differences in the way next-level managers and employees interpreted the challenge in the light of their own experience stunted the development of this integrative thinking capability. I myself (with a PhD in Systems Engineering) struggled to make sense of certain aspects of this capability. For instance, it took me almost three–four years to internalize the key ideas of systems consulting: (a) a holistic approach to handle complex problems, (b) through innovative use of IT, and (c) efficient ways of architecting and developing software. I understood the first and the third points, but could not relate to the second one, i.e., the way IT had been evolving and the innovative ways in which it could be used. While it may sound foolish in hindsight, my background, interest, and the nature of our everyday interactions at that time did not allow me to make sense of this aspect. For a majority of management consultants and IT professionals, integrative thinking seemed esoteric and unconnected with their everyday work. When there was a leadership change in late 1990s and the new leadership team could not see a market for such capabilities, they started treating such capabilities as NOTHING, i.e., not worth pursuing seriously. The success of IT leaders in quickly translating the global market demand for a skill into revenues and their own sense of business acumen probably dissuaded them from focusing on capabilities where the cause-effect linkages were fuzzy, would take time to evolve, were different from the concepts promoted by global consultants, and the possibility of closing the gap with global competition seemed improbable. In addition, their struggle to establish an identity independent of the earlier leader may have also inadvertently pushed them to foster and encourage a perception that such capabilities meant NOTHING. What I learnt by participating in these early initiatives was that developing higher level capabilities like systems thinking, consulting, business innovation, product development, and enhancing client access (executive level) was inextricably linked with the underlying patterns of relating, i.e., human interaction in workplace, with all its complexity and unpredictability. Therefore, instead of seeing such capabilities as worthless distractions or NOTHING it would be useful to pay attention to the underlying patterns of relating in the global IT services networks. Such a perspective can open up new ways of thinking about these challenges. This is the first element of Managing Nothing.

When I probed the underlying patterns of relating by participating in some of the strategic change initiatives launched by the new IT services leadership team (discussed in Section III), I got a sense of the highly constrained patterns of relating in the global IT service networks. In some cases, where I got to persist with these interactions, they created possibilities for changing the relationships and inducing more energy among people. However, I noticed that while senior managers who sponsored my work did speak positively about it in some forums; they did not try to participate in the emerging patterns of relating. Instead, they seemed to be consumed by the questions of the dominant paradigm, "How can we replicate this practice or replicate you?" In other words, the belief in finding the best practice or an individual who can somehow change the whole organization was deeply ingrained, even though most were aware that such practices rarely seem to work as expected. Why did managers have this belief (and continue to do so today)? One reason may be the market success that the firm was seeing. It may have made it extremely difficult for leaders to distinguish between the broader trend of outsourcing that was creating the demand and the effectiveness of their strategies. Another reason might be the political implications of accepting that the strategies were not working. It would be detrimental to their position and stakes. They could get excluded from the network. But, what did this belief and posturing do? It kept the leaders focused on the pre-conditions (plans, structures, processes and resources) and reduced the ordinary day-to-day interactions to NOTHING, i.e., time wasted in talking instead of getting work done. My work showed that ordinary day-to-day interactions had the potential to throw up instabilities that changed our ways of understanding and relating. In other words, it is important for managers to shift from focusing on abstract models (factors and relationships) and individuals to the process of human interaction, i.e., pay attention to ordinary day-to-day interactions. This is the second element of Managing Nothing. Instead of urging the workforce to be innovative, consultative and proactive,[33] leaders and managers should look deep into the capability that may be hidden in the current conversations and patterns of relating among the workforce. This is very important in an IT services business that is part of a complex evolving global service network where there is sufficient diversity to trigger movement in different directions.

However, what surprised me most in my exploration was that such a belief was held forth even in the extreme situation of GCS/TB, where the firm got disrupted and cut off from the global outsourcing trend for at least four years (as discussed in Chapters 9 and 10). Three years after the crisis there was a clear attempt to revive the dominant management belief through a process of specifying right financial targets, structure, resources and monitoring so that it would lead to desired results. When no big results were coming, people started saying that the strategy was not clear or the execution was not right. But, not many acknowledged that this thinking itself may be flawed.[34] The proposed solutions were always to find the right people or having a rigour in monitoring and measuring. While many leaders and employees felt the need to improve patterns of relating, there was no focused effort to understand and pay more attention to day-to-day interactions. In contrast, I have shown how when some of us focused on day-to-day interactions especially during the very fluid period of 2009–12 (three years immediately after the crisis), even

---

33 An example is the interview with the CEO of a leading Indian IT firm reported in Times of India (dated 5 December 2014). The CEO said that Indians need to not only solve problems, but also define the problem, be proactive and develop design thinking. He urges young people to speak up.

34 Peter-Brendon Samuel, CEO of Everest Group, makes a similar observation in his blog "Silver bullets don't drive growth in services" (12 February 2015). He observes that most service providers appear to do the same thing again and again and expect different results, which is insanity.

with very limited resources and knowledge levels, we were able to create some possibilities that helped rebuild the confidence among stakeholders. Instead of understanding and improving these patterns, leaders stuck in the dominant management paradigm knowingly or unknowingly disrupted these nascent patterns by using "No Results" as an instrument to include/exclude people.

Why is it extremely difficult for leaders to step out of the dominant paradigm of thinking? When I discussed these issues with leaders and employees, some of them said that they were aware of this problem, but felt that there was no viable alternative, i.e., another best practice, technique or the right people. Some went a step further and inquired how we could programme those interactions. Treating interaction as another best practice that needs to be institutionalized through training or hiring relevant people would be, like pointed out by a very experienced manager, an oxymoron—a least intended takeaway from this book. I hope that the narrative inquiry that I adopted might encourage some leaders and employees to collectively reflect and think about the dominant ideology, the indirect cost it involves in terms of getting a host of people to spend unaccounted time on these initiatives outside their regular work, and the anxiety it provokes among those who have to adopt these changes. I have shown through various examples that there are ways to facilitate change by participating in ongoing conversations and reflecting to make sense of what is emerging in a situation. A very simple yet powerful guidance for this comes from the theory of Complex Responsive Processes. We should stop our obsession with searching for another best practice. It will be more prudent to reflect on the practices that may be inhibiting us from making sense of what is emerging in front of us. Eliminating a number of inconsistent managerial abstractions or best practices will free people from doing a number of tasks that they do not believe in, and generate bandwidth and time to observe and reflect on what is really emerging. This is the third element of Managing Nothing.

In summary one can see from my reflexive inquiry that when it came to moving up the value chain and developing higher level capabilities like integrative thinking, consulting and innovation, even the most committed and visionary leaders failed to drive real qualitative change in the organization. On the other hand, leaders who were acclaimed for their business acumen in transforming the Indian IT firms into global firms and had more resources at their disposal also did not succeed in developing a truly differentiated capability. They may have also failed to observe and develop some new patterns of relating that were emerging during their tenure. For instance, through my work I noticed that there can be forms of participation which may not fall under any particular category like consulting, R&D, strategy or marketing and there can be different ways of responding to the new normal and the digital. We all seemed to be prisoners of the dominant managerial paradigm and struggled with the paradoxes created by the complexity of human interaction in global service networks. A few leaders who recognized the paradoxes and tried to adopt a "both … and" strategy realized that it led to integration problems at a later stage. Others who treated paradoxes as contradictions that need to be eliminated might have inadvertently created double binds and other contradictions for people at lower levels, thus reducing the capacity for change. I hope that this reflexive inquiry into my experience has provided sufficient "evidence" that the inherent complexity of global service networks not only constrains, but also provides scope for individuals to participate and explore new directions, even if it is not a success story in the traditional sense. This to me is the essence of managing nothing. Management thinkers and practitioners would do well to see if a deeper inquiry into managing nothing can broaden managerial thought in the same way that the concept of zero did for the number system.

> *"Nothing in all its guises has proved to be a key concept in many human inquiries, whose right conception has opened up new ways of thinking about the world."*

> **—John D. Barrow (2000)**

Interactions with Sample Accounts

Here I sketch the detailed interactions with three accounts over a period of one year. One of them is in the airlines industry; the second is in the financial services industry; and the third is a global data utility. The interaction notes highlight what happened during each of the meetings, how some shifts in thinking and perceptions happened in unexpected ways, and how the relationships evolved. A close look at the nature of responses in the three cases would also point to the different patterns of interactions in the global service networks.

Case #1: A large airlines account

1. 2 December 2005: My interaction with this account started after getting a go-ahead from the Sales Director (SD) for the transportation vertical. The SD had forwarded my mail to the Relationship Manager (RM) of the account. Subsequently, when I contacted the RM, he expressed an interest to talk and we arranged an initial meeting. I did not know much about the account apart from the fact that I had sat next to the previous RM during a pre-business planning session in December 2004. He had expressed doubts over doing a two-year plan. I guess this was the general state of affairs in most accounts at the point.

2. 13 December 2005: The RM was kind enough to invite his Engagement Manager (EM) and Project Managers (PMs) for

the meeting (unlike others who seemed to operate more like gate keepers). I tried to explain my role and gave some idea of my work at the utilities account. One of the PMs inquired if it was any different from Customer Value Management (CVM) and I gave him my perspective (but was not sure if it made any sense to him). The RM also queried about the frequency of strategic conversations with clients and I suggested that perhaps once in two/three weeks might be good. I was surprised to find the RM making sense of what I was saying, and thought there might be some hope in this account. At the end of the meeting they expressed an interest to discuss things further. We agreed to talk about the vision of the account during the next session. The RM took all of us out for a cup of coffee. While walking towards the café, one of the PMs mentioned that the RM was new to the account and was enthusiastic to try some new things (I thought that maybe this enthusiasm along with the newly launched Sales Force Training would probably help him establish new connections and break an existing pattern). During the informal chat over coffee I had also suggested that since this client was an industry leader there must be a lot of research literature about the client in the public domain and we could tap into it to get a good perspective. The RM replied that he himself had read many papers on the web (I took it as an indication that he may be seeing it as too intrusive). After the meeting I summarized my thoughts about various aspects of the account in a presentation and sent it to the RM suggesting that he could use the template to seek further inputs from his team and we could use it as a starter for our next meeting on account vision.

3. 6 January 2006: I met the team (RM, EM, PMs) to discuss the account vision. However, when we started talking about the vision, I came to know that the RM was actually preparing for a business planning presentation later during the week. So, I suggested that we use the session to talk about the opportunities that they had identified and we could subsequently use it to interpret the underlying strategy/vision. Then we spent time discussing about the difficulty associated with every opportunity and used a grid of

stakeholder complexity versus delivery complexity to plot these. The RM and the team were happy with the framework and output of the session. Later the RM called and told me that their story was well received by the audience in the business planning session, and they were impressed with the way opportunities were segmented and represented. He also sent me a copy of the presentation. I was surprised to note that they had acknowledged my contribution to the presentation (I haven't seen such open acknowledgement in 10 years of work in this firm). I was also wondering why he had done this and how others present in the planning session would have interpreted it (especially the Business Excellence Head, the Head of the Consulting Practice who was supposed to mentor the RM, the SD and the Europe Head). Would this change their interactions with me or the RM? Later I heard from the Business Excellence Head that the RM had found the discussions with me very useful.

4. 24 January 2006: This gave some impetus to our interaction and led us into our next session. This time we focused on interpreting the vision/strategy underlying various opportunities (present and future). I took them through each opportunity and asked them to look for the underlying meaning. Slowly they began to see the pattern. I had suggested an approach to structure it, but they indicated that they would take care of the strategy definition. I left it there.

5. 25 April 2006: I was on leave during February/March. When I returned, I sought time for a follow-up meeting. During this session we agreed to look into the organization to support their strategy (assuming they had worked it out). While the RM assembled all the PMs (there were some new ones), he also suggested that he had already made some decisions about the account organization. (I was surprised by the very lucid way in which he had explained my role to the PMs; this was the first RM who seemed to understand what I was trying to do—helping improve interactions with people, whether internal or external). I suggested that the span of attention may be too wide (more than

10?), but did not get into other details. Instead, I queried the PMs about their challenges and the discussion slowly veered towards mobilizing people at a micro level. I suggested some ways to do this through formal instruments such as translating their strategy into goals and aligning them at different levels. I thought this might give some clear directions. There was a newcomer (from a different firm) who expressed his concerns about our organization culture and pointed out that we were not addressing the real issues at the micro level. We seemed to be talking at a macro level and in his view that did not make sense. One PM joined late and when we ended the meeting inquired if there was a presentation that he could go through. I responded saying I did not have one. The RM responded saying this was the new style (no presentations). I assumed that it was said in a positive sense.

6. 26 May 2006: When we met this time, only a few PMs turned up. Maybe they had other appointments or may be some of them were losing interest in these conversations. But, we carried on and discussed the account from a Key Account Management (KAM) perspective. I suggested ways in which they could communicate the value of their services to the client and the importance of the account to internal management. I facilitated a quick session (using Interpretive Structural Modelling) to show them how they could extract the unique practices in the account and explain them to the client or to internal management. The sample exercise showed that one of their key strategies for getting projects was to retain key people and relationships, not the sales model that they were being trained in. I suggested that they could possibly use these kinds of outputs to do some joint development with the client which they could then try to publish in various forums. This could be one way of building a rapport with a strategic client. The meeting ended with them deciding that they would take up one of the projects (in Business Intelligence) to see how to construct a dialogue around it. The PM of the project was asked to have a follow-up session with me and work out the next steps. The RM remarked that it was good that some actions were now

beginning to emerge. During an informal chat, the RM and EM gave me pointers that their interactions with internal management were not going very smoothly; they appeared frustrated with the offshore leverage drive that the corporate office was pressing on, and generally referred to internal initiatives as the "flavour of the month".

7. 30 June 2006: While I was waiting for the project team to do some groundwork and get back to me, I had a call with the RM to get his feedback on key account metrics and the nature of interactions with macro groups. The RM pre-empted my explanation and said that there were fundamental issues with the metrics and the management style. He took off against the "establishment". He said that the offshore leverage issue was problematic. His view was that instead of looking at input parameters, the management should be concerned about output parameters like profitability. He felt that his account was a profitable account. But, it was different from another large telecom account (that was used as a reference for offshoring), and had to be recognized for the same. He indicated that there was no consensus at the senior management level (onsite/offshore) about what to expect from the account (even though he had presented his perspective in the business planning session). People from the delivery centre call and say, "Forget everything, enhance offshore leverage; we don't mind if you lose opportunities". This conversation also led into a discussion on the Sales Force Training (SFT). The RM suggested that they had encountered some problems in engaging the client (they had planned the meeting in advance, worked out the proposition as suggested in the SFT templates, engaged the relevant practices in developing it, but finally when they went to the presentation they found that the client had invited their IT counterpart and asked our team to focus on pending IT issues, and not bother telling them about their business). This experience led him to a conclusion that it is very difficult to change minds of clients in existing relationships. He also referred to a few other accounts facing similar issues (for example, our largest insurance account in

Europe). I was surprised by this reference because this insurance account was supposed to be one of the top accounts in the eyes of the senior management (and the client was recognized by industry analysts as a role model in multi-sourcing). He also said that he had discussed this with the SFT coach who had apparently agreed that it would be difficult to bring about change in existing relationships (I wondered what hope then the SFT programme had for DCTS where 98 per cent of the revenue comes from existing clients). The RM also indicated that the Business Excellence Head had asked him if he could share any of his positive experiences with others during the sales conference, but they were unwilling to discuss his concerns or negative experiences, and he refused to speak about his positive experiences. He indicated that he was planning to go back to offshore. I could feel his frustration and suggested that maybe he could assemble some RMs facing similar challenges and we could talk about it. He indicated that he would be willing to do so, and was going to be in the corporate office next week for a meeting with the Head of Consulting and could assemble a few people. But, the meeting with RMs did not happen. I was not sure why (I thought that even if he had tried, others wouldn't be keen to participate in such a conversation, especially since the SFT consultant was hired by the Europe Head to coach the RMs at a cost of 500 EUR per hour; who would dare to go against that?). I sent him some mails but got no response. (I was avoiding the accepted practice in DCTS and other IT firms—if you want a response, catch him over the phone—because I also knew that in the world of mobile phones, the other person can easily avoid taking the call and cite logical reasons for the same). I left it there feeling that another opportunity to create a real dialogue among RMs was lost.

8. 13 July 2006: Finally, the project team came back to me and we had an initial teleconference. The Project Leader (PL) who was assigned did not turn up, but a different set of people participated in it. We discussed how they might approach the problem and I sent some presentation material for them to have a look at.

9. 27 July 2006: Following this I had a more detailed session with the project team. The team said that we had played a strong role in this project (architecture, design, development and now involved in support). However, the client had recently hired a global consulting firm to review the whole programme. Our team was not involved in this and they were unaware about the recommendations being made by the consulting firm and the future implications of the programme (I remembered that this project area was one of the key opportunities in their business plan for the year, anticipating about 10 per cent of their revenue). The team was waiting for the client to make the decision and invite us (they were relying on an assumption that since they were involved in developing the solution earlier, they would be involved in any subsequent plans). I had suggested a few ways in which they could construct a story (using available information) and engage the client and find out what was happening in the programme and how they might participate in it in future. They promised to do some more work and get back.

10. 17 August 2006: We arranged for a follow-up session. The team presented their findings and we discussed the underlying data, ways to present the data, and also looked at other aspects that they could cover. There was still some work to be done and the team agreed to look at my comments/suggestions. Prior to this meeting, I sought some time with the RM to get his feedback on our interactions so far and understand his decision to go to offshore. The RM expressed his frustration with the leadership team of the account (Sales and Domain Practice) and the lack of trust/commitment. He was concerned that he did not have a role model to follow. He mentioned a situation where the SD apparently confided about how the CXO disapproved of the SD's leadership (this rang a bell for me about similar conversations between another SD and his RM). I thought maybe the SD did not have adequate listening spaces (bosses are also vulnerable and express it at different points in time). I felt that this was an opportunity for an RM to actually enhance trust by providing

this listening space. I wondered why this RM was not making use of the opportunity. Perhaps his discomfort with the SD or some implicit hierarchy in his mind that he must have a boss who was better than him was not allowing him to see this opportunity. Then the RM explained how he was brought into the account as a consultant (pre-sales), although his expertise was in a different domain, and was later made the RM. He said that the silver lining was that he was getting considerable support from the horizontals, and that conversations with me were his only source of learning. When I queried whether we could have done better, he said he did not think so. I was not sure why (since we only met once every month, and we could have pushed it to once every three weeks). He felt that the core activity offered very little learning and growth. In the absence of leaders who have experience and can lead the way (like in his former domain practice), he preferred to move out of this vertical itself. In any case he had taken this appointment as a last overseas attempt (on a personal front). I was wondering if there might be some scope for him to try to survive by giving him a sense of my experience in a similar situation and the way I had survived in the face of sabotage by the Head of the domain practice (in an earlier assignment). He mentioned that he had already spoken to the Europe Head, and had also sent his family back. There was no possibility of a rethink on his decision. In some ways this reinforced my perspective that introducing a fresh person or giving him cognitive inputs (SFT) would not be sufficient to break an existing pattern of relating either internally or externally. How do we then create new patterns of relating? I was hoping that the work on the identified project might illustrate a few points about my thought process.

11. 27 September 2006: We had a follow-up session to discuss the progress of the work on the identified project. I listened to the presentation and gave a few suggestions—for instance, using rhetoric to press their case (the client may know about the problem, but do they know the extent of the problem, i.e., shock them with facts that are available to the support team, akin to

the TV programme "You Are What You Eat"), or a punchline, or the five most important things to look at and so on. The team patiently agreed to try and improve the presentation and they said they would send me the final copy for review (but didn't; perhaps they did not have sufficient time). Subsequent to this meeting, I also took the opportunity to inquire how the account was shaping up (of both the RM and EM). The point made by the RM was that the client wanted our firm to engage at micro levels to get more opportunities, because the client policy appeared to be multi-sourcing at project level. My suggestion was to take this point seriously and ask what it meant (recursive thinking—get deeper understanding of it instead of ignoring the statement). I was not sure if he understood what I was suggesting. He also indicated that he was concerned about sustaining the conversations. The RM felt that the presentation would always be person-dependent and if the right person was not available, others could not engage the client. I sensed that the RM was of the view that it would be difficult to engage the client without complete knowledge. I suggested that it may be useful to partition the presentation in two ways: one part where the client specificity comes in and continues, and the second part where the generalized concept comes in. The account team could own the first part. It would be there in every presentation. Would this offer some flexibility?

12. 29 September 2006: The RM called me immediately after the meeting with the client and said that the discussion had created a lot of mindshare. They had a bigger audience than expected and the presentation was very well received. However, they were struggling with the next steps. I suggested that they could consider a follow-up workshop to prioritize the actions and then see if they could position somebody to look into the problem. I sent him an example and an excel tool to conduct such a session.

13. 10 October 2006: I had sent a mail to the RM (on 9 October 2006) inquiring if he would like to discuss the next steps. On 10 October 2006 I got a call from the RM stating that the client was extremely happy about the way the team had responded and

had agreed to kick-off two projects (with DCTS). I suggested that they could now ask the team to consolidate their experience and discuss it with other PMs. The RM suggested that he wanted to combine this with an HR awards programme (a corporate initiative) and also link it to the next RM (who was to replace him in a short time). For me this whole experience is another good example of what I managed to achieve at the utilities account, but now illustrated in a different context. It is about people breaking out of mental rigidities (thinking either/or, in discrete steps, with an exploitative mind, and expecting some outside help) and developing tendencies to live in the present, adopt a more continuous approach, exploring a little more and developing local connections.

14. 23 October 2006: The RM arranged a meeting with the new RM who was replacing him. I was keen to understand how a new RM would ease into his context. Before we started the meeting I happened to bump into the PM of the project on which we had worked. He asked if I had got the final presentation. When I said no, he said that he thought it would have been sent to me by the RM (I wondered why a PM was sticking to hierarchical protocol when there was no need for one. Why did he avoid an interaction in the name of hierarchy, even though in this case the RM happened to be more flexible than many others I had seen? How did this civilising happen?). When we started the actual meeting, the outgoing RM said that he was very excited about the outcome that he saw in one of the projects; he said he had not seen such a response from a client before. I was told that it manifested into projects worth 200,000 EUR and opened doors for future participation—at least ten per cent of their revenue target (frankly, I was surprised by this quick turnaround; I had facilitated similar things earlier in the utilities account, but seeing this happen in a different context without any major "external intervention" was a pleasant surprise, and that too it was flowing in a very logical form—vision, organization, capabilities). The RM said that the client had invited their entire design team and initially the clients

were a little uncomfortable, but when they started presenting the "magnitude of the problem" it made them sit up and take notice (shock tactics—rhetoric seemed to have helped sensitize them). He inquired if this "template" could be replicated in other areas with similar success especially since the client has always been receptive. His view was that we as an organization were not doing enough. I suggested that if this had given them the confidence that they can "talk the walk", then that would open up opportunities. There were some pauses in the conversation, almost like nothing more to say, but to reiterate same statements. I could sense that their interpretation was still a little different from my thinking; they still felt that the image of "the organization as an implementation partner" was enhanced (we don't just talk theory but give solutions to move things along as you wait for other strategic considerations. I thought we were still unable to connect on the key theme). But, instead of exploring this, I jumped to respond to how they could approach in other areas (thereby closing the opportunity). Sometime later when the discussion moved towards the new RM, I took the example of marketing to illustrate one aspect of my role. The outgoing RM gave an example of marketing intervention to change the client's perception. He pointed out that Marketing had sent sourcing brochures directly to the clients (without consulting the RM), and the clients (instead of calling up marketing and seeking an appointment and advice from the consultants assigned to the account, as anticipated) seemed upset; they couldn't connect the brochure with their experience on the ground. It reiterated my thinking that involving local people and local knowledge is critical for any marketing/corporate intervention in accounts. These interventions should be aimed at facilitating a shift in dialogue, not create a gap to be filled by the accounts (which are already struggling to fill existing gaps created by the growth ambition and competition). It probably reinforced my point that "client access and innovation have to co-evolve". The RM also made another observation about experts from other groups in the organization meeting clients directly without informing the RM, or looking to meet people whom the RM did not know. He indicated that he could only set up meetings with people whom he knew or could be approached through IT division of the client. The new RM brought up an important point about one of the projects where a sister concern was involved. He said that in another airlines account, they had to distance themselves from the fiasco related with a similar project since the client was seeing both as coming from the same group although they were different companies. They had to say that DCTS was a different company from the sister concern (this throws some light on how RMs work with partners or find ways to de-link when inappropriate). The outgoing RM was also feeling positive about the future of the account and at a personal level. When I discussed my plan to relocate and look at the offshore side of accounts, the RM indicated that he had some discussions with a friend in another global IT firm about their plan to improve onsite-offshore interactions. During this conversation I started noticing that responses were emerging for each utterance, but I was not exploring them sufficiently. Instead, I was jumping to another statement or aspect. Why was I doing this? Why didn't I stop and ask some questions to understand if we meant the same thing, especially when words had begun to lose their "standard" meaning and we needed to make sense in each context. It would also helped if I suppressed my own situation that had been forced on me through external targets/expectations and so on. I wondered, was this the nature of emergent work?

15. 10 November 2006: The first project's dialogue seemed to be expanding very rapidly. During a meeting with the PM, I was told that now the client shared the global consulting firm's report with them and had started requesting inputs on how to approach. It was also interesting to note that this exercise involved onsite and offshore staff, and took about five–six weeks (about two hours per week by five–six people). It seemed to have changed their interactions (within and with the client). I hoped they would build on it carefully without rushing into it with blinkers and rigidities in the paradigms of sales force training or consulting, otherwise

things could very soon turn into a situation of "sour grapes". The meeting was also used to start a conversation on their approach to a range of HR systems. DCTS was supporting two applications— Concessions Online and People Online (Oracle HRMS). One of the solutions had been developed by DCTS and there was some bitterness between the client and DCTS towards the end of the project. The team wondered how they might go back to them to seek a new opportunity. I suggested that it could be seen as a case of "repairing the relationship" and indicated some ways to start a dialogue in these two areas. I also gave them a flavour of how they could expand this to cover topics such as absence reporting, performance management (the client seemed to have brought a solution), and competency management/e-learning, and so on.[1] I also had a chance to meet the outgoing RM; he was about to leave the office and go back to offshore. I inquired about his next steps and he indicated that he had now taken up a pre-sales position in the domain practice (I was a little surprised given the stand he had taken some time back. I thought that may be this experience with one client in the transportation domain had given him a better appreciation of the domain and helped him make sense of his situation). Then I queried about new developments in his domain practice, especially the recent announcement of setting up an Innovation Lab. He said that it was all about making the right noises, and suggested that it was probably good to know how to make noise, when to make noise and where to make noise. I was reminded of the office jargon that I had read in a newspaper the previous day—"sea gull boss"—a boss who flies into a situation, makes lots of noise, dirties everything and leaves. I hoped he was not trying to be one of them. I wished him luck. But, this whole experience of interacting with him made clear to me the difficulty that bright young people face in breaking set patterns of relating, eventually either becoming part of it (and make more noise) or

---

1   I was unaware that I might be imposing our ideas on a client organization where HR practices could be different.

totally withdrawing from it (become silent). I couldn't possibly rescue him at that time, but I still hoped he would find a way out of this dominant discourse and look at his micro-interactions more deeply.

Case #2: A global financial services account

1. 23 November 2005: I sought a meeting with the Relationship Manager (RM). I had interacted with him earlier on the CVM (Customer Value Management) initiative. I had inquired if he would be interested to discuss things further. He checked with his Global Relationship Manager at offshore, and after getting his approval agreed that I could interact with the people from the account. He assembled his onsite EMs (two people who managed the delivery of IT services for two lines of business—Investment Management and Global Markets) and we exchanged initial thoughts. He suggested that one of the challenges that he was facing was how to respond to a situation where the client had hired an independent consultant to review their IT support programme in the Investment Management area. We agreed to have a meeting with others from this team to understand the situation. The RM shared some material on the account, and the findings of the survey conducted by the external consultants.

2. 30 November 2005: I then met the RM and the Project Leaders (PLs) from the Investment Management area to understand their situation and how they planned to respond to it. They expressed concerns that their clients were micro-managing their work, the fact that they were not involved in the survey, and the internal politics of the client. I felt that through their proposed response they were actually reinforcing the findings in the survey—that the company was reactive and defensive, they were not seeing a CMM-5 service, and there was not much trust in the relationship. I inquired why they were not using the CVM concept to respond to the situation, especially since the RM happened to be one of its champions. The RM said that they had tried it but, found it difficult to quantify value and were therefore struggling. I suggested

that before they get to measuring the value of their service, they could they try to bring more transparency into their service and also broaden the stakeholders to whom this information was sent so that there could be more balanced views.

3. 6 December 2005, 30 December 2005, 26 January 2006: We had three more sessions to discuss the type of information that could be presented and how it could be used to engage key stakeholders of an application support team (my earlier work on service management framework for the utilities account and analysing the production support metrics for an insurance product team came in handy here). The team went back and did some work at collecting the metrics, and prepared a template. We discussed and revised the template to reflect key patterns more clearly. The team revised it again and improved it.

4. 5 April 2006: Finally after several iterations they managed to bring out a framework that was consistent with what the clients were used to. They had, however, used only sample data and were planning to collect more realistic data. I had suggested that they should now have a session with the client and discuss this. At the same time, they should try to document this experience, look for joint publications, or presentations in some internal forums and so on. That seemed to generate some interest. One of them made an attempt, but I felt that others were not participating in developing the experience. The documentation was in a standard form and oriented towards internal audience. I sensed a keenness to impress the internal audience of the organization, especially where the team members had a strong offshore orientation. I suggested to them that they should look outward first, and also discuss the experience in a narrative form, like blogs.

5. 8 June 2006: In the meanwhile, they managed to present their scorecard to the client. Apparently the client had liked it and suggested that they could integrate it with the client's dashboard. I asked them how they felt doing this exercise. They did suggest that they came across new improvements due to this exercise, but did not comment much on internal relationships. I guess it was still

difficult because they struggled to get together to develop the case. Only one person seemed to show interest and despite repeated suggestions that they could involve others, it didn't seem to happen. I guess there was some concern about who would get the credit. However, the client context (in the Investment Management business) had started changing by then. This business was sold to another firm, and the focus shifted towards consolidation of staff and systems. As a result, this activity was put on hold. And the conversation lost momentum.

6. 12 June 2006, 13 June 2006, and 15 June 2006: The RM indicated he wanted to discuss some people issues in the account, especially relating to performance management. The HR partner had given him some feedback based on the internal climate survey conducted at a corporate level. He felt that the HR team's observations such as "your account is below average on these parameters" were not very useful. I also felt that as a line manager, he wasn't comfortable taking advice from the HR support staff. As a result the RM along with the account management team decided to launch an internal survey to understand what people felt and how it compared with the previous survey. I suggested that it might be useful to talk to people rather than conduct more surveys and take actions around the average opinion. I also shared some thoughts on goal definition and alignment (after looking at a few goal sheets), making performance management more interactive and frequent, and engaging people. I wondered if the account was struggling to grow and break barriers with clients, and therefore intelligent people were feeling stuck. The RM said that they had already initiated actions such as creating communities of practice and sent me the community charters. I inquired if I could participate in a community meeting to understand how they were making sense of the situation. I got a feeling that they were using these communities to push the SFT material to associates who were eager to get into sales roles. But, I wondered where the content was going to come from. Aren't relationships critical for generating meaningful content? I also felt uncomfortable with the

way the issues were discussed and actions formulated. Haste in doing this could result in a situation where you try to review the actions during the next meeting and the associate can easily say he had bandwidth problem and after a few iterations the whole thing disappears.

7. 27 June 2006: I had a session with the RM to get his perspective on key account management, metrics, and initiatives. He reiterated the point that they were not interested in questions from corporate groups. Instead, they would prefer advice from experienced people, who were willing to work with them. He clearly indicated that he did not have much confidence in the capability of support groups.

8. 11 July 2006, 19 July 2006, 25 July 2006: The conversation then slowly veered towards the Global Markets area of the account (partly because post sell-out of the Investment Management business to another firm, there was an intent to separate it into a new account, although this was not officially announced). I started by looking at what people felt about their life in the account (their responses to the recently conducted survey). It was clear that many could not connect their work with the overall vision or values of the organization. There was a case for understanding the vision or strategy at an account level and at least some discussion around that even if not a clear output. I suggested this to the RM.

9. 1 August 2006, 8 August 2006, 10 August 2006: The RM hijacked a weekly meeting to discuss these issues. He said that "not much happens during these weekly meetings in any case". We had a series of three meetings to articulate the strategy of the account (with a largely onsite team and a few people from offshore joining the call). The meetings had a variable audience, but a few were constant. The end result was a strategy map and we tried to relate this map to the underlying values and emotions. I could sense our difficulty in assigning an emotion, because of our limited vocabulary of emotions (or driving too much rationality into a fuzzy topic).

10. 15 August 2006: I then suggested that this model (of the Global Markets team) could be subjected to a review by the Investment Management team. It was clear that the Investment Management team was finding it difficult to relate to it. This meeting was followed by an informal session to celebrate India's Independence Day. I participated in the event and even in a skit and the following discussion. I noticed an interesting thing: the discussion that followed every skit was quickly summarized by the RM as the moral of the story. I felt that this was closing the conversation. For one of the skits, I tried to push the discussion slightly off course. It led to some interesting questions and finally somebody raised a topic that "managers seem to behave in one way with clients and in a different way with the associates"—a case of "inside/outside" differences? However, the discussion was shut down due to time constraints. I thought, however, that there was an opportunity to have a real conversation about the contradictions we encounter and use this to enhance trust in relationships. Conducting such skits and talking about them was a special skill of this particular RM, but he did not exploit it sufficiently. I am not sure if this kind of thing happened in other accounts. But, it did give an insight into the value of these organizational spaces. It took about eight months of interaction with the account to come close to a potential opportunity for transformation, but we could explore it.

11. 5 September 2006: I had a discussion with a PL from the Investment Management area about the way they gathered their Customer Satisfaction Index (CSI) data from the client. There was something interesting in their point about preparing the client for giving a CSI so that it was meaningful and consistent. I thought this could be converted into a good example of collecting feedback at different points of service purchase-delivery-post purchase using ethnographic methods—bringing to the surface critical feelings/words that represented the value vocabulary, instead of measuring some pre-set indicators of value. In the current form, it was a useful tool only for the service provider (but even they felt it was too inconsistent to

be taken seriously). I thought ethnographic perspectives would be important to communicate real value added by the service provider. They are the ones which have a more lasting impact on the mind (or facilitate mind change), than a rational model of quantified value (this is just one element of the story and could only make sense to the senior management). This was almost nine–ten months since I had initiated the discussion with this account (one of the original topics of interest for the RM was CVM). Now we were closer to some meaning of how this could be done in a situation like theirs.

12. 8 September 2006: This was followed by a lull, but later the RM and EM inquired if I could participate in a session with the client to talk about a joint workshop on the topic of enhancing agility in software delivery. When we met before the session, I had suggested that instead of pressing for a workshop straight away, they should seek to understand the client managers' willingness for such a thing, given that the client's CTO was interested and one of the client managers was already conducting some sessions in this regard. The meeting with the clients was stiff because they were neither sure about the purpose of the meeting nor about why I was involved, why I was talking about the notions of agility and so on. Nevertheless, they indicated that they would be interested in discussing it further with the RM. I suggested to the RM that they could use this as an opportunity to reinforce linkages with CTO, engage associates and use the details to engage clients. I am not sure what happened.

13. 12 September 2006: This was followed by a teleconference with the Global Markets team to explain the previous meeting with the client and also understand what had happened to the strategy map. As expected not many had thought it useful to look into it (the abstract object created by them did not make sense to them? Does it mean that unless the object translates into an immediate action such as a project or revenues or rewards, it is of no use? Why do people struggle to talk or relate to what is being said; why don't they say no or yes or question what is

being said—why do they just ignore it? Even long silences don't seem to work). The offshore team indicated that they had not even received the model, and some voiced their concern about where this discussion was headed: "We are not getting any vision statement". Clearly they were not able to see the connection between the discussion and what was emerging in their context; some withdrew, others were physically present (but mentally or emotionally absent). So, I suggested I could speak to each of them separately and help them make the connection between the model, their project and the client's strategy (was I getting into a coaching mode? I felt that interactions with this account were still in the traditional mode. They were sitting there to listen to me. They were not discussing their issues and using me as an interactionist. I was sort of getting into an advisory role. Instead, if I only talked to them about their concerns and left it there, would it spill over into their conversations in forums such as the Knowledge Sharing Sessions (KSS)? Should I tell them how to interact in KSS?).

14. 14 September 2006: When discussing with five PLs individually, I noticed how strongly the map represented their client's strategy (although some details were missing) and also explained their project strategy. I showed them how to extract details from their projects and use it as a medium to tease out key themes to engage clients and partners. We agreed to meet again to carry this forward. Some new themes emerged when I connected their work with the work being done at a research centre (WIT) in a leading university.

15. 19 September 2006: I had another session with the RM (EM of Investment Management was also present) to give feedback on my discussion with the Global Markets team and the potential in working with the map. I also touched on other aspects such as their participation in some client events (How did their clients perceive these? They indicated that it did not meet the client's expectation; the clients found it useful to connect among themselves). Also, they were not sure how such things could be

linked to the analysis of industry trends and implications. They indicated that thinking about the industry trends and positioning appropriate solutions was the job of Industry Practices (as per the discussion at the corporate level, where the RM participated in a workshop). I could sense that the sales team was now shifting part of the challenge to the Industry Practice. The Sales Force training programme was attempting to transform existing sales into Trusted Business Advisors.

16. 29 September 2006: I had a discussion with the Global Markets team on developing themes around the strategic objectives. I helped them in defining what agility meant in their project context, to move beyond the opportunity (resources) and delivery (project) dialogue, to connect the objectives to specific initiatives (objective 10, competency and knowledge management), to specific communities (agility/business projects/improvements to CVM), and sourcing/metrics to the Delivery Excellence initiative. Also, I suggested to the RM how they could use these discussions to feed into the discussion between senior management and client. I also felt that there may be options to link the agility idea to WIT and other centres in the organization. I inquired what this repeated interaction around the "strategy map" was doing in the case of this account. Some Team Members (TMs) mentioned that they were seeing some focus emerging. The RM felt that he was seeing some changes in the team. It was almost after 10 months of periodic interactions that this kind of positive view started emerging. This was bringing us close to the original intent of improving strategic alignment (corporate initiatives and account level issues). Why were they saying that it was generating some energy or they could see some change?

17. 6 October 2006: I participated in a KSS to understand how people in this account interacted at lower levels (who attends, why they attend, when they attend, how much preparation goes into it, how and what they talk, what actions flow out of this and how they use the output). The KSS was launched by the Learning and Development champion, stating that every

group should share its application knowledge and that those interested in becoming Business Analysts should attend this particular session. What I noticed was that in the beginning of the presentation, people sought a lot of clarifications to better understand the context of the solution and relate it to their own situation. But not much discussion happened later; some areas where there was insufficient knowledge got left out. The value for the presenter was that he got to better appreciate his system, but did that give him scope to find out more and create new linkages? I suggested to them that they could look at "contextualization—architectural, business and strategic", "creating a repository of doubtful areas—knowledge gaps", "identify strategic challenges for further conversation —roadmap of the solution", "value from the solution", and "maintain a hyperlinked note/blog of these" (instead of leaving them in a repository), thereby converting these sessions beyond "learning", to include "innovating" and link these to their "working". Can we look closely at the workday or work week of an individual (going one level below the job design), see if we can introduce elements of "exploitation and exploration", "mindful and mindless", individual (at the desk, in front of the computer) and social activity (meetings, workshops, chat), not with a view to look at the time and motion perspective.

18. 24 October 2006: I had two discussions: one with the Global Markets team to follow up on the strategy session, and the second with the RM and EM on the proposed presentation to the global client executives about how we as a firm intended to add value to the relationship (a response to a conversation between DCTS, COO and the client CIO). As far as the first one was concerned, we started talking from where we had left off. I sensed that some of them began talking and relating to me a little more compared to earlier meetings—a sign that some things were opening up (while they may still be stuck with the assumptions that we could not engage if we do not have information or relationships). There also appeared to be disconnects between the teams and their managers (how managers constructed their stories and engaged with clients)?

I suggested ways to make the account-specific knowledge a central focus. They did suggest that they engage with each other internally and inquired what I meant by engaging. I clarified to them the different forms of interactions (strategic conversations) and the power of sustaining these.

19. 7 November 2006: I had a discussion with the Investment Management team (that was now officially a new account)—EM+PLs—to understand how they were responding to the new situation and whether they could leverage what they had done earlier. I thought of improvizing this meeting (to avoid the traditional model of my asking questions and them responding and feeling that they were attending the meeting for my sake). I wanted to tell them that they had agreed to spend some time on this problem and therefore could use the time to discuss it (I would also participate in it). It didn't work that way, but I felt that they considered the discussion useful. The earlier work seemed to have lost meaning after the merger of the investment business with the new firm. The EM explained the present situation—some meetings had happened at the CEO level and our team seemed to have presented some propositions of how they could support the core solution of the new client or do performance enhancements on that solution (based on user complaints of the Investment Management business who were using the new system) or push people into the new client through client managers of the Investment Management business. These things had been met with a clear no. The team was concerned that they didn't seem to have relationships with the new client team and didn't seem to get any clear direction or visibility into what was happening. They also felt (management perception based on senior management meetings) that the new client was concerned about its intellectual property, was not sure if our firm would be interested in servicing a potentially low value account and were looking at setting up their own captive unit in India or exploring options to work with smaller Indian IT players. The client manager nominated to manage our relationship had apparently posed a challenge as

to how our firm could help reduce costs in a big way through a different contractual arrangement—how to reduce costs in supplier management, increase offshoring from the present 60 per cent, and bring in large-scale process improvements? He did not seem convinced that our firm was doing enough. I suggested that they should use this opportunity to start a dialogue and test whether it was worth developing the relationship. I also suggested to them that the client may currently be interested in "transitioning Investment Management applications into the new client's systems" and "reducing the cost of this transition", whereas our firm seemed to offer options that made inroads into their territory (and not address their pressing issue). I also indicated that they were probably reinforcing the image of our firm as not responsive to the needs of smaller clients. The best way to break this deadlock was to start a dialogue.

20. 9 November 2006: I had a discussion with two PLs from Global Markets business about how they could orchestrate "key themes/value" in their context and enhance strategic advantage for the account. A very interesting point came up during a discussion with one PL. The conversation went on—we were searching for what we could do in that context. There seemed to be too many constraints in the current set-up and things seemed too disconnected from our perspective. I suggested some ways to demonstrate differentiation in individual spaces and at a process or organization level instead of technology/solution level. Towards the end I was struck by a remark by the PL. He said, "Sorry for asking so many questions… it is not that I don't want to do it, but want to understand how to implement it…." At that time I did not pick up what he had said, and said that it was all right. But later, I realised the underlying thinking—if somebody asks too many questions, he was being uncooperative or not willing to get on with it—walk the talk … very interesting! Similarly "asking questions" could take on different meanings. When a superior asks a question of his subordinate, it reinforces his power. If the superior has to ask a question of his subordinate to clarify something then

he loses power (so does not show his vulnerability). A student can use questioning to close the gap with the teacher (regulative, accepted) or get the teacher thinking (generative). The other project members were telling me that there was scope for growth, good visibility and everything was fine. But, when I queried why there was a difficulty in their PM giving some indication of future resource requirements, things started to open up. I suggested that maybe the PM was having difficulty in predicting demand or selling the case to his managers to grow his team and so on. The team understood these problems and wanted to explore the two or three themes that could push the envelope in the relationship. They realized that they were not asking the question, "Why can't we accelerate propagation of this tool?"

21. 16 November 2006: The new EM sent me a draft of their proposed response. I suggested some changes so that they could focus on the client's problem and remove our interest from the picture. Please have a conversation on what the client should do, not how we could help.

22. 23 November 2006: I participated in a teleconference organized by one of the projects in the Global Markets business. I was happy with the outline provided by the Business Analyst (BA) who was coordinating the meeting. He gave a background of the strategy workshop and how we were trying to link it back with their particular project. During the conversation I asked the team what they thought were the differentiators for our firm in Business Analysis, development and support functions within the context of their project. One of them said they did not understand what I was saying. So I rephrased my statement—why would the client not stop taking the service from them? The support person said that they were already doing some work on process improvements at an account level. I asked if they could use it in the context of this project. Then I asked them about the development space. The person said that it was cost advantage and availability of some niche skills (although few in number). I probed whether they saw any value in application knowledge. There didn't seem to be much.

Then I queried the BA. He said that he did not see much scope for interacting with others in the organization until now, although he did interact with others in the team to get some inputs for his work. Then we turned our attention to the data that they might be collecting. The BA said that the client did not have a tool to systematically collect this data. Right now they were collecting some metrics, but it was not accurate. I asked them if it would be possible for them to collect some metrics from each side, then do some correlations and present the case to the client—whether the process needed to change or the tools or techniques to make the entire delivery process become more responsive. Perhaps, if they highlighted the magnitude of the problem, the client might sit up and take notice. The BA seemed excited. Others didn't seem much excited but said that they would have a follow-up session to discuss further. Then I suggested that they could leverage the work done in Investment Management on metrics and I suggested some names to contact. The BA said that one of them was now in Global Markets. Then I said they could seek his assistance.

23. 5 December 2006: I had a discussion with the RM to catch up on the developments in ML and also get a feedback on my paper. The RM said that subsequent to the meetings at the CEO-CIO/COO-CIO levels, the account management had put in a lot of effort to prepare a presentation for the CIO. The BFS domain practice, geography and a senior strategist have been involved and they planned to first test with EMEA and then present it to the CIO in the US. I made some queries on the context and the content. Then he said that all this was raising management expectations about the account's targets. He felt that it would be a challenge to do a follow-up to the presentation. It might open doors but how could we realize the value. I got a feeling that there was some disconnect. I asked him if the account had a strategy to realize the target and whether the presentation was reflecting that strategy. He said that it was being taken care of in the business planning session. This presentation was actually helping them in the business planning (It was the reverse of what I was thinking, we were showing the client

that we could do several things, and in some ways asking them to pick and choose, but we were not telling them what exactly we could do and why it was critical for our strategy as well). The RM then said that right now all this discussion was happening between four–five senior managers in the account and practice. I asked him how they planned to involve others in this, and whether the output that some PLs had generated was being used in this. He said that they were involved in working out specific details, and the discussions that we have had were useful. I wondered, however, if the PLs felt that their exercise was a waste of time. They had participated in discussions to think about a strategy, and now something else was happening from the top; would these two meet each other halfway? I could only hope that they didn't end up with this feeling. I asked the RM about the situation in the new account. He said that it was fine except for a small problem where they had to pay a penalty. Then he went on to explain the problem, where the offshore team had ignored an email that had been sent regularly, but the problem had not been fixed. He felt that there was inadequate ownership, even though there was a process in place. He inquired how one could resolve this situation. I suggested an interaction approach (to participate in the day-to-day onsite-offshore interactions) and create differences from within instead of only looking at the process or people. Then he gave an example of how they had planned the Diwali event. The team had come up with a traditional presentation/sweets format. But, he had tried to break that and introduce a dance event. After much reluctance the team had agreed and they had ended up making it a more interactive event with mehndi and rangoli. I thought this was another good example of shaking up existing patterns. Then the RM inquired about my next steps and how to work further on the situation. I told him that I would be moving offshore and possibly looking at the onsite-offshore issues more closely. He suggested that I should probably look at the input (because he felt that the quality was reducing day by day). I told him that I had started my journey there, and moved across the value chain before reaching my paradoxical conclusion. I clarified that I was concerned about our patterns of interactions that were inhibiting bright, young people from acting, and leaving them in a state of feeling stuck. I gave the example of another RM who had come with high hopes, but had to withdraw because he couldn't change the existing pattern of relating with clients or management. In the end the RM asked if I could share my feedback on interactions with the account and about him. I said that I would send him my notes. I left the meeting pondering how this conversation would shape our future interaction. The RM responded to my feedback soon saying, "The document is well compiled and I appreciate your detailed analysis and composition of each interaction. It takes a lot of dedication to do this on a daily basis—given your scope of managing multiple accounts, tiers of DCTS management and associates …. Your final sentence regarding the pondering of our future interaction was quite interesting. Rest assured, this document would only serve to ensure that our future interaction continues and improves."

24. 8 December 2006: I received an email from the EM of the new client with a subject line "a 1-1 mentoring requirement" (like the typical resource requirement mails). The email said "We have had an issue in our account, where the client is not satisfied with the soft skills of one of our Team Leads. Though the client has requested for a change, we have asked for six-weeks of time to turn things around. During this, we will be doing various mentoring and grooming sessions with him. … It might be helpful if you could have a few one-to-one sessions with this person, as you obviously have much more experience in understanding people's behaviour … Do you think this would be possible and helpful?" Though I was intrigued at this interpretation of my role, I suggested that I could speak to the concerned associate, without asking for any additional information. I wondered if it was the result of my previous interaction with the RM. The EM then thanked me for the offer and asked the associate to get in touch with me.

25. 12 December 2006: I waited for two days for the associate to contact me. When he didn't, I contacted him inquiring if he wanted

to meet. I wondered if he was usually like this. He responded to the email and we set up a time for a teleconference. I waited for his call for almost eight minutes when he called from his mobile. He said that he had met me earlier at Investment Management (was he seeking familiarity or was he saying that he knew what to expect?). Then I asked him if he would like me to call him. He said he had reserved a room and was going to call from there. I wondered why he didn't inform me that he would be late or try to apologize when he called. Then I asked him about his situation, the steps they were taking to resolve it, and his own interests. He explained that the situation emerged out of "not escalating" an issue around a mission critical application (I wondered if it was the 50K issue that the RM had pointed out). In response to the situation, they were now having regular meetings within the team and with the client, more ownership within the team, and understanding and closing knowledge gaps. I wondered how this would change perceptions at a micro level (this is actually leading to a micro-management situation that we tried to avoid through the earlier work on reporting metrics). He also said that he had taken over this project about five months back. The person who was earlier handling this system was now the EM at offshore. The team had sufficient experience (at least four of them), with two at onsite and four at offshore. He said that he wanted to take up this project because he wanted to handle larger teams and more critical systems. Personally he wanted to grow as a technical architect. I wondered if six people represented a large team compared to his earlier experience of working alone or with two–three people. I was struggling a little bit with the conversation because of the lack of clarity in the teleconference. Moreover, I felt that it would be good to have a face-to-face conversation. I suggested to him that we could meet the next day. He agreed but did not send me any invite or confirmation. The next day I sent him an email confirming my visit but did not get any response. I got a feeling that he was having some difficulty in relating/with attention to detail (day-to-day signals). Are our ambitions of growing fast in a dynamically changing world not allowing us to pay attention? I wondered what he had made of the email sent by his supervisor and about me What was his mind telling him about our interaction? Why did he want to continue this role? Could he turn it around in some way? Could the EM play some role? Was all this happening due to the wider context of the client (new contract, no growth)?

26. 13 December 2006: I was thinking about how to approach this conversation given that I was about to leave UK. I thought of three options: (a) Talk to him a little more to help him relate to his context—on the lines of "this is our time, what do you think we could do jointly now?", his understanding of how his work relates to his context and his own career, how he could improvize at a day-to-day level and shake up his patterns—how I saw myself versus how others saw me?, (b) Participate in one of their telecons—how do we interact as a group between onsite and offshore, (c) Keep in touch with him through email (increase his responsiveness in emails and F2F). All this without getting into a diagnostic or advisory mode? When I went to meet him, I quickly recognized his face. I had seen him before. He inquired if I would like to meet the EM. I said we could start talking (I could meet the EM later). Then we sat down to have a discussion. I asked him how he felt being in this situation, why people came to this conclusion that he required mentoring, and how did the situation develop. He said that he was not happy with the current situation. He was also shocked to note that he lacked soft skills. He had been working with the same colleagues for some time now. No one had presented this perspective. Now that a problem had been reported by the client, they were pointing fingers at him. Lack of escalation of issue was pointed to his soft skills, and when there is a fault with the team it is the team lead that has to bear the brunt. But, fault diagnosis had shown them that this problem was there even before he was nominated as a team lead (his nomination happened when the earlier team leads had to go offshore and clients had rejected other options within the team; his name was proposed since he had earlier worked on a module and had a good impression with

the clients, was even considered for development work). The particular scenario that had now occurred could have occurred any time. It had been reported to the third party, fixed once, and recurred again. Since people did not understand its criticality, they did not bother about it. This was not surfaced during knowledge transfer (KT) sessions. Even though he was new, his team had been there for a long time. So, why were they blaming him? Then I asked him how he felt after receiving the email from his EM and why he did not respond immediately. I told him what I had thought (my perception formation) when he had not responded. Then he said that he was waiting to check with his EM before responding to me. I asked him why. The email was sent by his EM, so why was he hesitating? Then he said that there were situations where their responses to client requests had created problems. He cited an example in this project when they had written to the business that the problem had been rectified and so on, but did not remove the email trace where there were some negative references to business teams. The business had raised an issue with the IT division who in turn complained to our management. This lack of sensitivity of how information might be used across different organizational boundaries (business/IT, supplier-customer) had led to a problem where the EM probably told him that he should not send any mails without their permission (I had witnessed similar situations in other accounts)—a good example of how behaviours are conditioned through small events (many times we are not aware of this). Then I gave him some suggestions on how he might change perceptions through day-to-day interactions with the team, account managers and clients: (a) See the situation in a positive light, i.e., what could you, the account and client gain from this situation?; (b) use interactions (F2F or email) with clients and teams more effectively; (c) start a weekly discussion on different business scenarios and its impact on the solution; (d) construct a holistic view of the system (as an architect); (e) blog one key lesson per day and share it with your team (and ask them to add one related thought). I summarized the key points in a mail for him. He replied saying he would try to implement the suggestions. Then I sent him my paper as a reference and also to get his feedback.

Case #3: A global consumer and financial data account

1. 22 December 2005: Based on our earlier interaction in the context of one of his accounts, I asked the Client Manager (CM) if I could start a similar conversation with this account. (I guess there was some value perceived by the Client Manager in the previous interaction). He agreed to introduce this account's RM to me.

2. 4 January 2006: He arranged a meeting with the RM and EM in his office. During this introductory meeting I tried to explain my role and also understand the account's context. I was told that the present SD was formerly associated with this client. The RM and EM gave me an overview of their account. They shared a document about the client's business (I had earlier accessed this from the client's website, and a few years back had done some groundwork on their business model). I was impressed that they had access to such documents. I became more curious and inquired about the uniqueness of the account. They indicated that one of the key aspects was "being a global account", but they also felt that it was the source of problems. The Europe component of the global account was suffering due to delivery problems associated with other geographies. They said they had good relationships with the business. In the CM's view, the client firm had a business model similar to ours (I realized they were referring to the outsourcing arm of the client, but the client's core business was different—information services). The client apparently leveraged DCTS to help them ramp up or down resources in relation to the demand from their customers. But, their outsourcing business was not doing well and therefore, the account anticipated some growth problems. The RM also mentioned that the client's sourcing strategy was causing difficulties. They said that the client was trying to encourage smaller players since they were not sure about the

interest of a large service provider such as DCTS in servicing them. It was also apparent that the client had stronger internal networking, and was sharing information of service failure across geographies. The account team was not keen to discuss the account strategy since they felt it has been well understood and also said that they were working with relevant teams (consulting and marketing) to change the client perception. They were interested to discuss governance and reporting (another account under the same CM had requested similar help). I summarized these observations and shared them with the team. But, in the back of my mind I was not sure if the team was really grasping the essential characteristic of their client (an information-based business, offering both products and services, and having deep linkages with the local context). I sensed that there was some difficulty on both sides in exploring what was emerging during the interaction.

3. 12 January 2006: I had a follow-up session with the RM to discuss his concerns about governance. I agreed to review their note. During this conversation I came to know that the client had asked a competing firm to help them with governance issues. I thought it was a great opportunity missed and could have undesirable implications.

4. 1 February 2006: We then had a follow-up session to review the RM's note on project governance. I presented some views on project-level governance and account-level governance and ways to enhance senior management interaction (through flexibility in the governance).

5. 12 April 2006: When I returned from vacation, I enquired about developments on their side. The RM said that they had shared their perspective with the client. But, they were yet to make any headway. He also mentioned that one of their projects which was in the red had been successfully completed. I suggested that they could leverage these recent positive experiences to emphasize key elements of project governance. This seemed to go down well with the team. Later the RM said that the client invited them to give a

presentation on governance, and they were leveraging a consultant from the Consulting Practice for the same.

6. 13 June 2006: Things cooled off after this for some time. I requested a meeting with the RM and EM to know how they were doing with the implementation of various initiatives. During the initial phase of the teleconference I sensed very little scope for a conversation. It was like a Q&A. I thought that they were viewing me as an assessor or perhaps I was not phrasing open-ended questions. So, I introduced a slightly different topic into the conversation. I inquired how their client was coping with being a products and a services firm at the same time. They responded saying there was a problem, but "they do not have much information to go with a proposition". I inquired if they could get the information without engaging. The RM then said that the topic was too sensitive, and the conversation was once again, over. (This reminded me of the rational problem solving perspective. I struggled to convey the interaction perspective by giving an example from the utilities account. While this was done to open the conversation, it may have inadvertently closed the conversation). Then I moved the conversation to client events. I pointed out that their client seemed to organize a number of events for their customers and inquired if we were invited to any of these events. They said that only their client's IT division had asked them to give a presentation on governance. I understood that their business relationships may not really be strategic. Later, the conversation moved to other initiatives. I confronted them with the findings from an HR survey—it was one of the few accounts where even the correlation between middle level and junior level staff was very low. Their response was that they had a lot of junior staff, who were struggling to cope with knowledge gaps and hence feeling stretched. They were trying to resolve this through KT sessions. I inquired if I could participate in some of their internal KT sessions to understand the challenges being faced (I asked them if they could invite me to their next session). This never happened. I wondered if they never had any KT

sessions after that or was it that I was out of sight, out of mind. I did not hear from them for some time.

7. 18 August 2006: One fine day, after almost two months, I received an email from the RM. He replied to my request for a meeting (after about a month). He wanted to know if he could speak to me urgently. I was not sure why he seemed so keen, but I agreed for a meeting (treating it as a delayed response to my earlier request). The RM expressed his concern about the lack of clarity on ownership of the account. He felt that this was affecting his prospects of winning business in Europe, and also the present opportunity in the US that involved replicating a solution implemented in Europe. He also said that this opportunity hinged on the support from delivery and that the clients were not happy with the Offshore Delivery Manager and were requesting for his replacement. After some discussions, his senior managers seemed to arrive at a conclusion that they could either persuade the client to work with the Delivery Manager or change the delivery centre (I was amused by this line of thinking). At that time, they seemed to be moving in the latter direction, with the Europe Head suggesting that the person at the other delivery centre would be the Global Delivery Manager (GDM). The RM said that clients in the US geography had expressed difficulty with the new GDM (they felt that there was no listening during teleconferences and it was like a monologue; the GDM kept the clients waiting during meetings, or not accomodate meetings at slightly odd hours). The RM was concerned that due to the above reasons there was a chance that the present deal may not go through (even though he was investing lot of effort from his side for a deal that would finally be billed to the US business). He wanted to know if I could speak to the Europe Head and ease the situation in some way (I thought this was the reason for the call, but I wondered why his line function was unable to do this). My suggestion to him was to look at consolidating sales (since Europe work was the core), work out a transition model for delivery, and speak to the GDM

so that ownership issues were taken care of. He felt that this was a good suggestion and thanked me.

8. 1 September 2006: We had a follow-up session to discuss the outcome. He indicated that he had spoken to the Europe Head and obtained an "assurance that he can spend some time on US sales opportunities". He felt that the GDM's position was more unsustainable and therefore did not speak to her.

9. 6 October 2006: I contacted the RM after some time to discuss how the global bid was coming up. He indicated that the delivery centre issue was being resolved (that Kolkata may most likely evolve as a more stable delivery centre in the future). I suggested to him that he could use this global programme to push the case for a global delivery centre and global sales component and set the stage for a global account. He agreed to discuss this in the second week of November. I inquired how other things were shaping up. He said that he was not entirely happy with the sales component but indicated that they were having some success in changing perceptions. I suggested that they could look at the Oracle ERP upgrade experience of another account. This might help in their bid as well. I also indicated to him that I could explain this to him if he was interested. I did not hear from him. Later I sent him a message saying I was likely to visit his city for a meeting at the business school and inquired if we could meet. There was no response; I am still wondering why.

10. November 2006: Towards the end of November I sent him my note and inquired if he could give me his feedback. I also requested a similar feedback from his superior. Later the RM responded, apologized for the delay, and said that he was busy, but gave me a date.

11. 6 December 2006: During the teleconference I asked him how the sale had gone off. He said that both opportunities were stuck to an extent. He said that the offshore team's presentation for the global support opportunity was not very impressive, and now the client was also looking at another Indian vendor as a potential alternative. All the same, he said that the person-in-charge for

the decision knew our organization very well (their strengths and weaknesses), and in order to keep his own situation safe might go with a known vendor than experiment with a new vendor. I wondered why this should be the case, especially since both are CMM companies and replacing one with another should not matter. Moreover, we all take over from the client at some stage, so would clients be really worried about a change in the service provider? Then the topic moved to the other opportunity. He said that it had got stuck because our proposal did not seem to meet the client's view that costs should be low because they were only replicating the Europe solution in the US. Our management felt that both technically and functionally there were some changes which would limit replicability. The RM pointed to some examples to emphasise this point. I then inquired how things were shaping in the account, especially in the context of the recent business planning session. What he said surprised me. He said that even though senior management felt that this client was a key account, he had suggested that it should be taken out of this list. His reasoning was that despite putting in a lot of effort as part of key account management (senior management meetings, marketing events, thought leadership, consulting presentations) the client did not seem to reciprocate their gestures. The client was still behaving in a very rigid manner and there was not enough respect. He quoted some examples where the client had abruptly stopped a presentation by a senior consultant on governance and change management saying, "We know all this, we don't want a lecture from you guys". The RM felt that this kind of customer behaviour was unacceptable, any self-respecting person would not take it, and it would not interest any internal groups to work with the client. (This reminded me of a similar situation in which I have been—"You are new to US, new to this firm, what are you going to tell us?" I had, at that time, felt agitated that there was no acknowledgement of my PhD or my broad range of capabilities. But, I had also felt that they were right in a way. That is how power-relating happens. There is no escape from power-relating.

The good thing in my case was that at the end of four months things had reversed). The RM also quoted another example, where they could not meet the delivery (after committing to aggressive timelines) on time due to one person falling sick. The client apparently was not willing to accommodate this request even though the RM had explained to him that it wouldn't have affected the client's workshops very much. Another example was that sometimes clients tended to adopt a partnership approach only to tease out some information from the supplier. (It is an aspect of power-relating, nothing wrong with that). The RM felt that this behaviour was prevalent at all customer touch-points. He felt that it was in their blood, and perhaps they needed psychiatric help (This rang a bell. It is not about communicating, it is about relating). He concluded that the customer was not responsive, and it may be better to spend the resources elsewhere. This experience reminded me of the sour grapes story and the conclusion reached in the Business Excellence Committee meeting not so long ago. But, I refrained from giving an opinion because I knew my experiences with micro-interactions would not make sense very easily. I had discussed in the paper that perception change happens through these micro-interactions, and not powerful frameworks or large presentations. Instead, I asked him what it would mean for the relationship. How would the account operate if it was not a key account? He said that one of the key changes would be that the growth target would be off, and the pressure to sell the five bubbles would reduce. I asked him if the client wouldn't see this lack of interest and switch to a different supplier. I wondered how the account would develop the relationship in this context (if our management feels there is revenue in this account). Would they consider change of people? Would that help? Can the new person change this pattern of relating? Then, I moved the conversation to my paper. The RM said that the key point in the paper was about the discussion regarding the Balanced Scorecard. He felt that management needs to listen to their people, otherwise, it is difficult to have a conversation. Most often managers try to ask questions or push for actions without actually helping them to move things. He quoted an example of Sales Force Training where it was suggested that "you have to give something to get something". Then I asked him if he saw similarities between his interactions with clients and internal managers. If clients were not responding, his view was that we should stop expending any extra effort. Would the same apply to management? He said there was a parallel between the situations. Towards the end he said that the interactions with me were useful. He felt that speaking to me was useful because there was some listening and he could talk freely. He also said that although things were not recorded, some of my suggestions had helped in moving things around a little bit. I said to him that I could send him a note summarizing our interactions. He could have a look at it and see if there were some elements to which he could give a re-look. I gave him an example of "if you want to be listened, may be you could start listening" As consultants or sales staff we don't realize this. In the end I pondered what our interactions did to our perceptions of each other, and what it would mean for our next interaction.

Patterns of interaction in different organizational spaces

Interactions between corporate teams at geography level and accounts:

1. <u>Talk in business planning sessions:</u> The general tendency of the RMs was to assume that "if numbers are good, then I am okay. No one would anyway understand the specific terms and initiatives relating to my client". Joint actions would emerge mainly in the case of clearly identified sales opportunities. Other proactive efforts would typically end up in the action items list. Most often the interaction in the planning session was seen as a means to reinforce the sales team's positioning with respect to other groups. For instance, after a session that covered accounts in one vertical, the SD said, "My 'boys' always do well" (as if it

was an exam and they had sustained their positioning). When listening to another account's business plan, I was struck by the "walk-the-talk" rhetoric presented by its Client Director. He was explaining to others that DCTS' differentiator was "walking the talk" and not just giving a report like a management consultant. I was amused by this rhetoric because a few years ago he was part of the management consulting unit in DCTS. I wondered how he got "civilized". I also wondered if DCTS knew how to "talk the walk". Otherwise, why would we need an initiative called Customer Value Management?

2. <u>Talk in the internal sales conference:</u> Management typically spelt out the strategy (usually a monologue) and highlighted issues that needed attention using some geography-level data. Sales people struggled to pay attention to presentations by different verticals—everybody was given the same template by the Business Excellence team (to ensure standardization). Some RMs (usually heroes) got an opportunity to showcase their best practices. The HR/Marketing team who managed the event would add its spin to it, like clean the street. Sales people started dropping out after the first day under some pretext (client escalation or the other). I wondered if such conferences energized them and created better networking.

3. <u>Talk on strategic initiatives:</u> In a growing organization, there were so many new initiatives all the time. So, even before an initiative got launched it would have been tagged as "another initiative". Some people jumped in as champions to pilot it in their accounts. They tried to present it in some forums and got some visibility out of it. Others responded by saying, "It is a good idea, but difficult to practice", "client needs to be educated", "we don't have bandwidth", "can only be done at offshore", "we are already doing elements of it", and "you have to take them and show them how to do it and they will see the value".

4. <u>Talk in external reviews:</u> Typically these happened once in a while—for instance, Business Excellence review or quality assessments. It is viewed as an examination and people prepare

(are given coaching) on how to answer, what to cover and so on. Since most of the questions are on specific parts, people find it easy to say that they have done it and have an example for each component. But, there is very little discussion on relationships. For instance, no one asks how one component has impacted the other—is there some correlation? The forum is not used to challenge the model itself; these concerns are seen as academic and a waste of time.

5. Talk in training sessions and Communities of Practice: The general pattern is that the people who attend are either those who get this information and are interested, or those who get nominated because they are unallocated. The feedback at the end of the session is that it is a good programme and everyone in DCTS should undergo this, but we were not sure if we will have bandwidth to practice it, i.e., we can do it if we get the right projects. The people who attend these do make some friends, but nothing persists once they leave the training room.

6. Talk between support groups and accounts: Corporate groups seek information (repeatedly in different formats) from accounts to monitor them or send reminders to comply against some corporate policies/requirements/billing queries.

7. Monthly teleconference with the Europe Head: People log in and keep quiet (attendance varies). They are afraid to express their view because either they might be shot down, stating lack of adequate preparation, or that somebody has already done it (so learn from them and don't say it cannot be done). The Europe Head observed that in his view people seem to join the bandwagon when someone's opinion is not shot down.

8. Talk in "open houses" or "town hall meetings": These terms are borrowed from local contexts, but we may not be cognizant of the underlying philosophy. They are usually viewed by senior managers as opportunities to give "darshan to devotees" and showcase their "strategic perspective". They expect associates to pose "questions that can showcase their intelligence" and not raise inconsequential operational issues. Accounts which comply with this are praised and

those that do not are moved out of their radar. Given the mismatch, it is no wonder that associates view them as an opportunity for enjoying a good meal and a free ticket to visit a new location.

9. Email etiquette internally: Mass emails seeking participation would never get a response. Even personalized mails were responded to only if sent by people who were close to power sources. Some PLs sent emails with warnings such as "if you don't attend the session (typically some corporate initiative) you will have to meet the RM in person". The responses of managers to resource requirements (for instance, sending an email about BA resource availability) are more prompt compared to other emails. Responses to internal emails do not have any element of salutation or giving thanks. The auto-generated text was used to the best effect for such routine internal mails.

Interactions between geography and clients:

Typically about eight different opportunities for interaction were explored. For instance, client events, invitations to special events such as industry awards or sports, thought leadership workshops, branded thought papers, reports in the media and CSAT survey.

1. Talk in client events (event managed by external parties): They were usually organized at an expensive location with good food and beverages. Some top academic institutions/professors were invited for a thought leadership session, leaving clients wondering "where is your stuff" or "we don't think this is a value add". Event organizers (marketing team) wondered, "What can we do to attract the right people from client organizations?", "the sales staff don't seem to have the right contacts", "next time we need to break the stranglehold of SDs/RMs over clients and reach out to the client executives directly".

2. CSAT survey: A different set of senior managers were sent to get feedback from clients. Meetings were coordinated by the RM. Most often the senior managers would request meetings at the highest level in the client organization, without realizing that the client executives at that level might not be aware of what DCTS

was doing with them. The typical conclusion that emerged from such interactions was the need to raise our visibility at the senior level and show them what value we are bringing. Therefore, we should practise CVM and open the doors for DCTS Senior managers or GPC to engage with client's senior managers. The SDs and RMs are impediments for further growth in the accounts. They have brought us here, but we need somebody else to take us from here to there.

3. <u>Thought leadership workshops:</u> Invites were sent directly to client managers. Some clients did not understand why they were getting this invite. Those who knew DCTS did not understand why it was talking about "thought leadership" when the teams that they interacted with every day did not seem to practise it in the client's context (making them more uncomfortable with DCTS). The clients who attended used them as an opportunity to catch up with colleagues from other firms rather than focus on the workshop.

Interactions between accounts and clients:

1. <u>Talk in sales proposals:</u> When an RFP was out, the RMs sent out emails seeking help and commitment of people from different groups for that proposal. The typical story line was "we know your problem", "we have been there, done that", and "we are the best", "we can walk the talk", "no one can beat us on price". In some cases, new terms were introduced into the conversation by sales coach or SDs—"understanding the pain areas or agendas of client managers", "socializing with them", and "get something out of the deal".

2. <u>Interactions with clients and competitors in client locations:</u> Typically there was a huge inside (DCTS)-outside (others) gap. They were secretive about their plans—a fear that the other would take away his/her job and onsite stay. But, through these "boundary separating" conversations, they would also pass on vital information to each other, which was used to improve their proposals.

3. <u>Interactions with clients in projects:</u> I looked closely at how

people interpret their situations, force/align/modify actions, and generate joint actions. Most of these interactions were seen as one-directional. Very often it was a reactive response to a client's request (even though clients have been pushing them to be proactive). They were not seen as opportunities to engage and seek further involvement of the client in generating a joint action such as "if you give me more info about a particular issue, I can come back to you with a better perspective". Even the customer satisfaction feedback was not seen as an opportunity to engage. It was a useful tool only for the service provider. But, as one senior DCTS manager says he wouldn't give much importance to the data (since there was so much variability).

4. <u>Email etiquette with clients:</u> Most leaders appeared to have picked up the salutation styles of the clients. But, the content and "thanking" left a lot to be desired.

Bibliography

Agrawal, N.M., Khatri, Naresh and Srinivasan, R. (2012), "Managing growth: Human resource management challenges facing the Indian software industry", *Journal of World Business*, 47(2), pp. 159–166.

Agrawal, N.M., Narayanaswamy, Ramesh, Ratan, Rashie and Devi, Renuka (2006), "Leadership challenges in Indian software industry", IIM Bangalore Research Paper No. 249.

Agrawal, N.M., Pandit, Rajesh and Menon, Divya (2012), "Strategy to usher in the next phase of growth in the Indian IT industry", *IIMB Management Review*, 24, pp. 164–179.

Allen, P.M. (1998), "Evolving complexity in social science", in Altman, G. and Koch, W.A. (eds) *Systems: New paradigms for the human sciences*, Walter de Gruyter, New York.

Alvesson, Matts (2004), *Knowledge Work and Knowledge-Intensive Firms*, Oxford University Press, Oxford.

Armbruster, Thomas (2006), *The Economics and Sociology of Management Consulting*, Cambridge University Press, Cambridge.

Athreye, Suma S. (2005), "The Indian software industry and its evolving service capability", *Industrial and Corporate Change*, 14(3), pp. 393–418.

Axelrod, Robert and Cohen, Michael D. (2001), *Harnessing Complexity*, Basic Books, New York.

Badreddin, Omar (2013), "Thematic review and analysis of Grounded Theory application in software engineering", *Advances in Software Engineering*, Article ID 468021.

Barnes, Thomas (2013), "The IT industry and economic development in India: A critical study", *Journal of South Asian Development*, 8(1), pp. 61–83.

Barrow, John D. (2000), *The Book of Nothing*, Vintage, London.

Beer, S. (1997), *The Heart of the Enterprise*, Wiley, Chichester.

Bhandari, B., Chintala, Prashanth Reddy, Gombar, Vandana, Jishnu, Latha, Majumdar, Shyamal and Pandey, Aanand (2009), *The Satyam Saga*, Business Standard Books, New Delhi.

Birkinshaw, Julian, Healey, Mark P., Suddaby, Roy and Weber, Klaus (2014), "Debating the future of management research", *Journal of Management Studies*, 51(1), pp. 38–55.

Blinder, Alan S. (2006), "Offshoring: The next industrial revolution?", *Foreign Affairs*, March/April, pp. 113–28.

Blumer, Herbert (1969), *Symbolic Interactionism: Perspective and Method*, University of California Press, Berkeley.

Bolton, Gillie (2010), *Reflective Practice: Writing and Professional Development*, Third Edition, Sage Publications, London.

Bowonder, B. and Sailesh, J.V. (2005), "ICT for the renewal of a traditional industry: a case study of Kancheepuram silk sarees", *International Journal of Services Technology and Management*, 6(3/4/5), pp. 342–55.

Brown, Junaita and Isaacs, David (2005), *World Café: Shaping Our Futures Through Conversations That Matter*, Berrett-Hoehler Publishers, San Francisco.

Bunyaratavej, Kraiwinee, Doh, Jonathan, Hahn, Eugene D., Lewin, Arie Y. and Massini, Silvia (2011), "Conceptual issues in services offshoring research: A multidisciplinary review", *Group Organization & Management*, 36(1), pp. 70–102.

Castells, M. (1996), *The Rise of the Network Society, The Information Age: Economy, Society and Culture, Vol. I.*, Cambridge, MA: Oxford, UK: Blackwell.

Cefkin, Melissa (2007), "Numbers may speak louder than words, but is anyone listening? The rhythmscape and sales pipeline management", *Ethnographic Praxis in Industry Conference*, pp. 188–200.

Cefkin, Melissa (ed.) (2009), *Ethnography and the Corporate Encounter: Reflections on Research in and of Corporations*, Berghahn Books, New York.

Chakrabarty, Subrata and Whitten, Dwayne (2011), "The side-lining of top IT executives in the governance of outsourcing: Antecedents, power struggles, and consequences", *IEEE Transactions on Engineering Management*, 58(4), pp. 799–814.

Collins, Randall (2004), *Interaction Ritual Chains*, Princeton University Press, Princeton.

Conway, Flo and Siegelman, Jim (2005), *Dark Hero of the Information Age: In Search of Norbert Wiener, the Father of Cybernetics*, Basic Books, New York.

Cook, David P., Goh, Chon-Huat and Chung, Chen H. (1999), "Service typologies: A state of the art survey", *Production and Operations Management Society*, 8(3), pp. 318–38.

Cooren, Francois (ed.) (2007), *Interacting and Organizing: Analyses of Management Meeting*, Lawrence Erlbaum Associates Publishers, Mahwah, New Jersey.

D'Costa, Anthony P. (2003), "The Indian software industry in the global division of labour", in D'Costa, A.P. and Sridharan, E. (eds), *India in the Global Software Industry: Innovation, Firm Strategies and Development*, pp. 1–26. Basingstoke: Palgrave MacMillan.

D'Costa, Anthony P. (2011), "Geography, uneven development and distributive justice: the political economy of IT growth in India", *Cambridge J Regions Econ Soc*, 4(2), pp. 237–51.

D'Mello, Marisa and Sahay, Sundeep (2008), "Betwixt and between? Exploring mobilities in a global workplace in India", in Upadhya, Carol and Vasavi, A.R. (ed.) (2008), *In an Outpost of the Global Economy: Work and Workers in India's Information Technology Industry*, pp. 76–100. Routledge, New Delhi.

Da Rold, C. and Karamouzis, F. (2009), "Case Study: Zurich Financial Services group delivers business value through its multisourcing strategy", Gartner Research, Stamford, CT.

Dalal, Farhad (2002), *Race, Colour and the Processes of Racialization*, Bruner-Routledge, London.

Dhar, Rajib Lochan (2009), "Cynicism in the Indian IT organizations: An exploration of the employees' perspectives", *Qualitative Sociology Review*, 5(1), pp. 152–75.

Doh, Jonathan P. (2005), "Offshore outsourcing: Implications for international business and strategic management theory and practice", *Journal of Management Studies*, 42(3), pp. 695–704.

Donnellon, Anne (1996), *Team Talk: The Power of Language in Team Dynamics*, Harvard Business School Press, Boston, MA.

Dossani, Raffiq (2005), "Globalization and the offshoring of services: The case of India", in Brainard, Lael and Collins, Susan M. (eds), *Offshoring White-Collar Work—The Issues and Implications*, The Brookings Trade Forum.

Dougherty, Deborah (2004), "Organizing practices in services: Capturing practice-based knowledge for innovation", *Strategic Organization*, 2(1), pp. 35–64.

Elias, Norbert (2001), *The Society of Individuals*, Continuum, New York.

Feuerstein, Patrick (2013), "Patterns of work reorganization in the course of the IT industry's internationalization", *Competition and Change*, 17(1), pp. 24–40.

Forrester, Jay (1961), *Industrial Dynamics*, MIT Press, Cambridge, MA.

Gibbs, Jennifer (2009), "Dialectics in a global software team: Negotiating tensions across time, space, and culture", *Human Relations*, 62(6), pp. 905–35.

Gibson, C. and Birkinshaw, J. (2004), "The antecedents, consequences, and mediating role of organizational ambidexterity", *Academy of Management Journal*, 47, pp. 209–26.

Gleick, James (1988), *Chaos: The Making of a New Science*, William Heinemann Limited, London.

Goffman, Ervin (1959), *The Presentation of Self in Everyday Life*, Doubleday, New York.

Goffman, Ervin (1967), *Interaction Ritual*, Doubleday, New York.

Gonzalez, Reyes, Llopis, Juan and Gasco, Jose (2006), "Information systems offshore outsourcing: A descriptive analysis", *Industrial Management & Data Systems*, 106(9), pp. 1233–248.

Gopalakrishnan, R. (2010), *When the Penny Drops: Learning What's Not Taught*, Portfolio Penguin, India.

Goyal, Rahul (2012), *Management in India: Grow from an Accidental to a Successful Manager in the IT & Knowledge Industry*, Packt Publishing. Kindle Edition.

Greiner, LE and Poulfelt, F (eds) (2009), *Management consulting today and tomorrow: Perspectives and advice from 27 leading world experts*, Routledge.

Hage, J.T (1999), "Organizational innovation and organizational change", *Annual Review of Sociology*, 25, pp. 597–622.

Haldane, Andrew and Bond, Peter (2004), "The use of KALiF[a] in the development of complex, emotioning, innovating, and polytechnical communities", http://www.lancaster.ac.uk/ias/documents/complexity%20 workshop/peterbond.pdf

Hamel, Gary and Breen, Bill (2007), *The Future of Management*, Harvard Business School Press, Boston.

Heintzman, Ralph (2003), "The dialectics of organizational design", in

Courchene, Thomas J. and Savoie, Donald J. (eds), *The Art of the State: Governance in a World Without Frontiers*, Institute for Research on Public Policy.

Heracleous, Loizos and Wirtz, Jochen (2014), "Singapore Airlines: Achieving sustainable advantage through mastering paradox", *The Journal of Applied Behavioral Science*, 50(2) pp. 150–70.

Hertog, Pim den (2000), "Knowledge intensive business services as co-producers of innovation", *International Journal of Innovation Management*, 4(4), pp. 491–528.

Ho, Karen (2009), *Liquidated: An Ethnography of Wall Street*, Duke University Press, Durham.

Holzweber, Markus, Mattsson, Jan, Chadee, Doren and Raman, Revti (2011), "Innovation strategy in the Indian IT service industry : User centred issues on innovation", in Sundbo, Jon and Toivonen, Marja (eds), *User-based Innovation in Services*, pp. 145–76, Edward Elgar Publishing Limited, Cheltenham, England.

Isaacs, William (1999), *Dialogue and the Art of Thinking Together*, Currency, New York.

Iyengar, Partha (2008), "India-3 are the emerging mega vendors", Gartner Research, https://www.gartner.com/doc/713207

Jacobs, Claus and Coghlan, David (2005), *Sound from silence: On listening in organizational learning, Human Relations*, 58(1), pp. 115–38.

Johnstone, Keith (1999), *Impro for Storytellers*, Faber and Faber Ltd., London.

Kahane, Adam (2004), *Solving Tough Problems*, Berret-Koehler Publishers, SanFrancisco.

Kamthania, D. (2014), *A Big Need for Indic-Language Solutions*, CSI Communications, 37(12), pp. 7–8.

Kanavi, Shivanand (ed.) (2007), *Research by Design: Innovation and TCS*, Rupa & Co., New Delhi.

Kauffman, Stuart, A. (1995), *At Home in the Universe: The Search for Laws of Self-Organization and Complexity*, Oxford University Press, Oxford.

Khetan, Parmeshwari Prasad (1992), *The Bhagavad Gita: With Text, Translation, and Commentary in the Words of Sri Aurobindo*, Sri Aurobindo Divine Life Trust, Rajasthan.

Kleiner, Art (2010), "Management by Reflection", *Strategy + Business*, March.

Kohli, F.C. (2005), *The IT Revolution in India: Selected Speeches and Writings*, Rupa & Co., New Delhi. Kindle Edition.

Kohli, F.C. (2014), Personal interview with Dr Kohli on 30 October 2014, Mumbai.

Kristoffersen, Steinar, "Programmers a-voiding complexity". Paper presented at 7th COOP 2006, Provence, France, May 9–12, 2006.

Langley, Ann, Smallman, Clive, Tsoukas, Haridimos and Van de Ven, Andrew H. (2013), "Process studies in change of organization and management: Unveiling temporality, activity and flow", *Academy of Management Journal*, 56(1), pp. 1–13.

Levy, David L. (2005), "Offshoring in the new global political economy", *Journal of Management Studies* 42(3), pp. 685–93.

Lewin, R. (1993), *Complexity: Life at the Edge of Chaos*, J.M.Dent, London.

Lind, M.R. and Zmud, R.W. (1991), "The influence of a convergence in understanding between technology providers and users of information technology innovativeness", *Organization Science*, 2(2), pp. 195–217.

Linn, Allison (2013), "The state of the American dream is uncertain", NBC News, http://www.nbcnews.com/feature/in-plain-sight/state-american-dream-uncertain-v19306579

Lovelock, Christopher and Gummesson, Evert (2004), "Whither services marketing? In search of a new paradigm and fresh perspectives", *Journal of Service Research*, 7(1), pp. 20–41.

Macdonald, Duff (2013), *The FIRM: The Inside Story of McKinsey*, Oneworld, London.

Maturana, Humberto and Varela, Francisco (1980), *Autopoiesis and Cognition: Realization of the Living*, Springer Science and Business Media.

McKenna, Christopher D. (2006), *The World's Newest Profession: Management Consulting in the Twentieth Century*, Cambridge University Press, Cambridge.

Mead, George Herbert (1932), *The Philosophy of the Present*, University of Chicago, Chicago.

Mead, George Herbert (1934), *Mind, Self and Society*, Chicago University Press, Chicago.

Meyer, Alan D., Gaba, Vibha and Colwell, Kenneth A. (2005), "Organizing far from equilibrium: Nonlinear change in organizational fields", *Organization Science*, 16(5), pp. 456–73.

Miller, James G. (1978), *Living systems*, McGraw-Hill, New York.

Mintzberg, Henry (2009), *Managing*, Barrett-Koehler Publishers, San Francisco.

Moore, Stephanie (2005), "The Forrester Wave™: Indian vendor consulting capabilities, Forrester Research", Q4.

Nadeem, Shehzad (2011), *Dead Ringers: How Outsourcing is Changing the Way Indians Understand Themselves*, Princeton University Press. Kindle Locations 253–57.

NASSCOM (2014), "Strategic review: The IT-BPM sector in India", NASSCOM.

Nelson, Richard R. and Winter, Sidney G. (1982), *An Evolutionary Theory of Economic Change*, Harvard University Press, Cambridge, MA.

Nurit, Zaidman and Brock, David M. (2009), "Knowledge transfer within multinationals and their foreign subsidiaries: A culture-context approach", *Group & Organization Management*, 34(3), pp.297–29.

Oshri, Ilan, Kotlarsky, Julia and Willcocks, Leslie (2009), *The Handbook of Global Outsourcing and Offshoring*, Palgrave Macmillan.

Palmisano, Samuel (2006), "The globally integrated enterprise", *Foreign Affairs*, 85(3), pp. 127–36.

Poole, M. S. and Van de Ven, A. H. (1989), "Using paradox to build management and organization theories", *Academy of Management Review*, 14, pp. 562–78.

Porter, Michael E. (1980), *Competitive Strategy*, Free Press, New York.

Prigogine, I. and Stengers, I. (1984), *Order Out of Chaos*, International Universities Press, New York.

Rahman, Was and Kurien, Priya (2007), *Blind Men and the Elephant*, Sage Publications, New Delhi.

Ramadorai, S. (2011), *The TCS Story & Beyond*, Penguin Books, New Delhi.

Ravishankar, M.N., Pan, Shan L. and Myers, Michael D. (2013), "Information technology offshoring in India: a postcolonial perspective", *European Journal of Information Systems*, 22, pp. 387–402.

Revuru, Ramesh (2012), *That's I.T.*, Amazon, Kindle Edition.

Rumelt, Richard (2011), *Good strategy, Bad Strategy*, Profile Books, London.

Sage, A.P. (1977), *Methodology for Large Scale Systems*, McGraw Hill, New York.

Sampson, S. E. and Froehle, C. M. (2006), "Foundations and implications of a proposed unified services theory", *Production and Operations Management*, 15(2), pp. 329–343.

Schon, D. (1983), *The Reflective Practitioner*, Basic Books, New York.

Senge, Peter M. (1990), *The Fifth Discipline*, Doubleday Currency, New York.

Sharma, Dinesh C. (2009), *The Long Revolution: The Birth and Growth of India's IT Industry*, HarperCollins Publishers, India.

Sharma, Dinesh C. (2014), "Indian IT outsourcing industry: Future threats and challenges", *Futures*, 56(2), pp. 73–80.

Shaw, Patricia (2002), *Changing Conversations in Organizations: A Complexity Approach to Change*, Routledge, London.

Shaw, Patricia and Stacey, Ralph (eds.) (2006), *Experience Risk, Spontaneity and Improvisation in Organizational Change: Working Live*, Routledge, UK.

Shotter, John (1993), *Conversational Realities: Constructing Life Through Language*, Sage Publications, London.

Shotter, John (2005), "'Inside the moment of managing': Wittgenstein and the everyday dynamics of our expressive-responsive activities", *Organization Studies*, 26(1), pp. 113–35

Sivakumar, Chitra and Sivakumar, S.S. (1996), "The meaning of social order in the Tamil country", in Robb, Peter, Yanagisawa, Haruka, and Sugihara, Kaoru (eds), *Local Agrarian Societies in Colonial India: Japanese Perspectives*, Richmond, Surrey: Curzon Press, New Delhi: Manohar, pp. 332–85.

Smith, W. K. and Lewis, M. W. (2011), "Towards a theory of paradox: A dynamic equilibrium model of organizing", *Academy of Management Review*, 36, pp. 381–403.

Smith, Wendy K., Binns, Andy and Tushman, Michael L. (2010), "Complex business models: Managing strategic paradoxes simultaneously", *Long Range Planning*, 43(2), pp. 448–61.

Søderberg, Anne-Marie, Krishna, S. and Bjørn, Pernille (2013), "Global software development: commitment, trust and cultural sensitivity in strategic partnerships", *Journal of International Management*, 19, pp. 347–61.

Stacey, Ralph (2001), *Complex Responsive Processes in Organizations: Learning and Knowledge Creation*, Routledge, London.

Stacey, Ralph (2003), *Complexity and Group Processes: A Radically Social Understanding of Individuals*, Brunner Routledge, Hove.

Stacey, Ralph (2012), *Tools and Techniques of Leadership and Management: Meeting the Challenge of Complexity*, Routledge, London.

Sundbo, J. and Gallouj, F. (2002), "Innovation as a loosely coupled system in services", in Metcalfe, J. S. and Miles, I. (eds.), *Innovation Systems in the Service Economy*, Norwell Mass. (Kluwer).

Sundbo, Jon, Johnston, Robert, Mattsson, Jan and Millett, Bruce (2001), "Innovation in service internationalization: the crucial role of the frantrepreneur", *Entrepreneurship & Regional Development*, 13(3), pp. 247–67.

Taganas, Rey AL and Kaul, Vijay Kumar (2006), "Innovation systems in India's IT industry: An empirical investigation", *Economic and Political Weekly*, 30, pp. 4178–186.

TCS (2009), "Case study on corporate social responsibility", http://www.tcs.com/SiteCollectionDocuments/Case%20Studies/CSR_Casestudy_Computer_Based_Functional_Literacy_08_09.pdf, TCS website, downloaded on 30 October 2014

Teece, David and Pisano, Gary (1994), "The dynamic capabilities of firms: An introduction", *Industrial and Corporate Change*, 3(3), pp. 537–556.

Teece, David J. (2000), *Managing Intellectual Capital*, Oxford University Press, Oxford.

Toppin, Gilbert and Czerniawska, Fiona (2005), *Business Consulting: A Guide to How it Works and How to Make it Work*, The Economist (with Profile Books), London.

Tracy, Sarah J. (2004), "Dialectic, contradiction, or double Bind? Analyzing and theorizing employee reactions to organizational tension", *Journal of Applied Communication Research*, 32(2), pp. 119–46.

Tsukasa, Mizushima (1986), "Nattar and the socio-economic change in South India in the 18th–19th centuries", *Study of Languages and Cultures of Asia and Africa*, Monograph Series 19, Tokyo University of Foreign Studies.

Ulrich, W (1983), *Critical Heuristics of Social Planning: A New Approach to Practical Philosophy*, Wiley, Chichester.

Umamaheswari, R. and Momaya, K. (2008), "Role of creative marketing in 10X Journey: Case of IT Firms from India", *IIMB Management Review*, 20(1), pp. 113–30.

Upadhya, Carol and Vasavi, A.R. (ed.) (2008), *In an Outpost of the Global Economy: Work and Workers in India's Information Technology Industry*, Routledge, New Delhi.

Urry, John (2005), "The complexities of the global", *Theory, Culture & Society*, 22(5), pp. 235–54.

Varma, Pavan (2005), *Being Indian*, Penguin Books, New Delhi.

Vidyasagar, M. (2007), "Indic computing, digital divide and citizen services", in Kanavi, Shivanand (ed.), *Research by Design: Innovation and TCS*, Rupa & Co., New Delhi.

Warfield, J. N. (1976), *Societal Systems: Planning, Policy, and Complexity*, Wiley Interscience, New York.

Webb, Jeremy (2013), *Nothing: From Absolute Zero to Cosmic Oblivion*, Profile Books (New Scientist).

Wiener, N. (1948), *Cybernetics: Or Control and Communication in the Animal and the Machine*, MIT Press, Cambridge, MA.

Williams, L. Christine (2006), "Shopping as symbolic interaction: Race, class and gender in the toy store", *Symbolic Interactionism*, 28(4), pp. 459–72.

Wilmott, Hugh and Alvesson, Mats (eds.) (1992), *Critical Management Studies*, Sage, London.

Winograd, T and Flores, F. (1986), *Understanding Computers and Cognition*, Ablex Publishing Corporation, Norwood, N.J.

About the Author

Sudhir Varadarajan, PhD in Systems Engineering and Management from IIT Madras, is a consultant-catalyst with specific interest in service design, innovation and strategy.

He has strong experience in identifying and developing new sources of differentiation for two leading Indian IT services firms through technical and managerial roles in software development, consulting, R&D, key account management, practice development, marketing and business strategy.

Beyond the call of duty, he has also actively contributed to governmental initiatives aimed at improving the quality of engineering education in India and been a guest faculty for "Contemporary Issues in Management" at IIT Madras since 2007.

The author can be contacted at vsudhirs@outlook.com.